RELIGION

An Obstacle to Human Progress

RELIGION

An Obstacle to Human Progress

Dr Chandra Sekhar Tiwary

MD PUBLICATIONS PVT LTD
NEW DELHI
www.mdppl.com

Published by :

MD Publications Pvt Ltd
"MD House", 11, Darya Ganj,
New Delhi - 110 002
Phone : +91-11-41563325 (Customer Service)
+91-11-41562846 (Editorial)
E-mail (orders): order@mdppl.com
Website: www.mdppl.com

ISBN: 978-81-7533-228-7

Published and Printed by Mr. Pranav Gupta on behalf of **MD Publications Pvt Ltd** at Times Press, New Delhi.

Preface

Human beings who were living tens of thousands of years ago were essentially modern humans with the same intellectual abilities that people have today and yet they lived a difficult existence as hunter gatherers in a dangerous world in which an injury or illness that could be easily treated today would have meant almost certain death. If one of those individuals could have been born in modern times they would easily have blended in and achieved anything that any one of us could achieve because they would have the benefit of the accumulation of knowledge from everyone who had lived before them.

Civilization began when human beings discovered agriculture, domesticating and breeding animals, and creating permanent settlements in which a social order was established and work was much more efficient and productive. This was also a period in our history in which the advances in every sort of activity could quickly be learned by everyone living in an organized society and could be passed down to the next generation.

Religious knowledge, according to religious practitioners, may be gained from religious leaders, sacred texts (scriptures), and/or personal revelation. Some religions view such knowledge as unlimited in scope and suitable to answer any question; others see religious knowledge as playing a more restricted role, often as a complement to knowledge gained through physical observation. Some religious people maintain that religious knowledge obtained in this way is absolute and infallible (religious cosmology).

Religion is an often talked about issue. Most people follow a particular religion because of what it teaches them and helps them attain. Many people are passionate about their religion because it lends them an identity. However, if it turns to extremism, progress in any sphere is hampered. Respect and tolerance are essential prerequisites for the functioning of a secular society like India.

Some might say that tradition holds no relevance in the modern day scenario, that they restrict the thinking capacity of people. But, according to me, traditions lend us individuality. They are essential if we have to understand our past any better, because our present is the result of the past. Traditions broaden our horizons and make us better rounded. They lend a broader outlook to our vision for a global village.

Many contemporary critics fault religion as being irrational. Some assert that dogmatic religions are in effect morally deficient, elevating to moral status ancient, arbitrary, and ill-informed rules—taboos on eating pork, for example, as well as dress codes and sexual practices—possibly designed for reasons of hygiene or even mere politics in a bygone era.

I am very grateful to Mr. Pranav Gupta, Director of MD Publications Pvt Ltd, New Delhi, for his kind cooperation and support for this book.

Dr Chandra Sekhar Tiwary

CONTENTS

1

Religion
An Introduction

In the frame of western religious thought, religions present a common quality, the "hallmark of patriarchal religious thought": the division of the world in two comprehensive domains, one sacred, the other profane. Religion is often described as a communal system for the coherence of belief focusing on a system of thought, unseen being, person, or object, that is considered to be supernatural, sacred, divine, or of the highest truth. Moral codes, practices, values, institutions, tradition, rituals, and scriptures are often traditionally associated with the core belief, and these may have some overlap with concepts in secular philosophy. Religion is also often described as a "way of life" or a life stance. A religion is an organized approach to human spirituality which usually encompasses a set of narratives, symbols, beliefs and practices, often with a supernatural or transcendent quality, that give meaning to the practitioner's experiences of life through reference to a higher power or truth.

It may be expressed through prayer, ritual, meditation, music and art, among other things. It may focus on specific supernatural, metaphysical, and moral claims about reality (the cosmos, and human nature) which may yield a set of religious laws, ethics, and a particular lifestyle. Religion also encompasses ancestral or cultural traditions, writings, history, and mythology, as well as personal faith and religious experience. The term "religion" refers to both the personal practices related to communal faith and to group rituals and communication stemming from shared conviction. "Religion" is sometimes used interchangeably with "faith" or "belief system," but it is more socially defined than personal convictions, and it entails specific behaviours, respectively. The development of religion has taken many forms in various cultures. It considers psychological and social roots, along with origins and historical development.

The English word religion has been in use since the 13th century, loaned from Anglo-French religiun (11th century), ultimately from the Latin religio, "reverence for God or the gods, careful pondering of divine things, piety, the res divinae". The ultimate origins of Latin religio are obscure. It is usually accepted to derive from ligare "bind, connect"; likely from a prefixed religare, i.e. re (again) + ligare or "to reconnect." This interpretation is favoured by modern scholars such as Tom Harpur and Joseph Campbell, but was made prominent by St. Augustine, following the interpretation of Lactantius. Another possibility is derivation from a reduplicated leligare. A historical interpretation due to Cicero on the other hand connects lego "read", i.e. re (again) + lego in the sense of "choose", "go over again" or "consider carefully". It may also be from Latin religiô, religiôn, perhaps from religâre, to tie fast. Religion has been defined in a wide variety of ways. Most definitions attempt to find a balance somewhere between overly sharp definition and meaningless generalities. Some sources have tried to use formalistic, doctrinal definitions while others have emphasized experiential, emotive, intuitive, volitional and ethical factors.

Definitions mostly include:

- A notion of the transcendent or numinous, often, but not always, in the form of theism.
- A cultural or behavioural aspect of ritual, liturgy and organized worship, often involving a priesthood, and societal norms of morality (ethos) and virtue (arete).
- A set of myths or sacred truths held in reverence or believed by adherents.

Sociologists and anthropologists tend to see religion as an abstract set of ideas, values, or experiences developed as part of a cultural matrix. For example, in Lindbeck's Nature of Doctrine, religion does not refer to belief in "God" or a transcendent Absolute. Instead, Lindbeck defines religion as, "a kind of cultural and/or linguistic framework or medium that shapes the entirety of life and thought... it is similar to an idiom that makes possible the description of realities, the formulation of beliefs, and the experiencing of inner attitudes, feelings, and sentiments." According to this definition, religion refers to one's primary worldview and how this dictates one's thoughts and actions. There is a tendency in the sociology of religion to emphasize the problems of any definition of religion. Talal Asad has gone so far as to say "there cannot be a universal definition of religion ... because that definition is itself the historical product of discursive processes"

Other religious scholars have put forward a definition of religion that avoids the reductionism of the various sociological and psychological disciplines that reduce religion to its component factors. Religion may be defined as the presence of a belief in the sacred or the holy. For example Rudolf Otto's "The Idea of the Holy," formulated in 1917, defines the essence of religious awareness as awe, a unique blend of fear and fascination before the divine. Friedrich Schleiermacher in the late 18th century defined religion as a "feeling of absolute dependence." Other encyclopedic definitions include: "A general term used... to designate all concepts concerning the belief in god(s) and goddess(es) as well as other spiritual beings or transcendental ultimate concerns" and "human beings' relation to that which they regard as holy, sacred, spiritual, or divine."

While superstitions and magical thinking refer to nonscientific causal reasoning, applied to specific things or actions, a religion is a more complex system about general or ultimate things, involving morality, history and community. Because religions may include and exploit certain superstitions or make use of magical thinking, while mixing them with broader considerations, the division between superstition and religious faith is hard to specify and subjective. Religious believers have often seen other religions as superstition. Likewise, some atheists, agnostics, deists, and skeptics regard religious belief as superstition. Religious practices are most likely to be labeled "superstitious" by outsiders when they include belief in extraordinary events (miracles), an afterlife, supernatural interventions, apparitions or the efficacy of prayer, charms, incantations, the meaningfulness of omens, and prognostications.

Greek and Roman pagans, who modeled their relations with the gods on political and social terms scorned the man who constantly trembled with fear at the thought of the gods, as a slave feared a cruel and capricious master. Such fear of the gods (deisidaimonia) was what the Romans meant by superstitio. Early Christianity was outlawed as a superstitio Iudaica, a "Jewish superstition", by Domitian in the 80s AD, and by AD 425, Theodosius II outlawed pagan traditions as superstitious. The Roman Catholic Church considers superstition to be sinful in the sense that it denotes a lack of trust in the divine providence of God and, as such, is a violation of the first of the Ten Commandments. The Catechism of the Catholic Church states superstition "in some sense represents a perverse excess of religion."

The history of religion refers to the written record of human religious experiences and ideas. This period of religious history typically begins with the invention of writing about 5,000 years ago (3,000 BCE) in the Near East. The prehistory of religion relates to the study of religious beliefs that existed prior to the advent of written records. The timeline of religion is a comparative chronology of religion. The nineteenth century saw a dramatic increase in knowledge about other cultures and religions, and also the establishment of economic and social histories of progress. The "history of religions" school sought to account for this religious diversity by connecting it with the social and economic situation of a particular group.

Typically religions are divided into stages of progression from more simple to more complex societies, especially from polytheistic to monotheistic and from extempore to organised. (There are now claims "that religion evolved from polytheism to monotheism has now been discredited". Thus, the starting point is the tribal band whose religion is animistic and involves shamans and totems. Since the group is tribal, there is no permanent sanctuary. Cultic rites centre on identification with wild animals and appeasing spirits, often of the hunted. As society developed into chiefdoms and small kingdoms, religious rites began to serve different functions. Agriculture became important and so fertility gods were introduced (often female, as it is the woman who has the power to produce life). The status of the "big man" (or chief) was supported with mythic tales of heroes and demigods, from whom he may be descended.

When these small kingdoms merged into larger groups (often through conquest), different cults merged. The conquest of one group by another is therefore recorded in an epic tale of the conquest of the conquered group's god by the victor's (e.g. some Hinduism and the Babylonian Marduk). Another solution was to syncretise different religious traditions, for example, the Romans' identification of their Gods with the Greeks and the Greeks' adoption of Anatolian myths and characters. Finally, the growth of the city state brought about progression to the most "civilised" level of religion, ethical monotheism. Students of the history of religions often learnt that this began in Egypt with Akhnaten and grew through 7th century BC Judaism, Persian Zoroastrianism and Greek Philosophy to endow Western society with the most progressive form of religion. The historical basis of this — that religion moved from polytheism to ethical monotheism — is now doubted.

Nevertheless, it is still widely held that ethical monotheism (e.g. Judaism, Christianity, Islam, some forms of Hinduism and Buddhism) was encouraged by the growth of city states. This was partly due to the role of a hierarchical society with a godlike absolute ruler. A more powerful social force was the isolation of the individual as he moved from the clan to a more cosmopolitan lifestyle. Questions of justice and value that had been previously answered by the family and small tribe were now to be pursued independently. The relative anonymity of the city afforded the opportunity for not only "sin" but also loneliness. Ethical monotheism answered society's need for a moral guide and motivation, whilst a unique personal God who was sovereign over all areas of life answered people's feelings of isolation and powerlessness. Good examples of this are the prophetic literature of the Jewish Tanakh (Old Testament), especially Isaiah, and the wisdom literature of the ancient near east dealing with apparently unjustified suffering. This includes Job, in the Judaeo-Christian Bible, and "The Dialogue of Pessimism", a Babylonian text.

The evolutionary origin of religions refers to the emergence of religious behaviour during the course of human evolution. When humans first became religious remains unknown, but there is credible evidence of religious behaviour from the Middle Paleolithic era (300-50 thousand years ago) and possibly earlier. Humanity's closest living relatives are common chimpanzees and bonobos. These primates share a common ancestor with humans who lived between four and six million years ago. It is for this reason that chimpanzees and bonobos are viewed as the best available surrogate for this common ancestor. Barbara King argues that while non-human primates are not religious, they do exhibit some traits that would have been necessary for the evolution of religion. These traits include high intelligence, a capacity for symbolic communication, a sense of social norms, and realization of "self" and a concept of continuity.

Dr. Frans de Waal and Barbara King both view human morality as having grown out of primate sociality. Though morality is a unique human trait, many social animals, such as primates, dolphins and whales, have been known to exhibit premoral sentiments. According to Michael Shermer, the following characteristics are shared by humans and other social animals, particularly the great apes:"attachment and bonding, cooperation and mutual aid, sympathy and empathy, direct and indirect reciprocity, altruism and reciprocal altruism, conflict resolution and peacemaking, deception and deception detection, community concern and caring about what others think about you, and awareness of and response to the social rules of the group".

De Waal contends that all social animals have had to restrain or alter their behaviour for group living to be worthwhile. Pre-moral sentiments evolved in primate societies as a method of restraining individual selfishness and building more cooperative groups. For any social species, the benefits of being part of an altruistic group should outweigh the benefits of individualism. For example, lack of group cohesion could make individuals more vulnerable to attack from outsiders. Being part of group may also improve the chances of finding food. This is evident among animals that hunt in packs to take down large or dangerous prey.

All social animals have hierarchical societies in which each member knows its own place. Social order is maintained by certain rules of expected behaviour and dominant group members enforce order through punishment. However, higher order primates also have a sense of reciprocity and fairness. Chimpanzees remember who did them favors and who did them wrong. For example, chimpanzees are more likely to share food with individuals who have previously groomed them. Chimpanzees live in fission-fusion groups that average 50 individuals. It is likely that early ancestors of humans lived in groups of similar size. Based on the size of extant hunter-gatherer societies, recent Paleolithic hominids lived in bands of a few hundred individuals. As community size increased over the course of human evolution, greater enforcement to achieve group cohesion would have been required. Morality may have evolved in these bands of 100 to 200 people as a means of social control, conflict resolution and group solidarity.

According to Dr. de Waal, human morality has two extra levels of sophistication that are not found in primate societies. Humans enforce their society's moral codes much more rigorously with rewards, punishments and reputation building. People also apply a degree of judgment and reason, not seen in the animal kingdom. Psychologist Matt J. Rossano argues that religion emerged after morality and built upon morality by expanding the social scrutiny of individual behaviour to include supernatural agents. By including everwatchful ancestors, spirits and gods in the social realm, humans discovered an effective strategy for restraining selfishness and building more cooperative groups. The adaptive value of religion would have enhanced group survival.

The religious mind is one consequence of a brain that is large enough to formulate religious and philosophical ideas. During human evolution, the hominid brain tripled in size, peaking 500,000 years ago. Much of the brain's expansion took place in the neocortex. This part of the brain is involved in processing higher order cognitive functions that are necessary for human religiosity. The neocortex is responsible for self consciousness, language and emotion. According to Dunbar's theory, the relative neocortex size of any species correlates with the level of social complexity of the particular species. The neocortex size correlates with a number of social variables that include social group size and complexity of mating behaviours.

In chimpanzees the neocortex occupies 50% of the brain, whereas in modern humans it occupies 80% of the brain. Robin Dunbar argues that the critical event in the evolution of the neocortex took place at the speciation of archaic Homo sapiens about 500 thousand years ago. His study indicates that only after the speciation event is the neocortex sufficiently large enough to process complex social phenomena such as language and religion. The study is based on a regression analysis of neocortex size plotted against a number of social behaviours of living and extinct hominids.

Lewis Wolpert argues that causal beliefs that emerged from tool use played a major role in the evolution of belief. The manufacture of complex tools requires creating a mental image of an object that does not exist naturally before actually making the artifact. Furthermore, one must understand how the tool would be used, which requires an understanding of causality. Accordingly, the level of sophistication of stone tools is a useful indicator of causal beliefs. Wolpert contends use of tools composed of more than one component, such as hand axes, represents an ability to understand cause and effect.

LANGUAGE AND RELIGION

Religion requires a system of symbolic communication, such as language, to be transmitted from one individual to another. Philip Lieberman states "human religious thought and moral sense clearly rest on a cognitive-linguistic base". From this premise science writer Nicholas Wade states:

"Like most behaviours that are found in societies throughout the world, religion must have been present in the ancestral human population before the dispersal from Africa 50,000 years ago. Although religious rituals usually involve dance and music, they are also very verbal, since the sacred truths have to be stated. If so, religion, at least in its modern form, cannot predate the emergence of language. It has been argued earlier that language attained its modern state shortly before the exodus from Africa. If religion had to await the evolution of modern, articulate language, then it too would have emerged shortly before 50,000 years ago.

Evolutionary Psychology of Religion

There is general agreement among cognitive scientists that religion is an outgrowth of brain architecture that evolved early in human history. However, there is disagreement on the exact mechanisms that drove the evolution of the religious mind. The two main schools of thought hold that either religion evolved due to natural selection and has selective advantage, or that religion is an evolutionary byproduct of other mental adaptations. Stephen Jay Gould, for example, believed that religion was exaltation or a spandrel, in other words that religion evolved as byproduct of psychological mechanisms that evolved for other reasons.

Such mechanisms may include the ability to infer the presence of organisms that might do harm (agent detection), the ability to come up with causal narratives for natural events (etiology), and the ability to recognize that other people have minds of their own with their own beliefs, desires and intentions (theory of mind). These three adaptations (among others) allow human beings to imagine purposeful agents behind many observations that could not readily be explained otherwise, e.g. thunder, lightning, movement of planets, complexity of life, etc. Some scholars have suggested that religion is genetically "hardwired" into the human condition. One controversial hypothesis, the God gene hypothesis, states that some human beings bear a gene which gives them a predisposition to episodes interpreted as religious revelation. One gene claimed to be of this nature is VMAT2.

The earliest evidence of religious thought is based on the ritual treatment of the dead. Most animals display only a casual interest in the dead of their own species. Ritual burial thus represents a significant advancement in human behaviour. Ritual burial represent an awareness of life and death and a possible belief in the afterlife. Philip Lieberman states "burials with grave goods clearly signify religious practices and concern for the dead that transcends daily life." The earliest evidence for treatment of the dead comes from Atapuerca in Spain. At this location the bones of 30 individuals believed to be Homo heidelbergensis have been found in a pit. Neanderthals are also contenders for the first hominids to intentionally bury the dead. They may have placed corpses into shallow graves along with stone tools and animal bones.

The presence of these grave goods may indicate an emotional connection with the deceased and possibly a belief in the afterlife. Neanderthal burial sites include Shanidar in Iraq and Krapina in Croatia and Kebara Cave in Israel. The earliest known burial of modern humans is from a cave in Israel located at Qafzeh. Human remains have been dated to 100,000 years ago. Human skeletons were found stained with red ochre. A variety of grave goods were found at the burial site. The mandible of a wild boar was found placed in the arms of one of the skeletons. Philip Lieberman states:

"Burial rituals incorporating grave goods may have been invented by the anatomically modern hominids who emigrated from Africa to the Middle East 100,000 years ago".

The use of symbolism in religion is a universal established phenomenon. Archeologist Steven Mithen contends that it is common for religious practices to involve the creation of images and symbols to represent supernatural beings and ideas. Because supernatural beings violate the principles of the natural world, there will always be difficulty in communicating and sharing supernatural concepts with others. This problem can be overcome by anchoring these supernatural beings in material form through representational art. When translated into material form, supernatural concepts become easier to communicate and understand. Due to the association of art and religion, evidence of symbolism in the fossil record is indicative of a mind capable of religious thoughts. Art and symbolism demonstrates a capacity for abstract thought and imagination necessary to construct religious ideas. Wentzel van Huyssteen states that the translation of the nonvisible through symbolism enabled early human ancestors to hold beliefs in abstract terms.

Some of the earliest evidence of symbolic behaviour is associated with Middle Stone Age sites in Africa. From at least 100,000 years ago, there is evidence of the use of pigments such as red ochre. Pigments are of little practical use to hunter gatherers, thus evidence of their use is interpreted as symbolic or for ritual purposes. Among extant hunter gatherer populations around the world, red ochre is still used extensively for ritual purposes. It has been argued that it is universal among human cultures for the color red to represent blood, sex, life and death. The use of red ochre as a proxy for symbolism is often criticized as being too indirect. Some scientists, such as Richard Klein and Steven Mithen, only recognize unambiguous forms of art as representative of abstract ideas. Upper Paleolithic cave art provides some of the most unambiguous evidence of religious thought from the Paleolithic. Cave paintings at Chauvet depict creatures that are half human and half animal, an example of anthropomorphism commonly associated among shamanistic practices.

Organized religion traces its roots to the Neolithic revolution that began 11,000 years ago in the Near East but may have occurred independently in several other locations around the world. The invention of agriculture transformed human societies from a hunter gatherer lifestyle to a sedentary lifestyle. The consequences of the Neolithic revolution included a population explosion and acceleration in the pace of technological development. The transition from foraging bands to states and empires precipitated more specialized and developed forms of religion that reflected the new social and political environment. While bands and small tribes possess supernatural beliefs, these beliefs do not serve to justify a central authority, justify transfer of wealth or maintain peace between unrelated individuals. Organized religion emerged as a means of providing social and economic stability through the following ways:

- Justifying the central authority, which in turn possessed the right to collect taxes in return for providing social and security services to the state?
- Bands and tribes consist of small number of related individuals. However states and nations are composed of thousands of unrelated individuals. Jared Diamond argues that organized religion served to provide a bond between unrelated individuals who would otherwise be more prone to enmity. He argues that the leading cause of death among hunter gatherer societies is murder.
- Religions that revolved around moralizing gods may have facilitated the rise of large, cooperative groups of unrelated individuals.

The states born out of the Neolithic revolution, such as those of Ancient Egypt and Mesopotamia, were theocracies with chiefs, kings and emperors playing dual roles of political and spiritual leaders. Anthropologists have found that virtually all state societies and chiefdoms from around the world have been found to justify political power through divine authority.

Following the Neolithic revolution, the pace of technological development intensified culminating in the invention of writing 3500 years ago. Writing is thought to have been first invented in either Sumeria or Ancient Egypt and was initially used for accounting. Soon after, writing was used to record myth. The first religious texts mark the beginning of religious history. The Pyramid Texts from ancient Egypt are one of the oldest known religious texts in the world dating to between 2400-2300 BCE. Writing played a major role in sustaining organized religion. In pre-literate societies, religious ideas were based on an oral tradition, the contents of which remain limited to the collective memories of the society's inhabitants. With the advent of writing, information that is not easy to remember could easily be stored in sacred texts. Humans could store and process large amounts of information with writing, that otherwise would have been forgotten. Writing therefore enabled religions to develop coherent and comprehensive doctrinal systems that remained independent of time and place.

THEORIES ON THE ORIGINS OF RELIGION

Groups of Theories on the Origin of Religion

There are two broad groups of theories about the origin of religion.

1. *Faith-based theories:* According to David Barrett et al, editors of the "World Christian Encyclopedia: A comparative survey of churches and religions - AD 30 to 2200," there are 19 major world religions which are subdivided into a total of 270 large religious groups, and many unique faith groups. Among this great religious diversity, there are probably hundreds of different religious creation stories which describe how humans, other species of life, the Earth, and the rest of the universe came to be. Many of these stories describe the origins of their particular religion. It was typically based on revelation from one or more deities — mainly gods and goddesses.

2. *Secular-based theories:* Anthropologists, evolutionary biologists, and other researchers have reached a near consensus that humans of the species Homo sapiens evolved from a species of proto-humans who originated somewhere in Africa. (This statement probably upsets any white supremacists who are reading this essay. That can't be helped; scientists consider the evidence to be conclusive; ultimately, we are all descended from Africans.) These proto-humans walked upright, and had an opposing thumb and little finger. Their internal brain structure represented a major advance over those of previous animals in terms of its flexibility, its ability to reason, and its ability to plan for the future. This gave proto-humans an improved ability to pass on their accumulated knowledge to their descendents, to form more advanced societies, and ultimately to create religions.

Nobody knows with accuracy how the first religions evolved. By the time that writing had developed, many religions had been in place for many millennia and the details of their origins had been forgotten. However, there is speculation that the first religions were a response to human fear. They were created to give people a feeling of security in an insecure world, and a feeling of control over the environment where there was little control. The developing abilities of proto-humans were a double-edge sword:

On the one hand, they aided their chances of surviving in a cruel and unpredictable world. They helped each successive generation of proto-humans to build upon the knowledge base of their ancestors.

This increased mental ability led to a terrifying piece of knowledge: personal mortality. For the first time, individual animals on earth became aware that their life was transient; they would die at some point in their future. This knowledge produced an intolerable emotional drain. During their evolution from proto-human to full human, they developed questions about themselves and their environment:

What controlled the seasonal cycles of nature — the daily motion of the sun; the motion of the stars, the passing of the seasons, etc.

What controlled their environment — what or who caused floods, rains, dry spells, storms, etc? What controls fertility — of the tribe, its domesticated animals, and its crops. What system of morality is needed to best promote the stability of the tribe? And above all: what happens to a person after they die?

Living in a prescientific society, people had no way to resolve these questions. Even today, with all of our scientific advances, we still debate about the second last question, and still have no way of reaching a consensus on the last. But the need for answers (particularly to the last question) was so important that some response was required, even if they were merely based on hunches. Some people within the tribe started to invent answers based on their personal guesses. Thus developed:

The first religious belief system

The first priesthood

The first set of rituals to appease the Goddess

Other rituals to control fertility and other aspects of the environment

A set of behavioural expectations for members of the tribe, and

A set of moral truths to govern human behaviour

These formed an oral tradition which was disseminated among the members of the tribe and was taught to each new generation. Much later, when writing was developed, the beliefs were generally recorded in written form. A major loss of flexibility resulted. Oral traditions can evolve over time; written documents tend to be more permanent. Unfortunately, because these belief systems were based on hunches, the various religions which developed in different areas of the world were all different. Their teachings were in conflict with each other. Because the followers of most religions considered their beliefs to be derived directly from God, they cannot be easily changed.

Thus, interreligious compromise is difficult or impossible. Also, because religious texts are often ambiguous, divisions developed within religions. Different denominations, schools, or traditions have derived different meanings from the same religious texts. Thus were laid the foundations for millennia of interreligious and intrareligious conflict.

The first organized religions appear to have been based on fertility. They were focused on the worship of the great Earth Goddess. Religion evolved to include male Gods who were gradually given increased importance by the priests. This development may have been caused by developing knowledge of the male's involvement in the process of reproduction. Today, most people follow either:

A monotheistic religion, in which a single male god is worshipped, or

A henotheistic religion which recognizes a single main deity but which recognizes other gods and goddesses, heroes, or saints as facets or manifestations or aspects of that supreme God.

Most religions teach that they were directly revealed by their deity/deities to humanity, and are unrelated to other world religions. However there is considerable historical evidence from ancient times that religions in the area from India to the Middle East shared many religious beliefs. One example of this are:

The many passages in the Hebrew Scriptures which contain concepts or passages taken from Egyptian, Babylonian and other nearby Pagan religions.

Many of the events in the life of Jesus as recorded in the Christian Scriptures (New Testament) appear to have been derived from earlier Hinduism and Pagan religious sources.

Religions were originally based on the particular beliefs of their founders and prophets. Thus, there were few points of similarity among the various spiritual paths:

In terms of their belief about supernatural being(s), various faith traditions have taught Agnosticism, Animism, Atheism, Deism, Duotheism, Henotheism, Monism, Monotheism,

Panentheism, Pantheism, Polytheism, Trinitarianism, and probably a few that we have missed. It is obvious from these conflicting ideas about deities that almost all religions are just plain wrong.

Few agreements exist among the world's religions about religious beliefs, sacred ritual, organizational structure, optimum family structure, limits on sexual behaviour, sexual orientation, the roles of women and men, other moral topics, the afterlife, etc.

Religions' traditional teachings in the area of science differ greatly from each other and from the findings of scientists. Examples from Judaism and Christianity are: how the universe was formed, where rainbows came from; the worldwide flood; talking animals; the sun standing still in the sky; the cause of epilepsy, deafness, blindness, and mental illnesses; virginal conception, demonic possession, walking on water, resurrection from the dead, ascension into the sky, etc.

RELIGIONS TODAY

Some observers believe that modern-day religions are largely a response to human fear. Their main function is to provide their followers with a feeling of security while living in a dangerous environment in which a person can be injured, killed or murdered at any time due to natural causes, accidents or human hatred and intolerance.

John Shelby Spong, retired bishop of the Episcopal Church, USA has written:

"Religion is primarily a search for security and not a search for truth. Religion is what we so often use to bank the fires of our anxiety. That is why religion tends toward becoming excessive, neurotic, controlling and even evil. That is why a religious government is always a cruel government. People need to understand that questioning and doubting are healthy, human activities to be encouraged not to be feared. Certainty is a vice not a virtue. Insecurity is something to be grasped and treasured. A true and healthy religious system will encourage each of these activities. A sick and fearful religious system will seek to remove them."

To paraphrase the remark of the French astronomer LaLande, the origin of religion is lost in the obscurity of the ages. The anthropologist Sir James G. Frazer wrote that religion began with belief in magic by primitive tribes. Neither of these statements gives a satisfactory explanation. Written language has only been here for some 10,000 years and men have been here 1-1/2 million years, with no written record of their activities, customs or possible religion for most of that time. Therefore, the only way we can speculate on how long they were receptive to religious beliefs and practices is by reason and logic.

To begin with, we have to state our axioms or selfevident facts on which we base our conclusions.

1. All things are natural; there is no supernatural.
2. All traits are the result of long ages of evolutionary development.
3. All present traits are the result of being favorable to survival.
4. All traits unfavorable to survival were eliminated by the process of natural selection.
5. It is possible to alter behaviour by education and training, but acquired characteristics cannot be inherited.

All mankind has a common origin, as primates for many ages and as Homo sapiens perhaps for a million years, they spread out, occupied different territories and continents and further changed in appearance and behaviour. At some time in their long journey they became receptive to religion. There are two ways to account for this: supernatural indoctrination or naturally by mutation. The first we will have to discard because of our axiom that everything is natural. The mutation must have occurred before the line split into the several races as all races have a religion of a sort, or there was a similar mutation in each race, which is improbable.

Religion persisted because it was favorable to survival. It held the family, the tribe and eventually the nation together and enabled them to defend themselves against animal and human predators. Time passed, and a few men were born without the religious gene. They made discoveries, the age of enlightenment began and with it the rise of science, and religion was no longer favorable to survival. It persisted as a vestige, like the muscles in the cheek that were there to flap the ears, or the wisdom teeth that have no utility, cause a deal of misery and eventually have to be pulled. Religion will continue until all who have that trait are eliminated by natural selection, and a new race of men is raised up with a genetic makeup fit to survive in the environment of that future age.

THE ORIGIN OF RELIGION IN THE RACE

The question of the origin of religion in the human race still remains one of the insoluble mysteries confronting the mind of man. Men have attempted to solve this problem through scientific research, only to find that the results lead to inevitable antinomies. Like all other questions of "origins," the origin of religion is more a matter of speculation than of investigation; or to make it less extreme, it will at all events be admitted that speculation is involved in a problem for which an entirely satisfactory solution cannot be found through historical investigation alone. We may trace a particular religion to its faint beginnings, we may even be able to determine the features which the most primitive form of religion presents, but we shall still be far from furnishing an answer to the question—How did religion arise? What is its source?

It is significant that the question of the origin of religion was not scientifically studied until modern times. Before we come to consider some modern theories it may be well to refer briefly to two views which were once widely prevalent, but which are now obsolete or at least absolescent.

The View of Divine Revelation

Jewish, Christian, and Mohammedan theologians, for a long time, assumed Divine Revelation as a necessary factor in the rise of religion, either in the form of a primitive Revelation vouchsafed to all mankind, or of a special Revelation to certain peoples singled out for the purpose. This view has usually taken the form of a belief in a primeval monotheism of divine origin, from which polytheism in its many forms is a later relapse. It is now usually held that the doctrine of revelation has explained the origin of religion in far too intellectual and mechanical a fashion, "as if religion began with the impartation to man of a set of ideas, readymade and finished ideas poured into a mind conceived as a kind of empty vessel." This is a crudely unpsychological view. Moreover, the theory of evolution has led us to conceive of primitive man as utterly incapable of receiving and retaining the highly developed ideas which primitive revelation was supposed to communicate to him.

The View of the English Deist

The English deist of the eighteenth century came on the scene rejecting the idea of revelation and found the origin of religion in human reason. Through the intellect, they claimed, such fundamental doctrines as the belief in a god and the immortality of the soul could be established with a certainty that could not be shaken. The religion of reason is natural to man and therefore known to him from the beginning. But through the cunning devices of the priests, whose one object was to exploit the fears and credulity of the masses in order to get them under their control, elaborate superstitious beliefs and ritual practices came everywhere to take the place of the simple religion of reason. Thus religion has a twofold origin—viz., reason as the source of pure natural religion, and willful deceit on the part of priest as the source of all the actual historical religions.

This theory of the English Deists is now quite obsolete. It has several very serious and obvious defects. (a) It exaggerates the place of reason as the originating source of religion, and underestimates the place of that emotional and intuitional illumination which is such a fruitful source of religious ideas and experience. (b) It attributes to primitive man mature ideas which it took centuries for man to be able to grasp and appreciate. (c) Most absurd of all is the idea that all the actual religions of history are simply calculating hypocrisies invented by priests in a spirit of selfish greed and power. Doubtless priests have frequently exploited the religious impulses of men to serve their own ends, but they could only exploit what already existed independently of them.

As Sabatier says, "When I hear it said, 'Priest made religion,' I simply ask, 'And who, pray, made the priest?' In order to invent a priesthood, and in order that that invention should find general acceptance with the people that were to be subject to it, must there not have been already in the hearts of men a religious sentiment that would clothe the institution with a sacred character? The terms must be reversed. It is not priesthood that explains religion, but religion that explains priesthood." After seeing the complete untinability of this theory Dr. Edwards concludes that "this shallow and cynical theory makes religion a matter of deliberate invention rather than a matter of spontaneous growth with its roots in the deep foundation of man's nature." At present this theory has been discredited by most scholars and probably has no supporters.

These older and pre-scientific views we may now put on one side and proceed to discuss some of the more important modern theories of the origin of religion. There are two ways in which the question may be approached—the way of the anthropologist and the way of the psychologist. The former is concerned with the historic, or rather prehistoric, origin of religion. The problem of the latter is, what is its source in man's spiritual nature, not at the beginning only, but everywhere and always? In other words, the former deals with the origin of religion in the human race while the latter deals with the origin of religion in the individual. Since this chapter only deals with the origin of religion in the Race we may be content to set forth the various anthropological theories with little reference to the psychological views.

The Animistic Theory of E. B. Taylor

This may be said to be the first theory of the origin of religion that was backed up by a thoroughly scientific study of the mind and habits of the primitive. In this momentous work Tylor shows that at a certain stage of culture men everywhere attribute a kind of soul to the phenomena of Nature—e.g., to trees, brooks, mountains, clouds, stones, stars. Primitive man regarded all he saw as possessing a life like unto his own. The movement of things around him he accounted for on the analogy of his own movements, which he knew by immediate experience were due to the activity of his spirit or will. To early man, as to the savage today, all Nature was alive, filled with innumerable spirits. Thus religion, Tylor believed, arose in an effort to propitiate these spirits by offerings and to win their favor by prayers.

Tylor's conclusions in anthropological researches have deeply influenced the direction taken by the study of religion. Yet as an account of the origin of religion it cannot be regarded as satisfactory. The chief objections to this theory are, first that the argument does not account in a satisfactory manner for undoubted cases of direct worship of natural phenomena; second that the most primitive savage does not possess so clear an idea of spirit in distinction from body as is here implied. The notion of a soul as a definite thing is a fairly advanced concept which must have been beyond the mental reach of primitive man. And so authorities have come to recognize what is called a preanimistic stage of religion.

The Ghost-Theory of Herbert Spencer

Brief reference may be made to Spencer's wellknown theory which finds the origin of religion in the worship of ancestors appearing in the form of ghosts. The awe inspired by {death}, and the fear created by the dead who had passed beyond the control of the living, constitute the two factors which arouse a new sense in man; and as far back as we can go men are seen offering sacrifices to the spirits of their ancestors. This Herbert Spencer believed to be the most primitive form of religion. Animism is not original but derivative, being a generalized form of the belief in the spirits of dead ancestors reappearing as ghosts and choosing certain objects in Nature as their dwelling-place.

The weakness of Spencer's theory is at the point of over simplicity. The deification of ancestors is far too narrow a basis on which to rear the structure of religion. "Religion is too complex a phenomenon to be accounted for by the growth and spread of a single custom. Worship, of however primitive a character, is not the expression of a single thought or a single emotion, but the product of thoughts so complex, so powerful, as to force an expression in the same way in which a river, swollen by streams coming down the mountains from various directions, overflows its banks."

Dr. Jevons expresses his view in unqualified terms thus: "It never happens that the spirits of the dead are conceived to be gods. Man is dependent on the gods, but the spirits of his dead ancestors are dependent on him . . . The worshipper's pride is that his ancestor was a god and not mere mortal . . . The fact is that ancestors known to be human were not worshipped as gods, and that ancestors worshipped as gods were not believed to be human." This might be a slight exaggeration, but it does come somewhat within the facts (e.g., the natives of Central Australia, a most primitive type of people, believe in the reappearance of the spirits of ancestors, but do not worship them). The worship of ghost has not been found to be nearly as prevalent among the lower peoples as Spencer imagined, and it certainly cannot be maintained that ancestor-worship is more primitive in character than the worship of the spirits of natural objects.

The Totemistic Theory

Some authorities have found the origin of religion in totemistic practices. So complex and intricate is the phenomenon surrounding Totemism that an adequate description of it cannot be given in so brief a compass. However we may briefly present its essential features. A totem is a species of animal or plant, or more rarely a class of inanimate objects, to which a social group (a clan) stands in an intimate and very special relation of friendship or kinship—frequently it is thought of as the ancestor of the clan—and which provides that social group with its name. The totem is not exactly a god, but a cognate being and one to be respected. It must not be used for common purposes, nor must it be slain or eaten except in some solemn and sacramental way. It is all ways the species and never an individual animal or plant that is regarded as a totem. This theory of the totemistic origin of religion has been highly advocated by W. Robertson Smith in his Religion of the Semites (1885) and F. B. Jevons in his Introduction to the History of Religion (1896). Although Smith's ingenious theory has greatly influenced the scientific study of religion, it is far from being adequate to the facts. Jevons maintains that totemism is "the most primitive form of society," that it "is or has been worldwide," that polytheism is a relapse from it.

In criticism of this theory it has been revealed through recent research that not every religion has passed through the totemistic stage. It is admitted that totemism is very ancient, but its universality is very far from being proved. There are many peoples of very low culture among whom it is unknown, or at least unrecognizable. It is not discerned, for instance, among the Veddas of Ceylon, or among the Andaman Islanders, or among the low Brazilian tribes. Other tribes have totems which yet are not worshipped and which are in no sense deities. A new form has been given to this theory by the French sociological school, of which Emile Durkheim is the most distinguished representative. Durkheim's theory assumes totemism {as the earlier form of religion although he insist that the importance of totemism} is absolutely independent of whether it was ever universal or not, yet it is practically assumed as the earliest form of society and of religion everywhere. The essence of all religious belief lies in the idea of a mysterious impersonal force controlling life, and this sense of force is derived from the authority of society over the individual.

It is this sense of the power of the social group over his life that becomes to man the consciousness of a mysterious power in the world. The totem is the visible emblem of this power; but the reality behind the totem, which the totem symbolized, is the might of tribal custom, emotion, and thought, which seems like an actually existing force weighing upon each individual and dominating his life. His real god is society; the power he really worships is the power of society. It seems quite clear at this point that Durkheim's interest in totenism is determined by his sociological theory of religion as essentially and wholly a social phenomenon. The further discussion of it cannot be undertaken here. We can only repeat that there are large parts of the world in which no traces of totemism have been found, and that strictly speaking, totemism is not a religion at all. "Although regarded with reverence and looked to for help, the totem is never, where totemism is not decadent, prayed to as a god or a person with powers which we call supernatural."

A more weighty criticism of this theory is set forth by Dr. Hopkins. He states: "The fundamental objection which will eventually overthrow this theory is that it ignores or minimizes beyond reason the individual in favor of the group. . . . While it must be admitted that religious ideas in general reflect a man's habitat and group, it is a serious error to imagine that the habitat or group in which he is born produces his religious state of mind. The French theory does not hesitate to insist that man does not think at all as an individual; there is no such thing as an individual mentality and consequently all religious thought is social. But it is pure assumption that the mind of the group is so overwhelmingly coercive that the individual mind is entirely subservient to it. All that can be affirmed is that the social atmosphere affects the religious consciousness." On the basis of fact Durkheim's theory cannot be accepted as totally valid. But Durkheim is probably right in seeking to trace religion back to something more primitive than the animistic belief in nature-spirits conceived as personal or in the ghosts of ancestors.

Pre-Animistic Religion

Any satisfactory theory of the origin of religion must be able to account, not only for the prominence of magic and mysticism in religion, but also for the connection of these, from the beginning, with a vital moral element. Recent anthropology tends more and more to find this satisfactory theory in the conception of mana. Here the origin of religion is found in a pre-animistic period or stage characterised by a sense of awe in the presence of a diffused, indefinable, mysterious power or powers not regarded as personal. This potency has been given many names, but for the sake of uniformity we may call it mana, as the Polynesians do, amongst whom this potency as such was first discovered by modern investigators.

It is believed that mana is everywhere, intangible and all-pervasive. All things have it: of course this does mean that mana is something universal or of abstract reality—the primitive has not risen high enough to generalize a universal reality—but it means that there is potency in every object to which man's attention is given. Mana by no means has any moral quality. It may be good or bad, favorable or dangerous, according to time or place. Here, then, we seem to have the common root of magic and religion. Here is an attitude of mind which supplies religion with its raw material.

It is obviously more primitive in character than animism, and may be assumed to be chronologically prior to it. It "may provide the basis on which an animistic doctrine is subsequently constructed . . . Of such powers (towards which awe is felt) spirits constitute but a single class among many; though, being powers in their own right, they finish a type to which the rest may become assimilated in the long run." Religion in its origin is thus seen to be a sense of awe and mystery in the presence of the indefinable and incalculable power manifested in things, persons, and events, together with the attendant effort on man's part to adjust him negatively and positively to that power, with a view to satisfying certain felt needs of his life.

Magic and Religion

It has been implied above that religion and magic have a common root. At this point we may state this position more fully. The question of the relation between these two attitudes or types of behaviour has often been discussed by anthropologists, and has an important bearing on the problem of the origin and nature of religion. In dealing with this relationship many questions inevitably arise. Have we sufficient grounds for assigning logical or chronological priority to the one rather than to the other? If so, to which of the two does priority belong? Can we place a genetic relation between them? Did the one spring from the other, by way of development or else by way of relapse? Or did they have independent origins? In an attempt to answer these questions at least three positions have emerged.

The first position holds that religion was prior to magic or, in the words of Dr. Jevons, "that belief in the supernatural (religion) was prior to the belief in magic, and that the latter whenever it sprang up was degradation or a relapse in the evolution of religion." This doctrine of relapse implying that man started with a relatively pure form of religion, recurs in other contexts in Jevon's book, for an instance he holds that polytheism is a relapse from a kind of monotheism. This view, however, has few, if any, supporters among modern anthropologists. He is an exception at this point. He set forth the theory that spiritual intuition rather than magic accounted for the rise of religion. He sees primitive monotheism as the root of religion out of which animism and myth grew.

A second position holds that magic was prior to religion, and that the latter evolved in some way out of the former. Sir James Frazer is the outstanding exponent of this view. His famous theory may be thus briefly summarized. "In the evolution of thought, magic as representing a lower intellectual stratum, has probably everywhere preceded religion." At first man sought adjustment through magic, but "a tardy recognition of the inherent falsehood and barrenness of magic set the more thoughtful part of mankind to cast about for a truer theory of Nature and a more fruitful method of turning her resources to account." Thus man's bitter experience of the failure of magic drove him to a different and better method of dealing with the unseen. "The age of magic" gradually gave way to the "age of religion." In a word, man's despair of magic is the genesis of religion.

Frazer's theory has proved quite suggestive and thought

provoking. But, though doubtless it contains elements of truth, it cannot be accepted in the sharp antithetical way in which he presented it. As Edwards laconically states, "It is far too intellectualistic a view of the origin of religion. It seems to represent early man (of the more 'sagacious' type) as almost a full-blown arm chair philosopher in search of a working theory of life and the world, and ignores the spontaneous emotional response to environment which played a much greater part in the life of primitive man than reflective thought did." Further, the theory only offers a negative explanation of the genesis of religion—the failure of magic. A positive motive for religion still needs to be found.

A third position maintains that magic and religion had a common root in man's experience of the mysterious forces of the world, but that in the course of human evolution they revealed their mutual incompatibility even to the extent of active hostility. In this theory, then, religion and magic are thought of as issuing out of common conditions, being the results of man's more or less conscious experiments with the unseen powers in his keen struggle for existence, and of his endeavour to utilize the mysterious potency around him which is generally called mana to help him in the battle of life. This, as indicated above, is the view accepted by most modern anthropologists, and from my way of thinking it is quite valid.

The above brief study of the origin of religion in the light of anthropological research seems to culminate in the view that the most primitive religious idea is that of mana, that this arises in the actual ceremonial performances of the primitive groups, and that subsequently, as Marett says, "Gods start, in fact, as no more than portions of the ritual apparatus." However we must not reject the other theories as totally untenable. There seems to be some truth in each of these theories; none of them can be accepted as absolute. Maybe after all we will never get all of the facts as to the origin of religion in the race. Like Troeltsch we will probable have to be content to deal with religion in terms of what it has become, rather than from whence it came. After all this is the true essence of religion.

If, however, it can be proved that the origin of religion in the race was very crude we need not despair. The question of origins is relatively independent of the question of values. If religion can be traced back to lowly origins, that should not in itself be regarded as prejudicial to its real value in the higher stages of its development, or to its relative value even at the lower stages, any more than the fact that science and art have sprung from most crude and unpromising beginnings should discredit the value of the final results or of the painful and often bungling efforts which have contributed to those results. It seems more rational to maintain that the final achievement enhances the worth of the crude beginnings than to say that the crudeness of the beginnings depreciates the value of the results.

Monotheism and the Origin of Religion

The God of the Bible is God over the whole Earth—Jew and Gentile, Christian and pagan, Muslim, Hindu, Buddhist, and atheist. He created the world and everything in it, and all of man's history traces back to that singular event. Christians assert this as an absolute truth, though not everyone agrees. Evolutionists and atheists have long struggled to solve the problem of the origin of religion, specifically of monotheism—the belief that God is One. According to David Barrett's World Christian Encyclopedia, approximately 85 percent of the world's population believes in some sort of god (of the remaining 15 percent who are atheists and agnostics, 14 percent reside in communist countries), and 53 percent of the world's population is monotheistic, claiming to derive their faith from Abraham (Christians, Jews, and Muslims) Such a ubiquitous belief demands an explanation, yet evolutionists are at a loss to explicate the origin of this pervasive phenomenon.

As long as there has been religion, there have been those who have attempted to explain its origin naturalistically. The rise of monotheistic religion generally has been described as an evolution, an outgrowth, of some more primitive religious belief that parallels the evolution of man. This theory was discussed most thoroughly in the years directly after Darwin published Origin of Species and Descent of Man, but it has been a source of controversy since at least the second century. The Roman philosopher Celsus, who was rabidly anti-Christian, set out to prove that the monotheism of the Jews began as pagan polytheism,. "Those herdsmen and shepherds who followed Moses as their leader, had their minds deluded by vulgar deceits, and so supposed that there was one God". Erasmus, writing during the Reformation, suggested that many heathen customs had been adopted by the Roman Catholic Church.

David Hume, in Natural History of Religion (1757), and Voltaire's Essay (1780), similarly denied revelation a place in the history of religion. It was not until the nineteenth century and the arrival of the German rationalists that the theory reached its full-grown proportions. Max Müller, orientalist and philologist at Oxford, was chief among them, with his theory that religion originated with "a henotheistic Nature Worship, degenerated into Polytheism, sank into Fetishism, and then rose in some cases to new forms of Pantheism or Theism". Tylor, a colleague of Müller's at Oxford, rejected this, and claimed that animism, the worship of spirit beings, was the well-spring from which all other religion flowed; Herbert Spencer, the English sociologist and close friend of Charles Darwin, readily accepted this evolutionary hypothesis in his Principles of Sociology (1877). Others thought totemism (the belief that there existed a mythical relationship between man and certain plants or animal), to be the original source of religious beliefs. Similar theories were submitted, though the aforementioned were the most popular.

The scholars' theories enjoyed the spotlight only for a few years, however. Like Darwin, they made assertions, expecting the hard evidence to confirm their theories at a later date. The various hypotheses were advanced because the materialists thought such to be the only possible explanation for the rise of religion; supernatural revelation was not an option for them. But the theories they proposed have subsequently fallen out of favor because proof was lacking. Despite the most rigorous scholarship, the sciences of anthropology and archaeology failed to yield proof for any of the various concepts. As a result, modern anthropologists generally avoid the question altogether by stating that the mystery is unsolvable. Ninian Smart, in The Religious Experience of Mankind, took this approach when he wrote:

Neither can we know how man first experienced the holy. It may have been that men, in becoming aware of themselves through the power of speech and in discovering their capacity to change the world...also felt a sense of rupture from the natural world about them. Others persist in the belief that monotheism evolved. Mark Smith, professor of Bible and Near Eastern studies at New York University, published a book in 2001, describing the original Jewish pantheon of gods and its eventual development into monotheism. Thus, the evolutionary model survives and thrives today, despite nearly one hundred years of evidence to the contrary.

This contrary evidence is the result of the research of both believers and nonbelievers. As far back as the second century, the monotheistic roots of world religion were defended. In his hortatory address to the Greeks, Justin Martyr used their own prophets and poets to show that Greek religion was fundamentally the worship of the One God. He quoted the great poet Orpheus of the sixth century B.C. as saying, "Look to the one and universal King—One, selfbegotten, and the only One, of whom all things and we ourselves are sprung... And other than the great King there is none". Likewise, the ancient Sibyl, considered a prophetess, said: "There is one only unbegotten God, Omnipotent, invisible, most high, All-seeing, but He has seen by no flesh". These are the most ancient sources he mentioned, but he also included Homer, Sophocles, and Plato.

More recent scholarship has vindicated Justin Martyr's thesis. George Rawlinson, professor of ancient history at Oxford, affirmed that a historical survey has shown us that in the early times, everywhere, or almost everywhere, belief in the unity of God existed—barbarous nations possessed it as well as civilized ones—it underlay polytheism that attempted to crush it—retained a hold on language and thought—had from time to time its special assertors, who never professed to have discovered it.

Sir Flinders Petrie, dubbed "the father of modern Egyptology," wrote in agreement:

> Were the conception of a god only an evolution from such spirit worship, we should find the worship of many gods preceding the worship of one god.... What we actually find is the contrary to this; monotheism is the first stage traceable in theology....

To quote all the authorities that have come to this conclusion would be tedious (and has been done many times over), but the message is clear. Evolutionists would do well to take the advice of one their own, Robert Lowie of the American Museum of Natural history, who said: "The time has come for eschewing the all-embracing and baseless theories of yore to settle down to sober historical research" . Every culture in the world originally worshipped only one God. This holds true for the ancient Chinese, Native Americans, the Australian Aborigines, the Bushmen of the Congo, as well as the better-documented civilizations of the Old World. The significance of this is twofold: evolutionists cannot explain the rise and degeneration of the world's religions from monotheism to various other types of worship, such as polytheism, pantheism, animism, and totemism. Second, the Genesis record, which states that all men originally knew God, but then rebelled against Him and were scattered over the Earth, is validated. That God was involved in the lives of all His people at one time cannot be doubted, and is confirmed both by revelation and by the science of anthropology.

2

Religion and Development

Religion is no panacea, but aspects of it can complement as well as motivate development. It can also obstruct or undermine. The avenues by which religion influences development activities in different faiths and regions are haunting in their complexity. The literature is likewise many-headed and multilingual. Religious people and institutions may be agents of advocacy, funding, innovation, empowerment, social movements, and service delivery. Equally, religious people and institutions can incite violence, model hierarchy, oppose empowerment (women should stay at home); deflect advocacy (we care about the next life); absorb funding (build a new worship hall); and cast aspersions on service delivery (they are trying to convert you). This complexity is further heightened by personal opinions on the topic, which can be powerful. The gusto of development experts who resonate with religion is enthusiastically matched by the repugnance of those who revile it.

To scan busy contemporary intersections between religion and development, as we will do, is to neglect the long and varied historical associations and literatures. As Amartya Sen points out, Ashoka, a convert to Buddhism in the 3rd century B.C., explicitly championed religious tolerance – as indeed did Moghul Emperor Akbar in a muslim state nearly two millennium later (while the Christian Inquisition was in full swing). Bartolomé de las Casas, a 15/16th century Dominican friar and Spanish missionary to Latin America, wrote in defence of indigenous persons' rights to selfdetermination. Abdullahi An-Naim reminds that Gandhi's 'secular' India intended to draw upon and incorporate spiritual insights rather than sideline them. Many less salutary writings and incidents could also be mentioned. The point is that religion and development have often been intimately interwoven (for good or ill). The intersections of religion and development can be examined and mapped from a variety of perspectives, which inevitably overlap to some degree.

INTRINSIC VALUE

Religious faith may open an independent route to serenity and meaning whether one is in prison or in penury, or suffering illness or exclusion or bereavement or other troubles. Thus religion may contribute directly to a person's flourishing or contentedness, and comprise a dimension of human wellbeing. Attention has been indirectly drawn to this facet of religion (among other forces) by Amartya Sen, who notes that instead of grumbling many of the extreme poor have reconciled themselves with their lot and seem 'grateful for small mercies'. While Sen regards such unnatural happiness to be a momentous achievement he points out that their happiness is a poor indicator of their quality of life in other respects. In this way, religious practices stand alongside and complement other aspects of human flourishing that are intrinsically valued – such as safety, health, knowledge, meaningful work and play, selfdirection, culture and the like.

The contribution of religion to happiness is empirically studied within psychology but in 'participatory' and 'multidimensional' development initiatives the religious factor also arises. For example, the Voices of the Poor study by the World Bank, which synthesized conceptions of wellbeing articulated by approximately 60,000 people in 60 countries, who consider themselves to be poor and are so considered by their community, found that "harmony" with transcendent matters (which might include a spiritual life and religious observance) was regularly considered to be part of wellbeing. If development aims at expanding the freedoms people value and have reason to value, and if religion is so valued, then religious freedoms should be part of development (alongside tolerance and democratic practices), as the 2004 Human Development Report argued.

VISION OF DEVELOPMENT

Visions of development from faith perspectives may differ significantly from economic development. As Goulet wrote, to religious groups, development experts may seem like "one-eyed giants" who "analyse, prescribe and act as if man could live by bread alone, as if human destiny could be stripped to its material dimensions alone." For example, Seyyed Hussein Nasr's writings critically evaluated modernization and development with respect to the extent to which it distracts Muslims from their true nature, or enables them to live out their true purposes better. The Roman catholic social teachings, and in particular those since Populorum Progressio, articulate a faith-based view of development in which the contributions of spiritual disciplines and of ethical action to a person's "vocation to human fulfillment" are addressed alongside contributions made by markets, public policy, and poverty reduction.

Further visions of development arise in the liberation theologies, which criticize structural injustice and call for greater religious engagement in political and economic institutions to ensure equitable development processes. While these began with the publication of Gustavo Gutierrez' Theology of Liberation, distinct liberation theologies have emerged on other major faiths. Popular books also explicate development to the faithful – such as Bernardo Klicksberg's Social Justice: A Jewish perspective or Buddhist Sulak Sivaraksa's Seeds of Peace. From the interfaith perspective, fora such as the World Faiths Development Dialogue (WFDD) have mapped areas of convergence among the faiths' visions of development agendas – relating to relationships of service and solidarity, harmony with the earth, and the vital but limited contribution of material progress. Obviously religious and secular ethical approaches to development also have strong commonalities – some of which have also been explored.

Resurgent Religion

Many had argued that religion would decline with the advent of secular development. Instead, religion has arguably surged in numbers as well as visibility. For example, over the last 100 years, "the share of the world's population that is Muslim has risen from 12.5 per cent to 20 per cent." Even in countries with low religious attendance and high levels of economic development such as the US and Switzerland, people have strong religious beliefs – they just spend less time on them. Such findings have given rise to a vigorous set of studies on the changes of religious values during development – many of which have been able to make use of substantial new data sets on religious affiliation and beliefs. Pragmatically, it has also underlined the need for the engagement between religion and development to be enduring.

Faith-based Organizations

Moving to more practical matters, local, national, and international faith-based organizations (FBOs - organizations whose motivation or funding sources derive partly from their faith) are, in some areas, significant purveyors of education, service delivery and other non-market goods. Islamic Relief, Catholic Relief Services, the Aga Khan Development Network and others deliver significant resources. The Christian evangelical development agency World Vision, with a 2003 cash budget of $819 million, and an effective budget of $1.25 billion due to in kind contributions, is among the largest and more studied of such international NGOs.

By far the greatest number of FBOs, however, is local or national. One famous example is the Sarvodaya Shramadana

Movement in Sri Lanka, founded by A. T. Ariyaratne in the 1950s, which awakened members to their inner person, and urged them then to change outer structures by common activities such as volunteer work camps – with the famous slogan "We build the road and the road builds us". In some cases religious institutions also deliver services directly; for example religious schools may be subsidized and run directly by churches or monasteries/convents. Some government programs are also faith-based – for the separation of religion and state in industrialized countries is not found in many developing countries.

The prevalence of FBOs has led to their scrutiny by development institutions but the literature is widely dispersed. Most are case studies with respect to a particular sector or region or organization. Some are countrywide – such as World Bank findings that for the poor "in Benin, church-affiliated organizations represent the most prominent and effective protection network" or that in Malawi "in the mid-1970s, it is claimed that the annual budget of a prominent ecumenical organisation, the Christian Service Committee of the Churches of Malawi, was 1.5 times the size of the entire government allocation for development.." The World Bank's World Development Report 2004: Making Services work for the poor refers frequently to religious schools and organizations as delivery mechanisms.

Religious Professionals

Professionals working in secular organizations and governments may also be motivated to in part by religion, and see their engagement with development as an outgrowth of their values. In some cases, their beliefs may impact their professional behaviour. A study of religious health care NGOs in Uganda found that despite being paid lower wages, staff of religious not for profit organizations were more likely to charge less, and to use additional funding to decrease fees and increase services, rather than to raise their own salaries. Thus the chapter concludes that staff seem partly driven by altruistic concerns, and that such behaviours quantitatively improve their performance.

In any institution (religious or secular), religious professionals may also stress the need for respect and dignity among staff and partners and thus an alternative process of collaboration. Thus faith may have an instrumental effect because people remain motivated although they witness imperfect progress. Indeed one of Gandhi's reasons for cultivating theism was pragmatic: that it sustains persons in times of failure.

Global Encounters

Interaction between poverty-focused development agencies and religious individuals and institutions is another busy intersection. For example in 1998 Jim Wolfensohn, president of the World Bank and then-Archbishop of Canterbury George Carey founded a 'World Faiths Development Dialogue' to promote dialogue between religious groups, and between the World Bank and IMF and religious groups.

It has supported case studies, and organized publications and workshops with faith and development leaders, on themes of the World Development Reports, on Poverty Reduction Strategy Papers (PRSPs) and, in 2002, on the Millennium Development Goals. Other fora include the Inter-American Development Bank's initiative on Social Capital, Ethics, and Development, the World Council of Churches Dialogues with the ILO the IMF, and the World Bank, and UNFPA's ongoing dialogue with faith leaders.

RELIGION VS. DEVELOPMENT

Religion may become a practical problem when religious leaders or institutions obstruct development, or when religious rhetoric is a veneer for other motives. Classic issues of value conflict surround family planning methods such as contraception and abortion, HIV/AIDS prevention and implicit messages related to sexual morality, and women's empowerment; other issues might relate to sacred sites, dress, or tolerance of outside groups. In development such values and practices may be addressed under the label of 'culture'. Organizations such as UNFPA have, in particular, actively cultivated respectful modes of cooperation with faith leaders and international religious institutions. Cooperation with donor countries must also navigate religious values.

For example, at the time of writing the popularity of the ABC (Abstinence, Being Faithful, and Condoms) approach to HIV/AIDS prevention was threatening US funding for condoms. Given that patriarchy is engrained in the cultural forms of many world religions, a separate literature has developed on women and religion. Many topics may relate not to development itself but rather to sexuality, prayer, family life, or violence. However an active interface occurs between religious groups and 'gender and development' agendas such as women's empowerment, reproductive health, education, or personal security. This interface is expressed in meetings as well as literature that draws attention to oppressive or theologically disputable practices towards women, and also of devout women in positions of leadership.

Religious Forces in Civil Society

Another literature addresses religion as a critical factor in civil society support for development priorities. The Global Civil Society Report 2004/5 argues that "There is no way we can understand the logic, strategies and dynamics of civil society anywhere in the Third World unless we bring the transcendental dimension back into our analysis. Religious devotion is a fundamental motive for many social movements in the South, from Latin America to Africa and South Asia." Political and social movements and advocacy campaigns have often drawn upon religious motivations and the support of religious leaders. The churches' mobilization in support of the antiapartheid campaign and the Jubilee campaign for debt forgiveness was arguably central to their political visibility; in Latin America, churches among mobilized in support of literacy.

Insofar as political parties set development agendas that can be exclusive or equity-enhancing, the religious influence on political movements is also important. In India, the rise of Hindu nationalism has been linked to the televised Hindu epic series Ramayana; and religious regimes and parties, whether in Bhutan or Iran or Arab States or Pakistan or Latin America or Europe influence development priorities to some extent. The international MDG campaigns are actively collaborating with faith groups to mobilize the faithful for advocacy and nonviolent symbolic actions.

Religious Extremism

However, benevolent and indeed inspiring some religious expressions may be, development is regularly stymied by conflict and violence – some of which is also caused by religious groups (or groups with a religious veneer). An enormous literature has blossomed, particularly after Sept 11th, on religious contributions to conflict and violence. Whether in Sri Lanka or Central Asia and Chechnya, the Middle East or Gujarat, or Bosnia or Southern Africa, armed groups have claimed religious support for their endeavours. Given that conflict both causes and exacerbates poverty, and interrupts development, careful attention needs to be paid to the possible negative consequences of cooperation with religious groups.

WEAKNESS OF WILL

The recognition of human imperfection may be the most distinctive feature of religions. While many approaches to development implicitly attribute human misbehaviour to misunderstanding, or to a lack of education, or to perverse incentives, religious groups calmly acknowledge human weakness of will, and have structured avenues for expressing sorrow and seeking and granting forgiveness among a community as well as before a deity.

Convergence or Divergence

Over the course of the 20th century, ethnic, racial and national prejudices have increasingly given way to the recognition that humankind is a single family and the earth its common homeland. The United Nations (UN), which was created in response to this dawning recognition, has worked tirelessly to bring about a world where all peoples and nations can live together in peace and harmony. To help bring about this world, the UN has crafted a remarkable framework of international institutions, processes, conventions and global action plans that have helped to prevent conflict and warfare, to protect human rights, to nurture equality between women and men, and to uplift the material conditions of countless individuals and communities.

Despite these significant achievements, the United Nations has yet to grasp fully both the constructive role that religion can play in creating a peaceful and prosperous global order, and the destructive impact that religious fanaticism can have on the stability and progress of the world. This lack of attention to religion can be clearly seen in the development realm, where the United Nations has, for the most part, viewed religious communities merely as channels for the delivery of goods and services, and as mechanisms to carry out development policies and programs. Moreover, while the United Nations' human rights machinery has been used to condemn religious intolerance and persecution, UN development policies and programs have hardly begun to address religious bigotry as a major obstacle to peace and wellbeing.

Religion as the Basis of Civilization and Progress

It is becoming increasingly clear that passage to the culminating stage in the millennia long process of the organization of the planet as one home for the entire human family cannot be accomplished in a spiritual vacuum. Religion, the Bahá'í Scriptures aver, "is the source of illumination, the cause of development and the animating impulse of all human advancement" and "has been the basis of all civilization and progress in the history of mankind." It is the source of meaning and hope for the vast majority of the planet's inhabitants, and it has a limitless power to inspire sacrifice, change and long-term commitment in its followers. It is, therefore, inconceivable that a peaceful and prosperous global society - a society which nourishes a spectacular diversity of cultures and nations - can be established and sustained without directly and substantively involving the world's great religions in its design and support.

At the same time, it cannot be denied that the power of religion has also been perverted to turn neighbor against neighbor. The Bahá'í Scriptures state that "religion must be the source of fellowship, the cause of unity and the nearness of God to man. If it rouses hatred and strife, it is evident that absence of religion is preferable and an irreligious man is better than one who professes it." So long as religious animosities are allowed to destabilize the world, it will be impossible to foster a global pattern of sustainable development: the central goal of this Summit.

INDIAN PHILOSOPHY AND RELIGION

The origin of religion in India has a long past. The deification of natural phenomena always has been seen to have a harmful influence on the religious thoughts and practice in India. The world has become alive as the Gods are possessed of the human sense of justice and they are also capable of being influenced by the human qualities like hate and love. In India, the Gods are usually presented in a more humanized manner, as they bear all the human organs like the hands, legs or even the fair skin and long beard. They also have all the human characteristics like happiness, worries, anger and they fight and feast, dance and drink, eat and rejoice, just like the human beings.

The Gods have been the symbols of the nature as well, as they are described as the owners of different natural things like rain, fire, thunderstorm, soil, wind etc. The history of the origin of religion in India therefore unveils the fact that the Indian people also used to fear the Gods, as they can become harmful and cruel, anytime when they are in great anger and they love those Gods, who are helpful in their daily pursuits. Having similarity with this view of Gods, though the Vedic worship of the natural powers is not quite sincere, it is utilitarian. The history of the origin of religion in India states that the Gods have actually become the sources of material prosperity to the Indian people and as there is a division of functions and attributes, they usually pray to the particular deities for getting some particular things.

The ancient Indian philosophers perceived the concept of Gods, as strong rather than good, powerful rather than moral and this type of a religion is quite incapable of satisfying the ethical aspirations of men. The highest religious aspiration of men to get united with the Supreme power has been recognized in the Indian philosophy and the numerous Gods, have been created to help in enabling the people to reach the Supreme. The origin of religioı. in India is therefore the saga of taming the masses. In Indian philosophy Gods were created to enable people to reach the supreme. The concept of sacrifices came to the Indian philosophy, as a consequence of the fear to God and also as a mean to satisfy the Gods, so that they do not cause any harm to the devotees. Sacrifices are seen as a symbol of the depth of one's affection towards God, as people usually sacrifice their best property or possessions to the God.

However, there have been a lot of debates about the question of human sacrifice, as many of the ancient Indian philosophers raised their voices against this, saying that the concept of human sacrifices is neither allowed nor encouraged in the Vedas. They quoted the Sama Veda that says, "O, Ye Gods! We use no sacrificial stake. We slay no victim. We worship entirely by the repetition of the sacred verses". The Upanishads and the Buddhist and Jaina schools did adopt this protesting nature at a later period. The sacrifices actually represent the second stage of the Vedic religion, as the first stage talked only about simple prayer. The Parasarasmriti says, "Meditation in the Krtayuga, sacrifices in the Treta, worship in the Dvapara, praises and prayers in Kali". The Vishnupurana also says that the rules of sacrifices have actually formulated in the Tretayuga. The growth of religious practice in India has been so far, like from meditation to sacrifice, from sacrifice to worship and then from worship to praise and prayer.

Another aspect of the Indian philosophy in the ancient times is that, the people in ancient India had direct communion with the Gods, without the requirements of any meditation. There were no temples for the Gods in that period and people used to look upon the Gods as friends, rather than worshippers. This is the main reason why the terms like "Father Heaven", "Mother Earth" or "Brother Agni", have emerged from the ancient time in India. The ancient people used to share an intimate personal relationship with the Gods and religion dominated their entire life. They were also completely dependant on the Gods even for the ordinary necessities of their daily life. The Vedic religion, which tells the origin of religion of India, also described the concept of Sin quite elaborately and according to the Vedic religion, Sin is actually the alienation from God.

This definition of Sin in the Vedic religion is quite similar to that in the Hebrew theory and the Vedic religion has described the will of God, as the standard of morality. The Vedic religion says that the human guilt is shortcoming and people usually commit a sin when they transgress the commands of God, as the Gods are the upholders of the moral order of the world. It is the Gods, who protect the good and punish the wicked. The Vedic religion also says that Sin is not merely the omission of the external duties, as there are both moral and ritual sins. According to the ancient Indian philosophy, the consciousness of sin usually calls for propitiatory sacrifices. As a rule, the Gods of the Rig-Veda are always regarded as the guardians of morality in the Indian philosophy.

STUDY OF WORLD RELIGIONS

From the earliest known evidence of human religion by Homo Sapiens Neanderthalensis around 100,000 years ago to the present day, religion continues to be a very influential aspect of human lives. Today, there are numerous challenges and problems faced by humans from every possible background, location and social class. Every day people must face issues of health, safety and mortality. It is because of these daily challenges that religion continues to exist. Religion is the universal tool for explaining things which we do not understand through the context of the known physical world. Although there are countless religions, each different from the other, they all serve the same purpose. Each answers questions which all humans seem to be programmed to ask: Why are we here? What happens when I die? How shall I live my life?

Religion helps us to transmit our values from one generation to another, and influences the way we interact with the natural environment. It teaches us how to see ourselves in light of the universe and gives purpose and meaning to life. The following pages serve as a brief introduction to several world religions. They are intended to whet your appetite for further study and to help you understand those around you better. With our global society, it is likely that in your lifetime you will meet people from every corner of the planet. Understanding the religious beliefs of these people is one of the many steps which mankind must take in order to someday prosper together in peace.

Hinduism

Hinduism is a term, for a wide variety of related religious traditions native to India. Historically, it encompasses the development of Religion in India since the Iron Age traditions, which in turn hark back to prehistoric religions such as that of the Bronze Age Indus Valley Civilization followed by the Vedic religion. Hindu philosophy had six branches, evolving from about the 2nd century BCE to the 6th century CE, viz. Samkhya, Yoga, Nyaya, Vaisheshika, Mimamsa, and Vedanta. Monotheistic religions like Shaivism and Vaishnavism developed during this same period through the Bhakti movement.

Classical Pauranic Hinduism is established in the middle Ages, as was Adi Shankara's Advaita Vedanta which reconciled the Vaishna and Shaiva sects, and gave rise to Smartism, while initiating the decline of the non-Vedantic schools of philosophy. Hinduism under the Islamic Rulers saw the increasing prominence of the Bhakti movement, which remains influential today. The colonial period saw the emergence of various Hindu reform movements partly inspired by western culture, such as spiritism (Theosophy). The Partition of India in 1947 was along religious lines, with the Republic of India emerging with a Hindu majority.

During the 20th century, due to the Indian diaspora, Hindu minorities have formed in all continents, with the largest communities in the United States and the United Kingdom. In the Republic of India, Hindu nationalism has emerged as a strong political force since the 1980s, the religious right Bharatiya Janata Party forming the Government of India from 1999 to 2004, and its first state government in southern India in 2006.

Evidence of prehistoric religion in India is found in the Bronze Age Indus Valley Civilization, showing the certain elements of Hinduism such as baths (assumed to serve a ritual purpose) and phallic symbols, compared to the Shiva lingam. There were also found Swastika signs. Many male and female figurines, the female figurines popularly dubbed "Mother Goddesses" have been found in the Indus Valley, although some have expressed doubt as to the divine character of these female figures. A seal discovered during excavation of the Mohenjo-daro archaeological site in the Indus Valley has drawn attention as a possible representation of a "yogi" or "proto-Shiva" figure.

This "Pashupati" (Lord of Animals, Sanskrit paœupati) seal shows a seated figure, possibly ithyphallic, surrounded by animals. Some observers describe the figure as sitting in a traditional cross-legged yoga pose with its hands resting on its knees. The discoverer of the seal, Sir John Marshall, and others have claimed that this figure is a prototype of Shiva, and have described the figure as having three faces, seated in a "yoga posture" with the knees out and feet joined.

Vedic Period

Vedism was the sacrificial religion of the early Indo-European-speaking peoples who entered India from about 1500 BC from the Iranian plateau via the Hindukush and mixed up with the local populations. The earliest literature of Hinduism is made up of the four Vedas: the Rig-Veda, Sama-Veda, Yajur-Veda and the Atharva-Veda. Of these, the Rig-Veda is the oldest surviving work. These texts were composed between ca. 1500 and 800 BC, and were transmitted by oral tradition alone until the advent of the Pallava and Gupta period and by a combination of written and oral tradition since then.

Rigvedic Religion

The earliest text of the Vedas is the Rigveda, a collection of poetic hymns used in the sacrificial rites of Vedic priesthood. Many Rigvedic hymns concern the fire ritual (Agnihotra) and especially the offering of Soma to the gods (Somayajna). Soma is both an intoxicant and a god itself, as is the sacrificial fire, Agni. The royal horse sacrifice (Ashvamedha) is a central rite in the Yajurveda. The gods in the Rig-Veda are mostly personified concepts, who fall into two categories: the devas, who were gods of nature, such as the King of the gods, the weather deity Indra, Agni ("fire"), and Ushas ("dawn"), Surya "sun", Apas "waters", and on the other hand, the asuras, gods of moral concepts, such as Mitra ("contract"), Aryaman (guardian of guest friendship and marriage), Bhaga "share" or Varuna, the supreme Asura (or Aditya). While Rigvedic deva is variously applied to most gods, including many of the Asuras, the Devas are characterized as Younger Gods while Asuras are the Older Gods (pûrve devâ%). In later Vedic texts, the Asuras become demons.

The Rigveda has 10 Mandalas ('books'). There is significant variation in the language and style between the family books (2-7), book 8, the "Soma Mandala" (RV 9), and the more recent books 1 and 10. The older book share many aspects of common Indo-Iranian religion and is an important source for the reconstruction of earlier common Indo-European traditions. Especially RV 8 has striking similarity to the Avesta, containing allusions to Afghan Flora and Fauna, e.g. to camels (úcmra- = Avestan uštra. Many of the central religious terms in Vedic Sanskrit have cognates in the religious vocabulary of other Indo-European languages (deva: Latin deus; hotar: Germanic god; asura: Germanic ansuz; yajna: Greek hagios; brahman: Norse Bragi (or perhaps Latin flamen) etc.). Especially notable is the fact, which in the Avesta Asura (Ahura) is known as good and Deva (Daeva) as evil entity, quite the opposite of the RigVeda.

Brahmanism

In Iron Age India, during a period roughly spanning the 10th to 6th centuries BC, the Mahajanapadas arise from the earlier petty kingdoms of the various Rigvedic tribes, and the failing remnants of the Late Harappan culture. In this period the mantra portions of the Vedas are largely completed, and a flowering industry of Vedic priesthood organized in numerous schools (shakha) develops exegetical literature, viz. the Brahmanas. These schools also edited the Vedic mantra portions into fixed recensions, which were to be preserved purely by oral tradition over the following two millennia. This period of dominance of priestly Brahmanic Hinduism declines with the appearance of mystical traditions (the oldest Upanishads, BAU, ChU and JUB besides the Shatapatha Brahmana) attacking the rigid ritualism available only to the elite, in favour of spiritual insight through asceticism and meditation.

The rise of Buddhism at this time, according to tradition originating with Gautama Buddha, a 6th century BC Hindu prince, renouncing his status for enlightenment, is exemplary of this tendency. Politically, the Mahajanapadas declined, in the west falling to the invasion of Darius the Great, and from the east absorbed into the Magadha Empire which as the Maurya Empire would encompass almost the whole subcontinent by the time of Ashoka.

Vedism Today

Vedism as the religious tradition of Hinduism of a priestly elite was marginalized by other traditions such as Jainism and Buddhism in the later Iron Age, but in the Middle Ages would rise to renewed prestige with the Mimamsa school, which as well as all other astika traditions of Hinduism, considered them authorless (apaurusheyatva) and eternal. Srauta tradition, following many major elements of Vedic religion and is prominent in Southern India, with communities in Tamil Nadu, Kerala, Karnataka, Andhra Pradesh, but also in some pockets of Uttar Pradesh, Maharashtra and other states; the best known of these groups are the Nambudiri of Kerala, whose traditions were notably documented by Frits Staal.

Hinduism in the narrow sense (to the exclusion of Vedism and Iron Age Brahmanism) is the new religious mainstream arising with the decline of Buddhism in India and from about the 4th century AD.

Mauryan and Sangam Period

The Mauryan period saw an early flowering of classical Sanskrit Sutra and Shastra literature and the scholarly exposition of the "circum-Vedic" fields of the Vedanga. However, during this time Buddhism was patronized by Ashoka, who ruled large parts of India, and Buddhism was also the mainstream religion 'til the Gupta empire period. The Sangam literature (300 BC - 300 AD) is a mostly secular body of classical literature in the Tamil language. Nonetheless there are some works, significantly Pattupathu and Paripaatal, wherein the personal devotion to god was written in form of devotional poems. Vishnu, Shiva and Murugan were mentioned gods. These works are therefore the earliest evidences of monotheistic Bhakti traditions, preceding the large bhakti movement, which will give great attention in later times.

Gupta and Pallava Period

The Pallavas (4th to 9th centuries) were alongside the Guptas patronizers of Sanskrit. The pallava reign saw the first Sankrit inscriptions in a script called Grantha. Early Pallavas had different connections to South-East Asian countries. The Pallavas used Dravidian architecture to build some very important Hindu temples and academies in Mamallapuram, Kanchipuram and other places, which saw famous poets like Kalidasa. The Gupta period (4th to 6th centuries) saw a flowering of scholarship, the emergence of the classical schools of Hindu philosophy, and of classical Sanskrit literature in general on topics ranging from medicine, veterinary science, mathematics, to astrology and astronomy and astrophysics.

The famous Aryabhata and Varahamihira belong to this age. The Gupta established a strong central government which also allowed a degree of local control. Gupta society was ordered in accordance with Hindu beliefs. This included a strict caste system, or class system. The peace and prosperity created under Gupta leadership enabled the pursuit of scientific and artistic endeavors. The practice of dedicating temples to different deities came into vogue followed by fine artistic temple architecture and sculpture.

Expansion in South-East Asia

From about the 1st century, India started to strongly influence Southeast Asian countries. Trade routes linked India with southern Burma, central and southern Siam, lower Cambodia and southern Vietnam and numerous urbanized coastal settlements were established there. For more than a thousand years, Indian Hindu/Buddhist influence was therefore the major factor that brought a certain level of cultural unity to the various countries of the region. The Pali and Sanskrit languages and the Indian script, together with Theravada and Mahayana Buddhism, Brahmanism and Hinduism, were transmitted from direct contact as well as through sacred texts and Indian literature, such as the Ramayana and the Mahabharata epics. From the 5th to the 13th century, South-East Asia had very powerful Indian colonial empires and became extremely active in Buddhist architectural and artistic creation.

The Sri Vijaya Empire to the south and the Khmer Empire to the north competed for influence. Langkasuka (langkha Sanskrit for "resplendent land" -sukkha of "bliss") was an ancient Hindu kingdom located in the Malay Peninsula. The kingdom, along with Old Kedah settlement, is probably the earliest territorial footholds founded on the Malay Peninsula. According to tradition, the founding of the kingdom happened in the 2nd century; Malay legends claim that Langkasuka was founded at Kedah, and later moved to Pattani. From the 5th-15th centuries Sri Vijayan empire, a maritime empire centered on the island of Sumatra in Indonesia, had adopted Mahayana and Vajrayana Buddhism under a line of rulers named the Sailendras.

The Empire of Sri Vijaya declined due to conflicts with the Chola rulers of India. The Majapahit Empire succeeded the Singhasari Empire. It was one of the last and greatest Hindu empires in the Malay Archipelago. Funan was a pre-Angkor Cambodian kingdom, located around the Mekong delta, probably established by Mon-Khmer settlers speaking an Austro-Asiatic language. According to reports by two Chinese envoys, K'ang T'ai and Chu Ying, the state was established by an Indian Brahmin named Kaundinya, who in the first century C.E. was given instruction in a dream to take a magic bow from a temple and defeat a Khmer queen, Soma. Soma, the daughter of the king of the Nagas, married Kaundinya and their lineage became the royal dynasty of Funan.

The myth had the advantage of providing the legitimacy of both an Indian Brahmin and the divinity of the cobras, who at that time were held in religious regard by the inhabitants of the region. The kingdom of Champa (or Lin-yi in Chinese records) controlled what is now south and central Vietnam from approximately 192 through 1697. The dominant religion of the Cham people was Hinduism and the culture was heavily influenced by India. Later, from the 9th to the 13th century, the Mahayana Buddhist and Hindu Khmer Empire dominated much of the South-East Asian peninsula. Under the Khmer, more than 900 temples were built in Cambodia and in neighboring Thailand. Angkor was at the center of this development, with a temple complex and urban organization able to support around one million urban dwellers. The largest temple complex of the world, Angkor Wat, stands here; built by the king Vishnuvardhan, a king of the dynasty that believed them to be incarnations of Vishnu.

By the 8th century, the "Hindu golden age" of the past millennium was over. The formerly rich philosophic literature tended to be reduced to scholastic quarreling and infighting between innumerable sects, notably between emerging traditions of Vaishnavism and Shaivism. Adi Shankara in the 8th century managed to reconcile the antagonistic sects and to establish Hinduism as a single, if diverse, religious tradition. The compilation of the Puranas provided a mythical backdrop for this tradition, and served as a means of acculturation of the various preliterate tribal societies to the new religious mainstream. Various reforms of the later middle Ages, notably the Bhakti movement, besides new Yogic schools (Jnana yoga, Karma yoga, Hatha yoga, Bhakti yoga) gave Hinduism its classical form as described by the 18th to 19th century pioneers of Indology.

Bhakti Movement

The Bhakti movement was a Hindu religious movement in which the main spiritual practice was the fostering of loving devotion to God, called bhakti. It was a monotheistic movement generally devoted to worship of Shiva, Vishnu or Shakti. The first documented bhakti movement was founded by Karaikkal-ammaiyar. She wrote poems in Tamil about her love for Shiva and probably lived around the 6th century CE.

The twelve Alvars who were Vaishnavite devotees and the sixty-three Nayanars who were Shaivite devotees nurtured the incipient bhakti movement in Tamil Nadu. They constitute South India's 75 Apostles of Bhakti. During the 12th century CE in Karnataka, the Bhakti movement took the form of the

Virashaiva movement. It was inspired by Basavanna, a Hindu reformer who created the sect of Lingayats or Shiva bhaktas. During this time, a unique and native form of Kannada literature-poetry called Vachanas was born.

Advaita Vedanta

The introduction of Advaita Vedanta by Adi Shankara unified the theistic sects into a common framework of Shanmata system. Shankara stressed the importance of the Vedas, introducing the concept of apaurusheyatva, and his efforts helped Hinduism regain strength and popularity. He is the main figure in the tradition of Advaita Vedanta. He is the founder of the Dashanami Sampradaya of Hindu monasticism and Shanmata tradition of worship. He travelled all over India (Kerala to Kashmir and Nepal) three times over and was a major cause in the revival and integration of Sanatana Dharma. Shankara's reform essentially eclipsed all earlier schools of Hindu philosophy and became the nucleus of the medieval traditions, including Smartism and Sant Mat lineages, that lead up to the current religion.

Adi Shankara, along with Madhva and Ramanuja, were instrumental in the revival of Hinduism. In their writings and debates, they provided polemics against the non-Vedantic schools of Sankhya, Vaisheshika etc. Thus, they paved the way for Vedanta to be the dominant and most widely followed tradition among the schools of Hindu philosophy.

Pauranic Hinduism

Brahmanic Hinduism evolves out of Vedism during Iron Age India, and in turn contributes to the development of Vedantic and eventually classical Pauranic Hinduism. The transformation of Brahmanism into Pauranic Hinduism in post-Gupta India was due to a process of acculturation. The Puranas helped establish a religious mainstream among the preliterate tribal societies undergoing acculturation. The tenets of Brahmanic Hinduism and of the Dharmashastras underwent a radical transformation at the hands of the Purana composers, resulting in the rise of a mainstream "Hinduism" that overshadowed all earlier traditions.

Muslim Conquests

Muslim rulers began to extend their rule across Hindu-Buddhist populated lands in the 8th century CE and the Abrahamic religion of Islam began to spread across the Indian-subcontinent over several centuries. Most converts were from Hinduism or Buddhism, the two dominant local religions. Bhakti poetry of lasting greatness was composed in northern India under the rule of Muslim emperors. The humble mystic saint Kabir, who established his own order, composed devotional verses in the Bhakti spirit, but in common-man's Hindi dialect and transcendenting Hindu-Muslim theocratic divide. Tulsidas, Mira Bai and Surdas composed immortal Hindu devotional poetry in Hindi-dialects in the Mughal period - it is reminiscent of the earlier Kannada and Tamil Bhakti poetry of South India.

In the 16th to 18th centuries, the Mughal Empire reduced its Hindu subjects to Dhimmitude throughout the 17th century; the empire had reached its zenith by 1700. But, Hinduism once again rose to political prestige, under the Maratha Empire, from 1707 to 1761. In the century from 1760 to 1860, India was once more divided into numerous petty and unstable kingdoms: the Sikh Confederacy; the "lesser Mughals" following Bahadur Shah I; the Kingdom of Mysore; Hyderabad State; the Durrani Empire; and the territories held by the British East India Company. The entire subcontinent fell under British rule (partly indirectly, via Princely states) following the Indian Rebellion of 1857.

The official State religion of the Mughal Empire was Islam, with the preference to the jurisprudence of the Hanafi Madhab (Mazhab). However, throughout its history, subjects had complete freedom to practice any religion of their choice, though Non-Muslim able-bodied adult males with income were obliged to pay the Jizya (poll-tax to be spent by the State only on protection of non-Muslims), which signified their status as Dhimmis (responsibility of the State, in regard to safety of life and property).

After the invasion of Persia by the Mongol Empire, a regional Turko-Persio-Mongol dynasty formed. Just as eastern Mongol dynasties inter-married with locals and adopted the local religion of Buddhism and the Chinese culture, this group adopted the local religion of Islam and the Persian culture. One of Akbar's most unusual ideas regarding religion was Din-i-Ilahi (Faith of God), which was an eclectic mix of Islam, Zoroastrianism, Hinduism, Jainism and Christianity. It was proclaimed the state religion until his death. These actions however met with stiff opposition from the Muslim clergy, especially the Sufi Shaykh Alf Sani Ahmad Sirhindi.

Akbar's abolition of poll-tax on non-Muslims, acceptance of ideas from other religious philosophies, toleration of public worship by all religions and his interest in other faiths showed an attitude of considerable religious tolerance, which, in the minds of his orthodox Muslim opponents, were tantamount to apostasy. The emperor Jahangir, half Rajput, was also a religious moderate, his mother being Hindu. The influence of his two Hindu queens (the Maharani Maanbai and Maharani Jagat) kept religious moderation as a centerpiece of state policy which was extended under his son, emperor Shah Jahan, who was by blood 75% Rajput and only 25% Moghul.

Religious orthodoxy would only play an important role during the reign of Shah Jahan's son and successor, Aurangzeb, a devout Sunni Muslim. Aurangzeb was comparatively less tolerant of other faiths than his predecessors had been, and his reign saw an increase in the number and importance of Islamic institutions and scholars. He led many military campaigns against the remaining non-Muslim powers of the Indian subcontinent - the Sikh states of the Punjab, the last independent Hindu Rajputs and the Maratha rebels - as also against the Shia Muslim kingdoms of the Deccan. He also virtually stamped out, from his empire, open proselytisation of Hindus and Muslims by foreign Christian Missionaries, who remained successfully active, however, in the adjoining regions: the present day Kerala, Tamil Nadu and Goa.

Portuguese missionaries had reached the Malabar Coast in the late 15th century, made contact with the St Thomas Christians in Kerala and sought to introduce the Latin Rite among them. Since the priests for St Thomas Christians were served by the Eastern Christian Churches, they were following Eastern Christian practices at that time. Throughout this period, foreign missionaries also made many new converts to Christianity. This led to the formation of the Latin Catholics in Kerala. The Goa Inquisition was the office of the Inquisition acting in the Indian city of Goa and the rest of the Portuguese empire in Asia. St. Francis Xavier, in a 1545 letter to John III, requested for an Inquisition to be installed in Goa. It was installed eight years after the death of Francis Xavier in 1552. Established in 1560 and operating until 1774, this highly controversial institution was aimed primarily at Hindus and wayward new converts.

The Hindu Marathas long had lived in the Desh region around Satara, in the western portion of the Deccan plateau, where the plateau meets the eastern slopes of the Western Ghats Mountains. They had resisted incursions into the region by the Muslim Mughal rulers of northern India. Under their ambitious leader Shivaji, the Maratha freed themselves from the Muslim sultans of Bijapur to the southeast and, becoming much more aggressive, began to frequently raid Mughal territory, eventually sacking the wealthy Mughal port of Surat in 1664. After substantial territorial gains, Shivaji was proclaimed 'Chatrapati' (Emperor) in 1674; the Marathas had spread and conquered much of central India by Shivaji's death in 1680.

During the 19th century, Hinduism developed a large number of new religious movements, partly inspired by the European Romanticism, nationalism, scientific racism and esotericism

(Theosophy) popular at the time (while conversely and contemporaneously, India had a similar effect on European culture with Orientalism, "Hindoo style" architecture, reception of Buddhism in the West and similar).

These reform movements are summarized under Hindu revivalism and continue into the present.

- Sahajanand Swami establishes the Swaminarayan Sampraday sect around 1800.
- Brahmo Samaj is a social and religious movement founded in Kolkata in 1828 by Raja Ram Mohan Roy. He was one of the first Indians to visit Europe and was influenced by western thought. He died in Bristol, England. The Brahmo Samaj movement thereafter resulted in the Brahmo religion in 1850 founded by Debendranath Tagore — better known as the father of Rabindranath Tagore.
- Sri Ramakrishna and his pupil Swami Vivekananda led a reform in Hinduism in late 19th century. Their ideals and sayings have inspired numerous Indians as well as non-Indians, Hindus as well as non-Hindus. Among the prominent figures whose ideals were very much influenced by them were Rabindranath Tagore, Gandhi, Subhas Bose, Satyendranath Bose, Megh Nad Saha, and Sister Nivedita.
- Arya Samaj ("Society of Nobles") is a Hindu reform movement in India that was founded by Swami Dayananda in 1875. He was a sannyasin (renouncer) who believed in the infallible authority of the Vedas. Dayananda advocated the doctrine of karma and reincarnation, and emphasised the ideals of brahmacharya (chastity) and sanyasa (renunciation). Dayananda claimed to be rejecting all non-Vedic beliefs altogether. Hence the Arya Samaj unequivocally condemned idolatry, animal sacrifices, ancestor worship, pilgrimages, priestcraft, offerings made in temples, the caste system, untouchability and child marriages, on the grounds that all these lacked Vedic sanction. It aimed to be a universal church based on the authority of the Vedas. Dayananda stated that he wanted 'to make the whole world Aryan', i.e. he wanted to develop

missionary Hinduism based on the universality of the Vedas. To this end, the Arya Samaj started Shuddhi movement in early 20th century to bring back to Hinduism people converted to Islam and Christianity, set up schools and missionary organisations, and extended its activities outside India. It now has branches around the world and has a disproportional number of adherents among people of Indian ancestry in Suriname and the Netherlands, in comparison with India.

An important aspect of 20th-century Hinduism has been its spread among non-Indians, who have accepted the religion voluntarily. This perhaps began with the sojourn of Vivekananda to the World Parliament of Religions in Chicago in 1893. He founded the Ramakrishna Mission, which today operates temples, ashrams, charitable hospitals, and schools worldwide.

Contemporary Hinduism

As of 2007, of an estimated 944 million Hindus, 98.5% live in South Asia. Of the remaining 1.5% or 14 million, 6 million live in Southeast Asia (mostly Indonesia), 2 million in Europe, 1.8 million in North America, 1.2 million in Southern Africa. Modern Hinduism is the reflection of continuity and progressive changes that occurred in various traditions and institutions of Hinduism during the 19th and 20th centuries. Its main divisions are into Vaishnavism (largely influenced by Bhakti), Shaivism, Shaktism and Smartism (Advaita Vedanta).

Besides these traditional denominations, movements of Hindu revivalism look to founders such as Swami Vivekananda, Swami Dayananda (Arya Samaj), Rabindranath Tagore, Ramana Maharshi, Aurobindo, Shriram Sharma Acharya, Swami Sivananda, Swami Rama Tirtha, Narayana Guru, Paramhansa Yogananda, Shrii Shrii Anandamurti, Pandurang Shastri Athavale (Swadhyay Movement) and others. Influential in spreading Hinduism to a western audience were A.C. Bhaktivedanta Swami Prabhupada (Hare

Krishna movement), Sri Aurobindo, Meher Baba, Jiddu Krishnamurti, Osho, Maharishi Mahesh Yogi (Transcendental Meditation), Sathya Sai Baba, Mother Meera, among others.

The Hindutva movement advocating Hindu nationalism originated in the 1920s and has remained a strong political force in India. The major party of the religious right, Bharatiya Janata Party, since its foundation in 1980 has won several elections, and after a defeat in 2004 remains the leading force of opposition against the current Congress Party government. The resurgence of Hinduism in Indonesia is occurring in all parts of the country. In the early seventies, the Toraja people of Sulawesi were the first to be identified under the umbrella of 'Hinduism', followed by the Karo Batak of Sumatra in 1977 and the Ngaju Dayak of Kalimantan in 1980.

The growth of Hinduism has been driven also by the famous Javanese prophesies of Sabdapalon and Jayabaya. Many recent converts to Hinduism had been members of the families of Sukarno's PNI, and now support Megawati Sukarnoputri. This return to the 'religion of Majapahit' (Hinduism) is a matter of nationalist pride. The new Hindu communities in Java tend to be concentrated around recently built temples (pura) or around archaeological temple sites (candi) which are being reclaimed as places of Hindu worship. An important new Hindu temple in eastern Java is Pura Mandaragiri Sumeru Agung, located on the slope of Mt. Semeru, Java's highest mountain.

Mass conversions have also occurred in the region around Pura Agung Blambangan, another new temple, built on a site with minor archaeological remnants attributed to the kingdom of Blambangan, the last Hindu polity on Java, and Pura Loka Moksa Jayabaya (in the village of Menang near Kediri), where the Hindu king and prophet Jayabaya is said to have achieved spiritual liberation (moksa). Another site is the new Pura Pucak Raung in East Java, which is mentioned in Balinese literature as the place from where Maharishi Markandeya took Hinduism to Bali in the fifth century CE.

Buddhism

Soon after Buddha's death or parinirvana, five hundred monks met at the first council at Rajagrha, under the leadership of Kashyapa. Upali recited the monastic code (Vinaya) as he remembered it. Ananda, Buddha's cousin, friend, and favorite disciple — and a man of prodigious memory! - recited Buddha's lessons (the Sutras). The monks debated details and voted on final versions. These were then committed to memory by other monks, to be translated into the many languages of the Indian plains. It should be noted that Buddhism remained an oral tradition for over 200 years. In the next few centuries, the original unity of Buddhism began to fragment. The most significant split occurred after the second council, held at Vaishali 100 years after the first.

After debates between a more liberal group and traditionalists, the liberal group left and labeled themselves the Mahasangha — "the great sangha." They would eventually evolve into the Mahayana tradition of northern Asia. The traditionalists, now referred to as Sthaviravada or "way of the elders" (or, in Pali, Theravada), developed a complex set of philosophical ideas beyond those elucidated by Buddha. These were collected into the Abhidharma or "higher teachings." But they, too, encouraged disagreements, so that one splinter groups after another left the fold. Ultimately, 18 schools developed, each with their own interpretations of various issues, and spread all over India and Southeast Asia. Today, only the school stemming from the Sri Lankan Theravadan survives.

Ashoka

One of the most significant events in the history of Buddhism is the chance encounter of the monk Nigrodha and the emperor Ashoka Maurya. Ashoka, succeeding his father after a bloody power struggle in 268 BC, found himself deeply disturbed by the carnage he caused while suppressing a revolt in the land of the Kalingas. Meeting Nigrodha convinced Emperor Ashoka to devote himself to peace. On his orders, thousands of rock pillars were erected, bearing the words of the Buddha, in the brahmi script — the first written evidence of Buddhism. The third council of monks was held at Pataliputra, the capital of Ashoka's empire.

There is a story that tells about a poor young boy who, having nothing to give the Buddha as a gift, collected a handful of dust and innocently presented it. The Buddha smiled and accepted it with the same graciousness he accepted the gifts of wealthy admirers. That boy, it is said, was reborn as the Emperor Ashoka. He sent missionaries all over India and beyond. Some went as far as Egypt, Palestine, and Greece. St. Origen even mentions them as having reached Britain.

The Greeks of one of the Alexandrian kingdoms of northern India adopted Buddhism, after their King Menan-dros (Pali: Milinda) was convinced by a monk named Nagasena — the conversation immortalized in the Milinda Pañha. A Kushan king of north India named Kanishka was also converted, and a council was held in Kashmir in about 100 AD. Greek Buddhists there recorded the Sutras on copper sheets which, unfortunately, were never recovered. It is interesting to note that there is a saint in Orthodox Christianity named Josaphat, an Indian king whose story is essentially that of the Buddha. Josaphat is thought to be a distortion of the word bodhisattva.

Sri Lanka and Theravada

Emperor Ashoka sent one of his sons, Mahinda, and one of his daughters, Sanghamitta, a monk and a nun, to Sri Lanka (Ceylon) around the year 240 BC. The king of Sri Lanka, King Devanampiyatissa, welcomed them and was converted. One of the gifts they brought with them was a branch of the bodhi tree, which was successfully transplanted. The descendants of this branch can still be found on the island.

The fourth council was held in Sri Lanka, in the Aloka Cave, in the first century BC. During this time as well, and for the first time, the entire set of Sutras were recorded in the Pali language on palm leaves. This became Theravada's Pali Canon, from which so much of our knowledge of Buddhism stems. It is also called the Tripitaka (Pali: Tipitaka), or three baskets: The three sections of the canon are the Vinaya Pitaka (the monastic law), the Sutta Pitaka (words of the Buddha), and the Abhidamma Pitaka (the philosophical commentaries).

In a very real sense, Sri Lanka's monks may be credited with saving the Theravada tradition: Although it had spread once from India all over Southeast Asia, it had nearly died out due to competition from Hinduism and Islam, as well as war and colonialism. Theravada monks spread their tradition from Sri Lanka to Burma, Thailand, Malaysia, Cambodia, and Laos, and from these lands to Europe and the west generally.

Mahayana

Mahayana began in the first century BC, as a development of the Mahasangha rebellion. Their more liberal attitudes toward monastic tradition allowed the lay community to have a greater voice in the nature of Buddhism. For better or worse, the simpler needs of the common folk were easier for the Mahayanists to meet. For example, the people were used to gods and heroes. So, the Trikaya (three bodies) doctrine came into being: Not only was Buddha a man who became enlightened, he was also represented by various godlike Buddhas in various appealing heavens, as well as by the Dharma itself, or Shunyata (emptiness), or Buddha-Mind, depending on which interpretation we look at — sort of a Buddhist Father, Son, and Holy Ghost!

More important, however, was the increased importance of the Bodhisattva. A Bodhisattva is someone who has attained enlightenment, but who chooses to remain in this world of Samsara in order to bring others to enlightenment. He is a lot like a saint, a spiritual hero, for the people to admire and appeal to. Along with new ideas came new scriptures. Also called Sutras, they are often attributed to Buddha himself, sometimes as special transmissions that Buddha supposedly felt were too difficult for his original listeners and therefore were hidden until the times were ripe. The most significant of these new

Sutras are these:

- Prajñaparamita or Perfection of Wisdom, an enormous collection of often esoteric texts, including the famous Heart Sutra and Diamond Sutra. The earliest known piece of printing in the world is, in fact, a copy of the Diamond Sutra, printed in China in 868 AD.
- Suddharma-pundarika or White Lotus of the True Dharma, also often esoteric, includes the Avalokiteshwara Sutra, a prayer to that Bodhisattva.
- Vimalakirti-nirdesha or Vimalakirti's Exposition is the teachings of and stories about the enlightened householder Vimalakirti.
- Shurangama-samadhi or Hero's Sutra provides a guide to meditation, shunyata, and the bodhisattva. It is most popular among Zen Buddhists
- Sukhavati-vyuha or Pure Land Sutra is the most important Sutra for the Pure Land Schools of Buddhism. The Buddha tells Ananda about Amitabha and his Pure Land or heaven, and how one can be reborn there.

There are many, many others. Finally, Mahayana is founded on two new philosophical interpretations of Buddhism: Madhyamaka and Yogachara.

Madhyamaka

Madhyamaka means "the middle way." You may recall that Buddha himself called his way the middle way in his very first sermon. He meant, at that time, the middle way between the extremes of hedonistic pleasure and extreme asceticism. But he may also have referred to the middle way between the competing philosophies of eternalism and annihilationism — the belief that the soul exists forever and that the soul is annihilated at death or between materialism and nihilism.... An Indian monk by the name of Nagarjuna took this idea and expanded on it to create the philosophy that would be known as Madhyamaka, in a book called the Mulamadhyamaka-karika, written about 150 AD.

Basically a treatise on logical argument, it concludes that nothing is absolute, everything is relative, nothing exists on its own, and everything is interdependent. All systems, beginning with the idea that each thing is what it is and not something else (Aristotle's law of the excluded middle), wind up contradicting themselves. Rigorous logic, in other words, leads one away from all systems, and to the concept of shunyata. Shunyata means emptiness. This doesn't mean that nothing exists. It means that nothing exists in and of itself, but only as a part of a universal web of being. This would become a central concept in all branches of Mahayana. Of course, it is actually a restatement of the central Buddhist concepts of anatman, anitya, and dukkha.

Yogachara

The second philosophical innovation, Yogachara, is credited to two brothers, Asanga and Vasubandhu, who lived in India in the 300's AD. They elaborated earlier movements in the direction of the philosophy of idealism or chitta-matra. Chitta-matra means literally mind only. Asanga and Vasubandhu believed that everything that exists is mind or consciousness. What we think of as physical things are just projections of our minds, delusions or hallucinations, if you like. To get rid of these delusions, we must meditate, which for the Yogachara School means the creation of pure consciousness, devoid of all content. In that way, we leave our deluded individual minds and join with the universal mind, or Buddha-mind.

Tantra

The last innovation was less philosophical and far more practical: Tantra. It refers to certain writings which are concerned, not with philosophical niceties, but with the basic how-to of enlightenment, and not just with enlightenment in several rebirths, but enlightenment here-and-now. In order to accomplish this feat, dramatic methods are needed ones which, to the uninitiated, may seem rather bizarre. Tantra was the domain of the siddhu, the adept — someone who knows the secrets, a magician in the ways of enlightenment. Tantra involves the use of various techniques, including the wellknown mandalas, mantras, and mudras. mandalas are paintings or other representations of higher awareness, usually in the form of a circular pattern of images, which may provide the focus of one-pointed meditation. Mantras are words or phrases that serve the same purpose, such as the famous "Om mani padme hum." Mudras are hand positions that symbolize certain qualities of enlightenment.

Less well known are the yidams. A yidam is the image of a god or goddess or other spiritual being, either physically represented or, more commonly, imagined clearly in the mind's eye. Again, these represent archetypal qualities of enlightenment, and one-pointed meditation on these complex images lead the adept to his or her goal. These ideas would have enormous impact on Mahayana. They are not without critics, however: Madhyamaka is sometimes criticized as word-play, and Yogachara is criticized as reintroducing atman, eternal soul or essence, to Buddhism. Tantra has been most often criticized, especially for its emphasis on secret methods and strong devotion to a guru. Nevertheless, these innovations led to a renewed flurry of activity in the first half of the first millenium, and provided the foundation for the kinds of Buddhism we find in China, Tibet, Japan, Korea, Vietnam, and elsewhere in East Asia.

China

Legend has it that the Chinese Emperor Ming Ti had a dream which led him to send his agents down the Silk Road — the ancient trade route between China and the west — to discover its meaning. The agents returned with a picture of the Buddha and a copy of the Sutra in 42 Sections. This Sutra would, in 67 AD, be the first of many to be translated into Chinese.

The first Buddhist community in China is thought to be one in Loyang, established by "foreigners" around 150 AD, in the Han dynasty. Only 100 years later, there emerges a native Chinese Sangha. And during the Period of Disunity (or Era of the Warring States, 220 to 589 ad), the number of Buddhist monks and nuns increase to as many as two million. Apparently, the uncertain times and the misery of the lower classes were fertile ground for the monastic traditions of Buddhism. Buddhism did not come to a land innocent of religion and philosophy, of course. China, in fact, had three main competing streams of thought: Confucianism, Taoism, and folk religion.

Confucianism is essentially a moral-political philosophy, involving a complex guide to human relationships. Taoism is a life-philosophy involving a return to simpler and more "natural" ways of being. And the folk religion — or, should we say, religions — consisted of rich mythologies, superstitions, astrology, reading of entrails, magic, folk medicine, and so on. Although these various streams sometimes competed with each other and with Buddhism, they also fed each other, enriched each other, and intertwined with each other. Over time, the Mahayana of India became the Mahayana of China and, later, of Korea, Japan, and Vietnam.

Pure Land

The first example historically is Pure Land Buddhism (Ching-T'u, J: Jodo). The peasants and working people of China were used to gods and goddesses, praying for rain and health, worrying about heaven and hell, and so on. It wasn't a great leap to find in Buddhism's cosmology and theology the bases for a religious tradition that catered to these needs and habits, while still providing a sophisticated philosophical foundation. The idea of this period of time as a fallen or inferior time — traditional in China — led to the idea that we are no longer able to reach enlightenment on our own power, but must rely on the intercession of higher beings. The transcendent Buddha Amitabha, and his western paradise ("pure land"), introduced in the Sukhavati-vyuha Sutra, was a perfect fit.

Ch'an

Another school that was to be particularly strongly influenced by Chinese thought was the Meditation School - Dhyana, Ch'an, Son, or Zen. Tradition has the Indian monk Bodhidharma coming from the west to China around 520 AD. It was Bodhidharma, it is said, and who carried the Silent Transmission to become the First Patriarch of the Ch'an School in China:

From the very beginning, Buddha had reservations about his ability to communicate his message to the people. Words simply could not carry such a sublime message. So, on one occasion, while the monks around him waited for a sermon, he said absolutely nothing. He simply held up a flower. The monks, of course, were confused, except for Kashyapa, who understood and smiled. The Buddha smiled back, and thus the Silent Transmission began.

Zen Buddhism focuses on developing the immediate awareness of Buddha-mind through meditation on emptiness. It is notorious for its dismissal of the written and spoken word and occasionally for his rough-house antics. It should be understood, however, that there is great reverence for the Buddha, the Dharma, and the Sangha, even when they are ostensibly ignoring, poking fun, or even turning them upside-down. Zen has contributed its own literature to the Buddhist melting-pot, including The Platform Sutra, written by Hui Neng, the Sixth Patriarch, around 700 AD., The Blue Cliff Record, written about 1000 AD., and The Gateless Gate, written about 1200 AD. And we shouldn't forget the famous Ten Ox-Herding Pictures that many see as containing the very essence of Zen's message.

The Blossoming of Schools

During the Sui dynasty (581-618) and T'ang dynasty (618-907), Chinese Buddhism experienced what is referred to as the "blossoming of schools." The philosophical inspirations of the Madhyamaka and Yogachara, as well as the Pure Land and

Ch'an Sutras, interacting with the already sophisticated philosophies of Confucianism and Taoism, led to a regular renaissance in religious and philosophical thought. We find the Realistic School, based on the "all things exist" Hinayana School; the Three-Treatises School, based on Madhyamaka; the Idealist School, based on Yogachara; the Tantric School; the Flower Adornment School (Hua-Yen, J: Kegon), which attempted to consolidate the various forms; and the White Lotus School (T'ien-T'ai, J: Tendai), which focused on the Lotus Sutra.

All the Chinese Schools had their representatives in neighboring countries. Korea was to develop its own powerful form of Ch'an called Son. Vietnam developed a form of Ch'an that incorporated aspects of Pure Land and Hinayana. But it was Japan that would have a field day with Chinese Buddhism, and pass the Mahayana traditions on to the US and the west generally.

Japan

Again, we begin with the legendary: A delegation arrived from Korea with gifts for the Emperor of Japan in 538 AD., including a bronze Buddha and various Sutras. Unfortunately a plague led the Emperor to believe that the traditional gods of Japan were annoyed, so he had the gifts thrown into a canal. But the imperial court on the 600's, in their constant effort to be as sophisticated as the courts of their distinguished neighbors, the Chinese, continued to be drawn to Buddhism. Although starting as a religion of the upper classes, in the 900's, Pure Land entered the picture as the favorite of the peasant and working classes. And in the 1200's, Ch'an, relabeled Zen, came into Japan, where it was enthusiastically adopted by, among others, the warrior class or Samurai.

Zen was introduced into Japan by two particularly talented monks who had gone to China for their educations: Eisai (1141-1215) brought Lin-chi (J: Rinzai) Ch'an, with its koans and occasionally outrageous antics; Dogen (1200-1253) brought the more sedate Ts'ao-tung (J: Soto) Ch'an. In addition, Dogen is particularly admired for his massive treatise, the Shobogenzo. Ch'an has always had an artistic side to it. In China and elsewhere, a certain simple, elegant style of writing and drawing developed among the monks. In Japan, this became an even more influential aspect of Zen. We have, for example, the poetry, calligraphy, and paintings of various monks – Bankei (1622-1698), Basho (1644-1694), Hakuin (1685-1768), and Ryokan (1758-1831) – which have become internationally beloved.

One last Japanese innovation is usually attributed to a somewhat unorthodox monk named Nichiren (1222-1282). Having been trained in the Tendai or White Lotus tradition, he came to believe that the Lotus Sutra carried all that was necessary for Buddhist life. More than that, he believed that even the name of the Sutra was enough! So he encouraged his students to chant this mantra: Namu-myoho-renge-kyo, which means "homage to the Lotus Sutra." This practice alone would ensure enlightenment in this life. In fact, he insisted, all other forms of Buddhism were of little worth. Needless to say, this was not appreciated by the Buddhist powers of the day. He spent the rest of his life in relative isolation. The Nichiren School nevertheless proved to be one of the most successful forms of Buddhism on the planet.

Tibet

Finally, let's turn out attention to the most mysterious site of Buddhism's history, Tibet. Its first encounter with Buddhism occurred in the 700's ad, when a Tantric master, Guru Rinpoché, came from India to battle the demons of Tibet for control. The demons submitted, but they remained forever a part of Tibetan Buddhism – as its protectors! During the 800's and 900's, Tibet went through a "dark age," during which Buddhism suffered something of a setback. But, in the 1000's, it returned in force. And in 1578, the Mongol overlords named the head of the Gelug School the Dalai Lama, meaning "guru as great as the ocean."

The title was made retroactive to two earlier heads of the school. The fifth Dalai Lama is noted for bringing all of Tibet under his religious and political control. The lineage continues down to the present 14th Dalai Lama, Tenzin Gyatso, born 1935. In 1989, he was awarded the Nobel Peace Prize for his efforts on behalf of his people and nation, which had been taken over by the Communist Chinese in 1951.

The West

It was in the latter half of the 1800's that Buddhism first came to be known in the west. The great European colonial empires brought the ancient cultures of India and China back to the attention of the intellectuals of Europe. Scholars began to learn Asian languages and translate Asian texts. Adventurers explored previously shut-off places and recorded the cultures. Religious enthusiasts enjoyed the exotic and mystical tone of the Asian traditions. In England, for example, societies sprang up for devotees of "orientalia," such as T. W. Rhys Davids' Pali Text Society and T. Christmas Humphreys' Buddhist Society. Books were published, such as Sir Edwin Arnold's epic poem The Light of Asia (1879). And the first western monks began to make themselves know, such as Allan Bennett, perhaps the very first, who took the name Ananda Metteya. In Germany and France as well, Buddhism was the rage.

In the United States, there was a similar flurry of interest. First of all, thousands of Chinese immigrants were coming to the west coast in the late 1800's, many to provide cheap labor for the railroads and other expanding industries. Also, on the east coast, intellectuals were reading about Buddhism in books by Europeans. One example was Henry Thoreau, who, among other things, translated a French translation of a Buddhist Sutra into English. A renewal of interest came during World War II, during which many Asian Buddhists — such as the Zen author D. T. Suzuki — came to England and the U.S., and many European Buddhists — such as the Zen author Alan Watts — came to the U.S. As these examples suggest, Zen Buddhism was particularly popular, especially in the U.S., where it became enmeshed in the Beatnik artistic and literary movement as "beat Zen."

One by one, European and Americans who studied in Asia returned with their knowledge and founded monasteries and societies, Asian masters came to Europe and America to found monasteries, and the Asian immigrant populations from China, Japan, Vietnam and elsewhere, quietly continued their Buddhist practices. Today, it is believed that there are more than 300 million Buddhists in the world, including at least a quarter million in Europe, and a half million each in North and South America. I say "at least" because other estimates go as high as three million in the U.S. alone! Whatever the numbers may be, Buddhism is the fourth largest religion in the world, after Christianity, Islam, and Hinduism. And, although it has suffered considerable setbacks over the centuries, it seems to be attracting more and more people, as a religion or a philosophy of life.

Judaism

Judaism traces its history back to the creation of mankind, but the explicitly Jewish historical origins begin with Abraham and the Hebrews. According to the Torah, Abraham's home was the northern Mesopotamian town of Harran. Under God's command, Abraham migrated to the region of Canaan, which is roughly equivalent to modern Israel and Lebanon and for a time the Hebrews lived in servitude in Egypt, and then returned to Canaan.

The ancient Hebrew people were semi nomadic herdsman and farmers, organized into tribes and living in Mesopotamia. Contributions of nearby cultures include a West Semitic concept of divine messengers, Old Babylonian and Hurro-Semite law, Mesopotamian cosmogony and primitive history, Canaanite language and mythological literature, and Egyptian hymns and wisdom literature. All of these cultures featured belief in creator and preserver gods, a system of ethics, and developed religious rituals. The head of the Canaanite pantheon was El, a powerful god depicted as both judgmental and compassionate.

Biblical Jewish History

The period of Jewish history designated by some historians as "Biblical Judaism" is the centuries covered by the narratives of the Tanakh, from the creation and primitive history of mankind to the last of the prophets in the 4th century BCE. The Tanakh tells the history of the Hebrew people from a religious viewpoint, beginning with the creation of mankind and ending with the words of the last of the prophets in the 4th century BCE. This period is often referred to by scholars as "Biblical Judaism." The Tanakh follows the Hebrew nation as it experiences cycles of favor and discipline by God. God establishes successive covenants with humanity (Adam, Noah and Abraham) and issues an extensive set of laws (through Moses) by which the Hebrew are to be set apart as God's people. When they stray, God sends prophets and invading armies to bring them back to him. "It is this particular claim-to has experienced God's presence in human events-and its subsequent development that is the differentiating factor in Jewish thought."

The biblical book of Genesis begins with a single, all-powerful God creating the world out of chaos in six days, with human beings created on the sixth day. Genesis goes on to chronicle an ancient history in which mankind repeatedly turns away from God and to immorality until God destroys the earth with a flood. God then makes a covenant with Noah, the one man saved from the flood, that he will never destroy the earth again. The specifically Hebrew element of biblical history begins with Abraham, who is considered the founder of the Jewish religion. However, he does not discover God but is rather called by the God who is already known into a covenant, in which God promises to many descendents and the land of Canaan.

Modern scholarship has identified significant differences between the religion of Abraham and the patriarchs and the later Israelite religion of Moses. Historians note that the God of Abraham is referred to using generic, not specifically Israelite terms (namely, various forms of El), the Mosaic issues of divine jealousy and idolatry are virtually absent, and God's role is as a kind of patron deity who has bestowed his favor on Abraham. The religion of the patriarchs was simple, and centered on the agreement between Abraham and God. Religious practice consisted of sacrifice and prayer at a sacred altar, stone pillar, or sacred tree. Circumcision was the defining mark of the religious community. Its eschatology was the promise of land and many descendents.

Moses and the Covenant

According to biblical tradition, a famine caused the Hebrew tribes to migrate to Egypt, where they were enslaved. God rescued them from bondage by afflicting the Egyptians with successive plagues then drowning the Egyptian army in the Red Sea to allow the Hebrews to escape. At Mount Sinai, God established the nation of Israel (named for Abraham's grandson Jacob) as his own, and gave them the terms of his covenant with them. He then sustains the Israelites through 40 years of journeying in the wilderness before leading them into Canaan, the land promised to Abraham. Central to all these events is Moses, who, like Muhammad, fulfills many leadership roles, including religious, political, legislative and military.

This general sequence of events is accepted by most scholars as historically reliable. As one source explains, "To disallow these events would make their centrality as articles of faith in the later religious beliefs of Israel inexplicable." Mosaic religion centers on the covenant between God and the people of Israel. The covenant required exclusive loyalty to Yahweh, who rescued them from bondage in Egypt. Worship of other gods, veneration of idols (even of Yahweh), and magical practices are prohibited. Rituals and festivals are established to celebrate God's historical and continuing provision.

The conquest of Canaan is narrated in the biblical book of Joshua, with miraculous events (walls fell at a shout, the sun stood still) rivaling those of the Exodus. The process of occupation has been judged by scholars as more complex than that described in Joshua, incorporating a combination of military victories and treaty agreements. After the conquest of Canaan, Israel was led by leaders called "judges," during which time the Israelites are described as repeatedly falling into idolatry and apostasy. Figurines discovered in the Israelite levels of archeological digs in Palestine support such a report. At the same time, numerous altars to the God of Israel sprung up, and the Levites rose to the priesthood to conduct sacrifices at many of them. The Ark of the Covenant was housed and carefully protected at the Shiloh sanctuary, which was staffed by priests of the family of Eli.

To maintain occupation of the Promised Land, it became necessary to have centralized authority and organized armies that could hold off external enemies. Two diverging views of the prospect of a monarchy arose: a rejection of God's kingship (1 Sam. 8-12) or a God-given way to defend Israel (1 Sam. 9:16). The former view is represented by the prophet-judge Samuel, who reluctantly crowned the first king. Saul, of the tribe of Benjamin, was made king (in c. 1020 BCE) after defeating the Ammonites. He ruled from his hometown of Gibeah, a few miles north of Jerusalem. Saul's reign was marred by conflicts with the prophet Samuel, who held ongoing authority over the kingship. King David, Saul's successor, solved these problems by combining religious and political authority in one person (David and his descendents) and in one place (the city of Jerusalem).

David was succeeded by his son Solomon, whose history is recorded in 1 Kings 1-11 and 2 Chronicles 1-9. Solomon succeeded his father on the throne in early manhood, probably about sixteen or eighteen years of age. His father chose him as his successor, passing over the claims of his elder sons. His elevation to the throne took place before his father's death, and is hastened on mainly by Nathan and Bathsheba, in consequence of the rebellion of Adonijah. During Solomon's long reign of 40 years the Hebrew monarchy gained its highest splendour. This period has well been called the "Augustan age" of the Jewish annals. In a single year he collected tribute amounting to 666 talents of gold, according to 1 Kings 10:13. The first half of his reign was, however, by far the brighter and more prosperous; the latter half was clouded by the idolatries into which he fell, mainly, according to the scribes, from his intermarriages.

According to 1 Kings 11:3, he had 700 wives and 300 concubines. As soon as he had settled himself in his kingdom, and arranged the affairs of his extensive empire, he entered into an alliance with Egypt by a marriage with the daughter of Pharaoh.

After Solomon's reign the nation split into two kingdoms, Israel (in the north) and Judah (in the south). Israel was conquered by the Assyrian ruler Shalmaneser V in the 8th century BCE. The kingdom of Judah was conquered by a Babylonian army in the early 6th century BCE. The Judahite elite was exiled to Babylon, but later at least a part of them returned to their homeland, led by prophets Ezra and Nehemiah, after the subsequent conquest of Babylonia by the Persians. Already at this point the extreme fragmentation among the Israelites was apparent, with the formation of political-religious factions, the most important of which would later be called Sadducees and Pharisees.

After the Persians were defeated by Alexander the Great, his demise, and the division of Alexander's empire among his generals, the Seleucid Kingdom was formed. A deterioration of relations between hellenized Jews and religious Jews led the Seleucid king Antiochus IV Epiphanes to impose decrees banning certain Jewish religious rites and traditions. Consequently, the orthodox Jews revolted under the leadership of the Hasmonean family, (also known as the Maccabees). This revolt eventually led to the formation of an independent Jewish kingdom, known as the Hasmonaean Dynasty, which lasted from 165 BC to 63 BC. The Hasmonean Dynasty eventually disintegrated as a result of civil war between the sons of Salome Alexandra, Hyrcanus II and Aristobulus II.

The people, who did not want to be governed by a king but by theocratic clergy, made appeals in this spirit to the Roman authorities. A Roman campaign of conquest and annexation, led by Pompey, soon followed. Judea under Roman rule was at first an independent Jewish kingdom, but gradually the rule over Judea became less and less Jewish, until it became under the direct rule of Roman administration (and renamed the province of Judaea), which was often callous and brutal in its treatment of its Judean subjects. In AD 66, Judeans began to revolt against the Roman rulers of Judea. The revolt was defeated by the Roman emperors Vesesapian and Titus Flavius.

The Romans destroyed much of the Temple in Jerusalem and, according to some accounts, stole artifacts from the temple, such as the Menorah. Judeans continued to live in their land in significant numbers, and were allowed to practice their religion, until the 2nd century when Julius Severus ravaged Judea while putting down the bar Kokhba revolt. After 135, Jews were not allowed to enter the city of Jerusalem, although this ban must have been at least partially lifted, since at the destruction of the rebuilt city by the Persians in the 7th century, Jews are said to have lived there. Various responses developed to Roman rule, ranging from armed revolt (the Zealots) or withdrawal from the world (the Essenes) to a renewed focus on preserving tradition in a new situation (the Pharisees), to integration with Greek society (the Sadducees) and thought (Jewish Neoplatonists).

Rabbinical Judaism developed out of the Pharasiac movement and in response to the destruction of the Second Temple in 70 CE. The rabbis sought to reinterpret Jewish concepts and practices in the absence of the Temple and for a people in exile. Aside from some small side movements (such as the Karaites), Rabbinical Judaism was the dominant form of the Jewish religion for nearly 18 centuries. It produced the Talmud, the Midrash, and the great figures of medieval Jewish philosophy.

The Eastern Roman Empire, under assault from barbarian invasion, passed a number of laws in the early middle Ages, including the legislation of Justinian which culminated in the principle of taking away civil rights from heretics and unbelievers and of making their existence as difficult as possible. The restrictive laws of Constantine and Theodosius were renewed with increased rigor. The public observance of their religion was forbidden the Jews. The loss of their civil rights was followed by disregard for their personal freedom. In the wars waged by the Iconoclasts (eighth and ninth centuries) the Jews especially had to suffer, and mostly at the hands of iconoclastic emperors who were suspected of being heretics with Jewish tendencies.

Many Jews fled to the neighboring states of the Slavs and Tatars, which were just coming into existence, and found refuge and protection on the lower Volga and on the northern shores of the Black Sea in the realm of the Khazars. While the East-Roman empire was prolonging its inglorious existence by perpetual warfare with neighbors who were ever growing stronger, the Western Roman Empire fell prey to the barbarians. With the exception of the restrictive laws of the first Christian emperors, which still remained in force, the Jews were not troubled on account of their faith.

Not until the beginning of the ninth century did the Church succeed in drawing all humanity within her jurisdiction, and in bringing together and definitely settling the regulations in canonical law which the authority of the Church ordained for believers and their treatment of non-believers. Intercourse with Jews was almost entirely forbidden to believers, and thereby a chasm was created between the adherents of the two religions, which could not be bridged. On the other hand, the Church found herself compelled to make the Jew a fellow citizen of the believer; for she enforced upon her own communities the Biblical prohibition against usury; and thus the only way left open to her of conducting financial operations was to seek loans at a legally determined rate of interest from the adherents of another faith.

Through these peculiar conditions the Jews rapidly acquired influence. At the same time they were compelled to find their pleasures at home and in their own circles only. Their sole intellectual food came from their own literature, to which they devoted themselves with all the strength of their nature. This was the general condition of the Jews in Western lands. Their fate in each particular country depended on the changing political conditions. In Italy they experienced dark days during the endless wars waged by the Heruli, Rugii, Ostrogoths, and Longobardi. The severe laws of the Roman emperors were in general more mildly administered than elsewhere; the Arian confession, of which the Germanic conquerors of Italy were adherents, being in contrast with the Catholic characterized by its tolerance. Among the Burgundians and Franks, who professed the Catholic faith, the ecclesiastical sentiment, fortunately for the Jews, made but slow progress, and the Merovingian rulers rendered only a listless and indifferent support to the demands of the Church, the influence of which they had no inclination to increase.

In the Pyrenean peninsula, from the most ancient times, Jews had lived peaceably in greater numbers than in the land of the Franks. The same modest good fortune remained to them when the Suevi, Alani, Vandals, and Visigoths occupied the land. It came to a sudden end when the Visigothic kings embraced Catholicism and wished to convert all their subjects to the same faith. Many Jews yielded to compulsion in the secret hope that the severe measures would be of short duration. But they soon bitterly repented this hasty step; for the Visigothic legislation insisted with inexorable severity that those who had been baptized by force should remain true to the Christian faith. Consequently the Jews eagerly welcomed the Arabs when the latter conquered the peninsula in 711. Those Jews who still wished to remain true to the faith of their fathers were protected by the Church herself from compulsory conversion. There was no change in this policy even later, when the pope called for the support of the Carolingians in protecting his ideal kingdom with their temporal power.

Charlemagne, moreover, was glad to use the Church for the purpose of welding together the loosely connected elements of his kingdom when he transformed the old Roman Empire into a Christian one, and united under the imperial crown all the German races at that time firmly settled. When, a few decades after his death, his world-empire fell apart (843), the rulers of Italy, France, and Germany left the Church free scope in her dealings with the Jews, and under the influence of religious zeal hatred toward the unbelievers ripened into deeds of horror.

The trials which the Jews endured from time to time in the different kingdoms of the Christian West were only indications of the catastrophe which broke over them at the time of the Crusades. A wild, unrestrained throng, for which the crusade was only an excuse to indulge its rapacity, fell upon the peaceful Jews and sacrificed them to its fanaticism. In the First Crusade (1096) flourishing communities on the Rhine and the Danube were utterly destroyed. In the Second Crusade (1147) the Jews in France suffered especially. Philip Augustus treated them with exceptional severity. In his days the Third Crusade took place (1188); and the preparations for it proved to be momentous for the English Jews. After unspeakable trials Jews were banished from England in 1290; and 365 years passed before they were allowed to settle again in the British Isles. The Jews were also subjected to attacks by the Shepherds' Crusades of 1251 and 1320.

The justification for these deeds was found in crimes laid to the charge of the Jews. They were held responsible for the crime imputed to them a thousand years before this; and the false charge was circulated that they wished to dishonor the host which was supposed to represent Jesus' body. They were further charged with being the cause of every calamity. In 1240 the plundering raids of the Mongols were laid at their door. When, a hundred years later, the Black Death raged through Europe, the tale was invented that the Jews had poisoned the wells. The only court of appeal that regarded itself as their appointed protector, according to historical conceptions, was the "Roman emperor of the German nation."

The emperor, as legal successor to Titus, who had acquired the Jews for his special property through the destruction of the Temple, claimed the rights of possession and protection over all the Jews in the former Roman Empire. They thus became imperial "servi cameræ." He might present them and their possessions to princes or to cities. That the Jews were not utterly destroyed was due to two circumstances: (1) the envy, distrust, and greed of princes and peoples toward one another, and (2) the moral strength which was infused into the Jews by a suffering which was undeserved but which enabled them to resist persecution. The abilities which could find no expression in the service of country or of humanity at large were directed with all the more zeal toward the study of the Bible and Talmud, toward ordering communal affairs, toward building up a happy family life, and toward bettering the condition of the Jewish race in general.

Everywhere in the Christian Occident an equally gloomy picture was presented. The Jews, who were driven out of England in 1290, out of France in 1394, and out of numerous districts of Germany, Italy, and the Balkan peninsula between 1350 and 1450, were scattered in all directions, and fled preferably to the new Slavic kingdoms, where for the time being other confessions were still tolerated. Here they found a sure refuge under benevolent rulers and acquired a certain prosperity, in the enjoyment of which the study of the Talmud was followed with renewed vigor. Together with their faith, they took with them the German language and customs, which they have cultivated in a Slavic environment with unexampled faithfulness up to the present time.

As in Slavic countries, so also under Muslim rule the persecuted Jews often found a humane reception, especially from the eighth century onward in the Pyrenean peninsula. But even as early as the thirteenth century the Arabs could no longer offer a real resistance to the advancing force of Christian kings; and with the fall of political power Arabic culture declined, after having been transmitted to the Occident at about the same period, chiefly through the Jews in the north of Spain and in the south of France. At that time there was no field of learning which the Spanish Jews did not cultivate. They studied the secular sciences with the same zeal as the Bible and Talmud.

But the growing influence of the Church gradually crowded them out of this advantageous position. At first the attempt was made to win them to Christianity through writings and religious disputations; and when these attempts failed they were ever more and more restricted in the exercise of their civil rights. Soon they were obliged to live in separate quarters of the cities and to wear humiliating badges on their clothing. Thereby they were made a prey to the scorn and hatred of their fellow citizens. In 1391, when a fanatical mob killed thirty thousand Jews in Seville alone, many in their fright sought refuge in baptism.

And although they often continued to observe in secret the laws of their fathers the Inquisition soon rooted out these pretended Christians or Maranos. Thousands were thrown into prison, tortured, and burned, until a project was formed to sweep all Spain clean of unbelievers. The plan matured when in 1492 the last Moorish fortress fell into the hands of the Christians. Several hundred thousand Jews were forced from the country which had been their home for 1,500 years. Many of them fled to the Balkan Peninsula, where a few decades before the Crescent had won a victory over the Cross through the Osmanli Turks. These exiles have faithfully preserved the language of the country they were forced to leave; and today, after a lapse of more than 400 years, Spanish is still the mother tongue of their descendants.

During the period of the European Renaissance and Enlightenment, significant changes were happening within the Jewish community. The Haskalah movement paralelled the wider Enlightenment, as Jews began in the 1700s to campaign for emancipation from restrictive laws and integration into the wider European society. Secular and scientific education was added to the traditional religious instruction received by students, and interest in a national Jewish identity, including a revival in the study of Jewish history and Hebrew, started to grow. Haskalah gave birth to the Reform and Conservative movements and planted the seeds of Zionism while at the same time encouraging cultural assimilation into the countries in which Jews resided.

At around the same time another movement was born, one preaching almost the opposite of Haskalah, Hasidic Judaism. Hasidic Judiasm began in the 1700s by Rabbi Israel Baal Shem Tov, and quickly gained a following with its more exubarent, mystical approach to religion. These two movements, and the traditional orthodox approach to Judiasm from which they spring, formed the basis for the modern divisions within Jewish observance. At the same time, the outside world was changing. Though persecution still existed in some European countries (hundreds of thousands of Jews were killed in pogroms in the 18th and 19th centuries), Napoleon invited Jews to leave the Jewish ghettos in Europe and seek refuge in the newly created tolerant political regimes that offered equality under Napoleonic Law. At the same time, Jewish migration to the United States created a new community in large part freed of the restrictions of Europe.

Christianity

The history of Christianity concerns the Christian religion and the Christian Church, from the ministry of Jesus and his Twelve Apostles, to contemporary times and denominations. Christianity is an Abrahamic religion. It differs most significantly from the others in the claim that Jesus Christ is God the Son. The vast majority of Christians believe in a triune God consisting of three unified and distinct persons: God the Father, God the Son and the Holy Spirit. There have been significant theological differences among Christians regarding the divine and human natures of Jesus and the triune nature of God. These differences continue today.

In many Christian denominations "The Church" is understood theologically as the institution founded by Jesus for the salvation of humankind. This understanding is shared between Catholic and Orthodox traditions. They see in the Church a foundation of Christ, who continues to live in it, through the Holy Spirit. In the Catholic tradition, the Catholic Church is the Body of Christ. Protestant churches generally view all Christians to be the Body of Christ. Some Protestant theologians call this High Church. In contrast, Low Church denominations generally emphasise the personal relationship between a believer and Jesus Christ. Other Christians, however, would say that the Church is not an institution at all.

Instead, it is the gathering of believers, individually, and ultimately in heaven where all believers from all nations and times will be gathered together; so, church history is not just about the history of institutions, but the major happenings amongst believers throughout the world, throughout time. Christianity began in 1st century AD Jerusalem. It ultimately became the state religion of Armenia in either 301 or 314, the state religion of Ethiopia in 325, the state religion of Georgia in 337, and then the state religion of the Roman Empire in 380. During the Age of Exploration (15th to 17th cent.), Christianity expanded throughout the world, becoming the world's largest religion. Throughout its history, the religion has weathered schisms and theological disputes that have resulted in many distinct churches. The largest branches of Christianity are the Roman Catholic Church and the Eastern Orthodox Church, and the Protestant churches.

Scholars generally agree that Jesus was born to a Jewish mother named Mary in 6-4 B.C. and that he was raised in Nazareth, Galilee and possibly lived for a short time in Egypt. Scholars further believe Jesus began his ministry around the age of thirty and that it included recruiting disciples who regarded him as a wonderworker, healer and/or the Son of God. He was eventually executed by crucifixion in Jerusalem circa AD 33 on orders of the Roman Governor of Iudaea Province, Pontius Pilate; and after his crucifixion, Jesus was buried in a tomb.

Christians believe that three days after his death, Jesus and his body rose from the dead and that the empty tomb story is a historical fact. Early works by Jesus's followers document a number of resurrection appearances and the resurrection of Jesus formed the basis and impetus of the Christian faith. His followers wrote that he appeared to the disciples in Galilee and Jerusalem and that Jesus was on the earth for 40 days before his Ascension to heaven and that he will return to earth again to fulfill aspects of Messianic prophecy, such as the resurrection of the dead, the last judgment and the full establishment of the Kingdom of God. The main sources of information regarding Jesus' life and teachings are the four canonical Gospels, and to a lesser extent the Acts of the Apostles and writings of Paul. Christianity's popularity is largely founded and based on one central point found in these Gospels that Jesus died and rose from death as God's sacrifice for human sins.

Early Christianity refers to the period when the religion spread in the Greek/Roman world and beyond, from its beginnings as a 1st century Jewish sect, to the end of imperial persecution of Christians after the ascension of Constantine the Great in AD 313, to the First Council of Nicaea in 325. It may be divided into two distinct phases: the apostolic period, when the first apostles were alive and organising the Church, and the post-apostolic period, when an early episcopal structure developed, whereby bishoprics were governed by bishops (overseers). However, the latter case was greatly frowned upon until the eras of Constantine, Gregory, and Pope Boniface II.

The Apostolic Church, called by some the Primitive Church, was the community led by Jesus' apostles and his relatives. According to the Great Commission, the resurrected Jesus commanded the disciples to spread his teachings to the entire world. The principal source of information for this period is the Acts of the Apostles, which gives a history of the Church from the Great Commission, Pentecost and the establishment of the Jerusalem Church to the spread of the religion among the gentiles, Paul's conversion and eventual imprisonment in Rome in the mid-first century. However, the historical accuracy of Acts is also disputed and may conflict with accounts in the Epistles of Paul.

The first Christians were essentially all ethnically Jewish or Jewish Proselytes. In other words, Jesus preached to the Jewish people and called from them his first disciples, though the earliest documented "group" of appointed evangelisers, called the Seventy Disciples, was not specifically ethnically Jewish. An early difficulty arose concerning the matter of Gentile (non-Jewish) converts as to whether they had to "become Jewish" (usually referring to circumcision and adherence to dietary law) as part of becoming Christian. Circumcision was considered repulsive during the period of Hellenization of the Eastern Mediterranean. The decision of Peter, as evidenced by conversion of the Centurion Cornelius, was that they did not, and the matter was further addressed with the Council of Jerusalem, see also Primacy of Simon Peter.

The doctrines of the apostles brought the Early Church into conflict with some Jewish religious authorities. This eventually led to their expulsion from the synagogues; acts records the martyrdom of SS. Stephen and James the Great. Thus, Christianity acquired an identity distinct from Rabbinic Judaism. The name "Christian" (Greek Χριστιανο'ζ) was first applied to the disciples in Antioch, as recorded in Acts 11:26.

The sources for the beliefs of the apostolic community include the Gospels and New Testament Epistles. The very earliest accounts are contained in these texts, such as early Christian creeds and hymns, as well as accounts of the Passion, the empty tomb, and Resurrection appearances; often these are dated to within a decade or so of the crucifixion of Jesus, originating within the Jerusalem Church. The earliest Christian creeds and hymns express belief in the risen Jesus, e.g., that preserved in 1 Corinthians 15:3–4 quoted by Paul: "For I delivered to you first of all that which I also received: that Christ died for our sins according to the Scriptures, that he was buried, that he was raised on the third day according to the Scriptures."

The antiquity of the creed has been located by many scholars to less than a decade after Jesus' death, originating from the Jerusalem apostolic community, and no scholar dates it later than the 40s.Other relevant and very early creeds include 1 John 4:2, 2 Timothy 2:8, Romans 1:3–4, and 1 Timothy 3:16, an early creedal hymn. Early Christianity retained some of the doctrines and practices of first-century Judaism while rejecting others. They held the Jewish scriptures to be authoritative and sacred, employing mostly the Septuagint or Targum translations, later called the Old Testament, and added other texts as the New Testament canon developed. Christianity also continued other Judaic practices: baptism, liturgical worship, including the use of incense, an altar, a set of scriptural readings adapted from synagogue practice, use of sacred music in hymns and prayer, and a religious calendar, as well as other distinctive features such as an exclusively male priesthood, and ascetic practices (fasting etc.).

Circumcision was rejected as a requirement at the Council of Jerusalem. Quartodecimanism (the day of preparation for Passover) was rejected at the First Council of Nicaea and Sabbath observance was modified. The early Christians in first century believed Yahweh to be the only true God, the God of Israel, and considered Jesus to be the Messiah (Christ) prophesied in the Old Testament. Alister McGrath, a proponent of palaeoorthodoxy, claimed that many of the Jewish Christians were fully faithful religious Jews, only differing in their acceptance of Jesus as the Messiah.

The Apostolic Church hierarchy was organised into Overseers (Bishop, Elder, Presbyter) and Servants (Deacons. Clement, a Bishop of Rome, refers to the leaders of the Corinthian church as bishops and presbyters indifferently. He writes that the bishops are to lead God's flock by virtue of the chief Shepherd - Jesus Christ. Important bishops of the Apostolic Era include Clement of Rome and Ignatius of Antioch, who, along with Polycarp of Smyrna, reportedly knew and studied under the apostles personally and are therefore called Apostolic Fathers.

The post-apostolic period concerns the time roughly after the death of the apostles when bishops emerged as overseers of urban Christian populations, and continues during the time of persecutions until the legalisation of Christian worship with the advent of Constantine the Great and the earliest recorded use of the terms Christianity and Catholic dates to this period attributed to Ignatius of Antioch c. 107. From the beginning, Christians were subject to various persecutions. This involved even death for Christians such as Stephen (Acts 7:59) and James, son of Zebedee (12:2). Larger-scale persecutions followed at the hands of the authorities of the Roman Empire, beginning with the year 64, when, as reported by the Roman historian Tacitus, the Emperor Nero blamed them for that year's great Fire of Rome.

According to Church tradition, it was under Nero's persecution that SS. Peter and Paul were each martyred in Rome. Similarly, several of the New Testament writings mention persecutions and stress endurance through them. For 250 years Christians suffered from sporadic persecutions for their refusal to worship the Roman emperor, considered treasonous and punishable by execution. In spite of these at-times intense persecutions, the Christian religion continued its spread throughout the Mediterranean Basin. By the late first and early second century, a hierarchical and episcopal structure becomes clearly visible. Post-apostolic bishops of importance are SS Polycarp of Smyrna and Irenaeus of Lyons.

This structure was based on the doctrine of Apostolic Succession where, by the ritual of the laying on of hands, a bishop becomes the spiritual successor of the previous bishop in a line tracing back to the apostles themselves. Each Christian community also had presbyters, as was the case with Jewish communities, who were also ordained and assisted the bishop; as Christianity spread, especially in rural areas, the presbyters exercised more responsibilities and took distinctive shape as priests. Lastly, deacons also performed certain duties, such as tending to the poor and sick. As Christianity spread, it acquired certain members from well-educated circles of the Hellenistic world; they sometimes became bishops but not always. They produced two sorts of works: theological and "apologetic", the latter being works aimed at defending the faith by using reason to refute arguments against the veracity of Christianity. These authors are known as the Church Fathers, and study of them is called Patristics. Notable early Fathers include Ignatius of Antioch, Polycarp, Justin Martyr, Irenaeus of Lyons, Tertullian, Clement of Alexandria, Origen of Alexandria, etc.

Christian art only emerged relatively late, and the first known Christian images emerge from about 200 AD, though there is some literary evidence that small domestic images were used earlier. Although many Hellenised Jews seem, as at the Dura-Europos synagogue, to have had images of religious figures, the traditional Mosaic prohibition of "graven images" no doubt retained some effect. This early rejection of images, although never proclaimed by theologians, and the necessity to hide Christian practise from persecution, leaves us with few archaeological records regarding early Christianity and its evolution. The oldest Christian paintings are from the Roman Catacombs, dated to about 200 AD, and the oldest Christian sculptures are from sarcophagi, dating to the beginning of the 3rd century.

The New Testament itself speaks of the importance of maintaining orthodox doctrine and refuting heresies, showing the antiquity of the concern. Because of the biblical proscription against false prophets (notably the Gospels of Matthew and Mark) Christianity has always been preoccupied with the "correct", or orthodox, interpretation of the faith. Indeed one of the main roles of the bishops in the early Church was to determine the correct interpretations and refute contrarian opinions (referred to as heresy). As there were differing opinions among the bishops, defining orthodoxy would consume the Church for some time (and still does, hence, "denominations").

In his book Orthodoxy, Christian Apologist and writer G. K. Chesterton asserts that there have been substantial disagreements about faith from the time of the New Testament and Jesus. He pointed out that the Apostles all argued against changing the teachings of Christ as did the earliest church fathers including Ignatius of Antioch, Irenaeus, Justin Martyr and Polycarp. Jesus also refers to false prophets (Mark 13:21–23) and the "darnei" (Matthew 13:25–30, 13:36–43) of the flock and how their distortion of the Christian faith is to be rejected. The earliest controversies were generally Christological in nature; that is, they were related to Jesus' (eternal) divinity or humanity. Docetism held that Jesus' humanity was merely an illusion, thus denying the incarnation.

Arianism held that Jesus, while not merely mortal, was not eternally divine and was, therefore, of lesser status than God the Father (John 14:28). Trinitarianism held that God the Father, God the Son and the Holy Spirit were all strictly one being with three hypostases. Many groups held dualistic beliefs, maintaining that reality was composed into two radically opposing parts: matter, usually seen as evil, and spirit, seen as good. Others held that both the material and spiritual worlds were created by God and were therefore both good, and that this was represented in the unified divine and human natures of Christ.

The development of doctrine, the position of orthodoxy, and the relationship between the various opinions is a matter of continuing academic debate. Since most Christians today subscribe to the doctrines established by the Nicene Creed, modern Christian theologians tend to regard the early debates as a unified orthodox position against a minority of heretics. Other scholars, drawing upon, among other things, distinctions between Jewish Christians, Pauline Christians, and other groups such as Gnostics and Marcionites, argue that early Christianity was fragmented, with contemporaneous competing orthodoxies.

The Biblical canon is the set of books Christians regard as divinely inspired and thus constituting the Christian Bible. Though the Early Church used the Old Testament according to the canon of the Septuagint (LXX), the apostles did not otherwise leave a defined set of new scriptures; instead the New Testament developed over time. The writings attributed to the apostles circulated amongst the earliest Christian communities. The Pauline epistles were circulating in collected form by the end of the first century AD. Justin Martyr, in the early second century, mentions the "memoirs of the apostles", which Christians called "gospels" and which were regarded as on par with the Old Testament. A four gospel canon (the Tetramorph) was in place by the time of Ireanaeus, c. 160, who refers to it directly.

By the early 200's, Origen of Alexandria may have been using the same 27 books as in the modern New Testament, though there were still disputes over the canonicity of Hebrews, James, II Peter, II and III John, and Revelation see also Antilegomena. Likewise the Muratorian fragment shows that by 200 there existed a set of Christian writings somewhat similar to what is now the New Testament, which included the four gospels. Thus, while there was a good measure of debate in the Early Church over the New Testament canon, the major writings were accepted by almost all Christians by the middle of the second century. In his Easter letter of 367, Athanasius, Bishop of Alexandria, gave a list of exactly the same books as what would become the New Testament canon, and he used the word "canonised" (kanonizomena) in regards to them. The African Synod of Hippo, in 393, approved the New Testament, as it stands today, together with the Septuagint books, a decision that was repeated by Councils of Carthage in 397 and 419.

These councils were under the authority of St. Augustine, who regarded the canon as already closed. Pope Damasus I's Council of Rome in 382, if the Decretum Gelasianum is correctly associated with it, issued a biblical canon identical to that mentioned above, or if not the list is at least a sixth century compilation. Likewise, Damasus's commissioning of the Latin Vulgate edition of the Bible, c. 383, was instrumental in the fixation of the canon in the West. In 405, Pope Innocent I sent a list of the sacred books to a Gallic bishop, Exsuperius of Toulouse. When these bishops and councils spoke on the matter, however, they were not defining something new, but instead "were ratifying what had already become the mind of the Church.

"Thus, from the fourth century, there existed unanimity in the West concerning the New Testament canon (as it is today), and by the fifth century the East, with a few exceptions, had come to accept the Book of Revelation and thus had come into harmony on the matter of the canon. Nonetheless, a full dogmatic articulation of the canon was not made until the Council of Trent of 1546 for Roman Catholicism, the Thirty-Nine Articles of 1563 for the Church of England, the Westminster Confession of Faith of 1647 for Calvinism, and the Synod of Jerusalem of 1672 for the Greek Orthodox.

The cracks and fissures in Christian unity which led to the Great Schism started to become evident as early as the fourth century. Although 1054 is the date usually given for the beginning of the Great Schism, there is, in fact, no specific date on which the schism occurred. What really happened was a complex chain of events whose climax culminated with the sacking of Constantinople by the Fourth Crusade in 1204. The events leading to schism were not exclusively theological in nature. Cultural, political, and linguistic differences were often mixed with the theological. Any narrative of the schism which emphasizes one at the expense of the other will be fragmentary.

Unlike the Copts or Armenians who broke from the Church in the fifth century, the eastern and western parts of the Church remained loyal to the faith, from their perspective, and to the authority of the seven ecumenical councils. They were united, by virtue of their common faith and tradition, in one Church. Nonetheless, the transfer of the Roman capital to

Constantinople inevitably brought mistrust, rivalry, and even jealousy to the relations of the two great sees, Rome and Constantinople. It was easy for Rome to be jealous of Constantinople at a time when it was rapidly losing its political prominence. In fact, Rome refused to recognise the conciliar legislation which promoted Constantinople to second rank. But the estrangement was also helped along by the German invasions in the West, which effectively weakened contacts.

The rise of Islam with its conquest of most of the Mediterranean coastline (not to mention the arrival of the pagan Slavs in the Balkans at the same time) further intensified this separation by driving a physical wedge between the two worlds. The once homogenous unified world of the Mediterranean was fast vanishing. Communication between the Greek East and the Latin West by the 600s had become dangerous and practically ceased. Two basic problems — the primacy of the bishop of Rome and the procession of the Holy Spirit — were involved. These doctrinal novelties were first openly discussed in Photius's patriarchate.

By the fifth century, Christendom was divided into a pentarchy of five sees with Rome holding the primacy. This was determined by canonical decision and did not entail hegemony of any one local church or patriarchate over the others. However, Rome began to interpret her primacy in terms of sovereignty, as a God-given right involving universal jurisdiction in the Church. The collegial and conciliar nature of the Church, in effect, was gradually abandoned in favour of supremacy of unlimited papal power over the entire Church. These ideas were finally given systematic expression in the West during the Gregorian Reform movement of the eleventh century. The Eastern churches viewed Rome's understanding of the nature of episcopal power as being in direct opposition to the Church's essentially conciliar structure and thus saw the two ecclesiologies as mutually antithetical.

This fundamental difference in ecclesiology would cause all attempts to heal the schism and bridge the divisions to fail.

Rome based her claims to "true and proper jurisdiction" (as the Vatican Council of 1870 put it) on St. Peter. This "Roman" exegesis of Mathew 16:18, however, was unacceptable to the patriarchs of Eastern Orthodoxy. For them, specifically, St. Peter's primacy could never be the exclusive prerogative of any one bishop. All bishops must, like St. Peter, confess Jesus as the Christ and, as such, all are St. Peter's successors. The churches of the East gave the Roman See, primacy but not supremacy and the Pope being the first among equals, but not infallible and not with absolute authority.

The other major irritant to Eastern Orthodoxy was the Western interpretation of the procession of the Holy Spirit. Like the primacy, this too developed gradually and entered the Creed in the West almost unnoticed. This theologically complex issue involved the addition by the West of the Latin phrase filioque ("and from the Son") to the Creed. The original Creed sanctioned by the councils and still used today by the Orthodox Church did not contain this phrase; the text simply states "the Holy Spirit, the Lord and Giver of Life, who proceeds from the Father." Theologically, the Latin interpolation was unacceptable to Eastern Orthodoxy since it implied that the Spirit now had two sources of origin and procession, the Father and the Son, rather than the Father alone. In short, the balance between the three persons of the Trinity was altered and the understanding of the Trinity and God confused.

The result, the Orthodox Church believed, then and now, was theologically indefensible. But in addition to the dogmatic issue raised by the filioque, the Byzantines argued that the phrase had been added unilaterally and, therefore, illegitimately, since the East had never been consulted. In the final analysis, only another ecumenical council could introduce such an alteration. Indeed the councils, which drew up the original Creed, had expressly forbidden any subtraction or addition to the text. In 1453, Constantinople fell to the Ottoman Empire. By this time Egypt had been under Muslim control for some seven centuries, but Orthodoxy was very strong in Russia which had recently acquired an autocephalous status; and thus Moscow called itself the Third Rome, as the cultural heir of Constantinople. Under Ottoman rule, the Greek Orthodox Church acquired substantial power as autonomous millet. The ecumenical patriarch was the religious and administrative ruler of the entire "Greek Orthodox nation" (Ottoman administrative unit), which encompassed all the Eastern Orthodox subjects of the Empire.

As a result of the Ottoman conquest of the Byzantine Empire in 1453, and the Fall of Constantinople, the entire Orthodox communion of the Balkans and the Near East became suddenly isolated from the West. For the next four hundred years, it would be confined within a hostile Islamic world, with which it had little in common religiously or culturally. The Russian Orthodox Church was the only part of the Orthodox communion which remained outside the control of the Ottoman Empire. It is, in part, due to this geographical and intellectual confinement that the voice of Eastern Orthodoxy was not heard during the Reformation in sixteenth century Europe. As a result, this important theological debate often seems strange and distorted to the Orthodox. They never took part in it and thus neither Reformation nor Counter-Reformation is part of their theological framework.

3

Religion in Society

There is no doubt about it, in a society of gross imbalances somebody has to ask, "What is the role of religion? Should it be a private refuge or a public presence and how will we ever know?" The Vietnamese tell a folk tale that I think goes right to the point of the question. The Vietnamese say that there is only one difference between heaven and hell. In hell, they have chopsticks three feet long and the people can't eat. In heaven, they have chopsticks three feet long but the people feed each another. The purpose of holiness is not to protect us from our world. The purpose of holiness is to change the way we live in the world, not for our own sake but for the sake of others. Jesus demands the same thing. For some reason or other, we often miss that point. We are more inclined to want a religion that comforts us than challenges us. Why? Where did we ever get that idea? Maybe it is because we have misunderstood, or at least forgotten, the meaning of Sabbath, the importance of mountain symbolism in religious literature and the effect of the very placement of gospel text.

Let's look at each for a minute. Sabbath, the rabbis teach us, doesn't exist because God needed rest. God doesn't need rest. That is heresy. The rabbis tell us that the Sabbath exists because God demanded rest. God wanted Sabbath to equalize the rich and the poor, so that the poor could be free for at least one day and the rich could no longer oppress them. God wanted Sabbath to give us time to evaluate our work as God evaluated God's work, to see if our work was equally good. Finally, God gave us Sabbath to give us time to reflect on the meaning of life. Sabbath is one-seventh of every week. It is one-seventh of every life. Sabbath is fifty-two days a year, over 3,500 days in a lifetime of seventy years, or over ten years of the average life. Sabbath is thinking time designed to change us. Sabbath is important, then, to all of us in our worlds.

Week after week after week, we have to ask the questions, "What changes are demanded of us now?" That answer, I think, depends on how we see the role of religion. There is a scripture story about the Transfiguration of Christ that gives us an idea, perhaps, of the answer. In the story of the Transfiguration, remember, Jesus takes Peter, James and John up a high mountain. Mountains, you may well know, in Greek, Hebrew, Roman and Asian religious literature, were always places where the human could touch the divine. Sure enough, at the top of that mountain with Jesus, a wonderful thing happened. The apostles began to see Jesus a new way. The apostles got a brand-new insight into whom this Jesus really was — dazzling, consuming, literally enlightening. They began to see Jesus differently.

What they see at the top of that mountain is, at least, unexpected and certainly disturbing. You see, at the top of that mountain before those apostles, Jesus does not appear with Aaron the priest, who was the interpreter of the law. Jesus doesn't appear there with David the King, the defender of the state. No, Jesus does not appear with symbols of royalty or ritualism. Jesus appears to those apostles with Moses, Elijah, the prophets. Moses, who led the people out of oppression; Elijah, whom King Ahab had called, "that trouble of Israel," because he condemned the people's compromise between true and false gods as the underlying cause of their problems. In a gospel apparently about the mystical dimension of religion, there is a troubling, teeming under-current of turmoil, a struggle between piety and real Christianity, a struggle between religion for real and religion for show. The gospel shows us that Peter, in your name and mine, opted for piety. "Let's settle down here, Jesus, and build three booths."

I'm not really sure, but I think what he had in mind been a chancery, a seminary and a college. Peter, in other words, was opting for a religion of temples, institutions and shrines. Peter was opting for a religion that transcends the world, but the scripture reads that before he could even finish speaking, God interrupted and said, "Listen." Then something happens that we too often forget. The gospel is completed by a portion that is usually unread, too little remembered, too much unfulfilled. At the very moment, when it would seem that Jesus is emphasizing the mystical and transcendent dimension of religion, Jesus himself takes the apostles away from visions, away from privatized religion, to meet the ones who needed them most in the town.

Jesus takes them to the man whose son was possessed by a demon. Jesus himself leads them down to the bottom of that mountain to the hurting people, unbelieving officials, the ineffective institutions and the demons below. Real religion is not about building temples and keeping shrines. Real religion is about healing hurts, speaking for and being with the poor, the helpless, the voiceless and the forgotten who are at the silent bottom of every pinnacle, every hierarchy and every system in both state and church, church and state. Real religion, the scripture insists, is not about transcending life; real religion is about our transforming life. The gospel of the transfiguration calls us to Sabbath; calls us to become enlightened; calls us to change our attitudes about the role of religion; calls us to understand the nature of religion itself; because the so-called rational has failed.

For instance, they say that militarism is rational. How else can we defend ourselves? Never before in history have we spent so much money on defense and never before in history, have been so vulnerable because of it. The people below, the people at the bottom of our mountains, wait to be healed of the diseases that spring from our spiritual darkness. The poor wait for jobs; the homeless wait for shelter; children are waiting for food; young people are waiting for education and job training; the elderly are waiting for care that we say that we can't afford in the richest nation in the world.

Every year we go on in peace time spending more money on instruments of destruction than on the development of peoples. We create the end of the world and store it in the corn fields of Kansas while the working poor, the people who suffer under part-time pay for part-time work or double-time work for part-time pay, get poorer and poorer in this country and around the globe. Religion, you see, does not call us to the rational. Religion calls us to the Beatitudes, to the works of mercy, to the casting out of demons, to the doing of miracles for those in need, to the being and act of irrational love and burning justice of God. That is what the Transfiguration is about, that is what religion is really about, changing ourselves so we can change the world.

Once upon a time a group of disciples asked an elder, "Does your God work miracles?" The elder said, "Well, it all depends on what you mean by a miracle. Some people say it's a miracle that God does the will of the people. We say, it's a miracle when people do the will of God." What is the role of religion in society, private refuge or public presence? Transfiguration means that the role of religion demands enlightenment. The role of religion is to bring us to an awareness of life. The role of religion is to transform the world, to come to see the world as God sees the world and to bring it as close to the vision of God as we possibly can. Why? Scripture is very clear. What God changes, God changes through us.

THE VIEW OF RELIGION IN CLASSICAL SOCIOLOGY

Durkheim, Marx, and Weber had very complex and developed theories about the nature and effects of religion. Durkheim and Weber specifically are often difficult to understand, especially in light of the lack of context and examples in their primary texts. Religion was considered to be an extremely important social variable in the work of all three:

Karl Marx

Despite his later influence, Karl Marx did not view his work as an ethical or ideological response to nineteenth-century capitalism (as most later commentators have). His efforts were, in his mind, based solely on what can be called applied science. Marx saw himself as doing morally-neutral sociology and economic theory for the sake of human development. As Christiano states, "Marx did not believe in science for science's sake...he believed that he was also advancing a theory that would...be a useful tool...[in] effecting a revolutionary upheaval of the capitalist system in favor of socialism." As such, the crux of his arguments was that humans are best guided by reason. Religion, Marx held, was a significant hindrance to reason, inherently masking the truth and misguiding followers. As we will later see, Marx viewed social alienation as the heart of social inequality. The antithesis to this alienation is freedom. Thus, to propagate freedom means to present individuals with the truth and give them a choice to accept or deny it. In this, "Marx never suggested that religion ought to be prohibited."

Central to Marx's theories was the oppressive economic situation in which he dwelt. With the rise of European industrialism, Marx and his colleague Friedrich Engels witnessed and responded to the growth of what he called "surplus value." Marx's view of capitalism saw rich capitalists getting richer and their workers getting poorer (the gap, the exploitation, was the "surplus value"). Not only were workers getting exploited, but in the process they were being further detached from the products they helped create. By simply selling their work for wages, "workers simultaneously lose connection with the object of labor and become objects themselves. Workers are devalued to the level of a commodity – a thing..." From this objectification comes alienation. The common worker is told he or she is a replaceable tool, alienated to the point of extreme discontent. Here, in Marx's eyes, religion enters.

Emile Durkheim

Émile Durkheim placed himself in the positivist tradition, meaning that he thought of his study of society as dispassionate and scientific. He was deeply interested in the problem of what held complex modern societies together. Religion, he argued, was an expression of social cohesion. In the fieldwork that led to his famous Elementary Forms of Religious Life, Durkheim, a secular Frenchman, spent fifteen years studying primitive religion among the Indigenous Australians. His underlying interest was to understand the basic forms of religious life for all societies. In Elementary Forms, Durkheim argues that the totems the aborigines venerate are actually expressions of their own conceptions of society itself.

This is true not only for the aborigines, he argues, but for all societies. Religion, for Durkheim, is not "imaginary," although he does deprive it of what many believers find essential. Religion is very real; it is an expression of society itself, and indeed, there is no society that does not have religion. We perceive as individuals a force greater than ourselves, which is our social life, and give that perception a supernatural face. We then express ourselves religiously in groups, which for Durkheim makes the symbolic power greater. Religion is an expression of our collective consciousness, which is the fusion of all of our individual consciousnesses, which then creates a reality of its own.

It follows, then, that less complex societies, such as the Australian aborigines, have less complex religious systems, involving totems associated with particular clans. The more complex the society, the more complex the religious system. As societies come in contact with other societies, there is a tendency for religious systems to emphasize universalism to a greater and greater extent. However, as the division of labor makes the individual seem more important (a subject that Durkheim treats extensively in his famous Division of Labor in Society), religious systems increasingly focus on individual salvation and conscience.

Durkheim's definition of religion, from Elementary Forms, is as follows: "A religion is a unified system of beliefs and practices relative to sacred things, that is to say, things set apart and forbidden – beliefs and practices which unite into one single moral community called a Church, all those who adhere to them." This is a functional definition of religion, meaning that it explains what religion does in social life: essentially, it unites societies. Durkheim defined religion as a clear distinction between the sacred and the profane; in effect this can be paralleled with the distinction between God and humans.

This definition also does not stipulate what exactly may be considered sacred. Thus later sociologists of religion (notably Robert Bellah) have extended Durkheimian insights to talk about notions of civil religion, or the religion of a state. American civil religion, for example, might be said to have its own set of sacred "things": the Flag of the United States, Abraham Lincoln, Martin Luther King Jr., etc. Other sociologists have taken Durkheim in the direction of the religion of professional sports, the military, or of rock music.

Max Weber

Max Weber differed from Karl Marx and Emile Durkheim in that he focused his work on the effects of religious action and inaction. Instead of discussing religion as a kind of misapprehension (an "opiate of the people,") or as social cohesion, Weber did not attempt to reduce religion to its essence. Instead, he examines how religious ideas and groups interacted with other aspects of social life (notably the economy). In doing so, Weber often attempts to get at religion's subjective meaning to the individual.

In his sociology, Weber uses the German term "Verstehen" to describe his method of interpretation of the intention and context of human action. Weber is not a positivist – in the sense that he does not believe we can find out "facts" in sociology that can be causally linked. Although he believes some generalized statements about social life can be made, he is not interested in hard positivist claims, but instead in linkages and sequences, in historical narratives and particular cases.

Weber argues for making sense of religious action on its own terms. A religious group or individual is influenced by all kinds of things, he says, but if they claim to be acting in the name of religion, we should attempt to understand their perspective on religious grounds first. Weber gives religion credit for shaping a person's image of the world, and this image of the world can affect their view of their interests, and ultimately how they decide to take action.

For Weber, religion is best understood as it responds to the human need for theodicy and soteriology. Human beings are troubled, he says, with the question of theodicy – the question of how the extraordinary power of a divine god may be reconciled with the imperfection of the world that he has created and rules over. People need to know, for example, why there is undeserved good fortune and suffering in the world. Religion offers people soteriological answers, or answers that provide opportunities for salvation – relief from suffering, and reassuring meaning. The pursuit of salvation, like the pursuit of wealth, becomes a part of human motivation.

Because religion helps to define motivation, Weber believed that religion (and specifically Protestant Calvinism) actually helped to give rise to modern capitalism, as he asserted in his most famous and controversial work, The Protestant Ethic and the Spirit of Capitalism. In The Protestant Ethic, Weber argues that capitalism arose in Europe in part because of how the belief in predestination was interpreted by everyday English Puritans. Puritan theology was based on the Calvinist notion that not everyone would be saved; there was only a specific number of the elect who would avoid damnation, and this was based sheerly on God's predetermined will and not on any action you could perform in this life. Official doctrine held that one could not ever really know whether one was among the elect.

Practically, Weber noted, this was difficult psychologically: people were (understandably) anxious to know whether they would be eternally damned or not. Thus Puritan leaders began assuring members that if they began doing well financially in their businesses, this would be one unofficial sign they had God's approval and were among the saved – but only if they used the fruits of their labor well. This led to the development of rational bookkeeping and the calculated pursuit of financial success beyond what one needed simply to live – and this is the "spirit of capitalism." Over time, the habits associated with the spirit of capitalism lost their religious significance, and rational pursuit of profit became its own aim. The Protestant Ethic thesis has been much critiqued, refined, and disputed, but is still a lively source of theoretical debate in sociology of religion. Weber also did considerable work in world religions, including Hinduism and Buddhism.

Religion is a pillar of society. Throughout history it has played a major role in many cultures, influencing art, music, philosophy, and moral codes of many people. Some religions have spread well beyond their place of origin, while others stayed in the areas they emerged. Of all the religions that have impacted different cultures, Christianity, Islam, and Hinduism are the major world contributors. Although Christianity has many denominations, it consists of two major churches: the Catholic and the Eastern Orthodox. While Catholicism is widespread in Europe, North and South America, Orthodox predominates in Greece, Russia, other Slavic countries, and in many areas of the United States. Among those countries, Russia is seen as the leader of the Orthodox Church. While Christianity and Islam share similarities, Hinduism, on the other hand, is a very different realm. It does not have a particular founder like Jesus or Mohamed.

Religion's contribution to the development of a society can be classified into several levels or categories. The major factor is the role it plays in a society: history, politics, and many other factors. Religion can also play a chief function in the lives of individuals of a particular society. It also defines standards for acceptable behaviour by creating taboos. Mythology, ritual, and imagery are an essential part of any large religion. Imagery, although can be used to tell the mythology of a particular belief system, can also be used as a constructive or a destructive force. The mythology of both Christianity and Hinduism play an important role in carrying the traditions of each religion. Christianity derives its myths from Judaism, mainly through Torah, reinterpreting them and adding original ones in the New Testament.

Similarly, Hinduism relies on the Vedic traditions and its mythology to define the rituals and traditions. Both of these religions use myths to show examples of certain behaviour, or to explain where certain traditions come from. Christianity is deeply rooted in Judaism. It has two key features that clearly define it: eternal salvation and forgiveness of all sins. The only price one has to pay for them is to follow Jesus Christ, which means to live by his commandments. The concept of complete forgiveness of sins perhaps has played one of the major roles in the success of the spread of Christianity, although bloody conversions have also taken place throughout history.

Christianity reached Russia in the tenth Century. At that point Russia was ruled by Prince Vladimir. Vladimir had several religions to choose from. There were the pagan religions among the Slavs, which were fully developed and spread across the territory. Other religions such as Judaism and Islam were also part of the picture for the Prince. However, there are two major factors that contributed to Vladimir's decision. On the one hand, he needed a strong ally who can help him in gaining total control of the land. Vladimir saw this in the face of the Byzantine Empire. The second was more mystical in nature. According to early writings, Vladimir was becoming blind. A princess suggested that he get baptized as soon as possible. After his baptism, Vladimir regained his vision; this influenced his decision in accepting Orthodox Christianity as the state religion.

In the mind of Russian people this legend has contributed to setting a strong example of the greatness of Christianity. The historical choice also reflects upon the morale and nationalism of Russia today. Russia not only adopted Orthodoxy, it made it its own to a point where it became known as Pravoslavie, or the right to worship. Unable to completely get rid of the Slavic pagan traditions, the Church absorbed them and declared them Christian. Ever since, Orthodox Christianity has been a key factor in early Russian politics, from uniting the people to conquering other lands. Whereas Christianity was very successful in spreading across the world, other religions, such as Hinduism, for the most part, remained within its territory spreading only into Southeast Asia (Encarta).

Unlike Christianity, which has a founding figure, Hinduism does not. Nor does it have a single concept that can define it. Rather, it can be perceived as a religion of humanity, human nature, and the entire world. According to Monier-Williams, Hinduism "has no difficulty in including all other religions within its all-embracing arms and ever-widening fold". Hinduism, just as Christianity, had its predicator. It is the Vedic traditions of the Vedic India. Vedas consist of four major parts and thousands of texts. The age of its origin has been speculated to be around 1500-500 B.C.E. Most of the evidence for Vedic India is textural. These writings had influenced several cults, each named after a certain text: the Brahmanas, the Srauta Sutras, the Aranyakas, and the Upanisads. Throughout centuries the Vedic culture has been changing, eventually becoming what is known today as Hinduism.

Although certain beliefs, rituals, and myths have remained in Christianity as well as Hinduism, they both have evolved over the centuries and each adapting to a particular culture and time period. A good example of the adaptation of Christianity to a culture can be seen in Russian Orthodox traditions. Pravoslavie has played a significant role in the lives of the Russian people. It has survived from its establishment in the tenth century, to the Bolshevik revolution of 1917, through the Soviet regime, and to the modern day Russia. Ever since the fall of the Soviet Union in 1991, Russia has been experiencing a great spiritual revival. Even though Russian Church experienced an enormous prosecution under the Soviet rule, it was able to survive and maintain its traditions. The role the church plays in Russian society has become much greater in the past couple of decades. With Yeltsin, religion returned to the upper ranks of political spectrum. He was also directly responsible for rebuilding the Cathedral of Christ the Saviour.

It is important to mention that the Cathedral has been completely demolished by Stalin's order in 1931. It was the main Russian Cathedral that signified Russia's victory over Napoleon. With its destruction, communists hoped to diminish people's spirit. The rebuild of the Cathedral can be seen as a significant social event that reestablished Orthodox traditions back into the lives of the Russian people. After the fall of the Soviet Union, people began to search for new symbols and identity. The number of believers has been growing in the past few decades. For example, according to VTsIOM (a research group based in Russia), in 1991, 45 percent of people believed in God. In a similar report of 2002, the number of believers rose to 60 percent, and another 20 percent declared that they are not religious, but do believe in a higher power.

The Soviet regime tried to mould people according to their doctrines. The church, on the other hand, became a symbol of not only religion, but of the free spirit as well. With the idea of Pravoslavie as the main Russian religion, nationalism began to rise. Largely, many people blended the "National Idea" with the Russian Orthodox traditions. Historically, the church and state were inseparable. Even today, the role of the church in the society is seen as second to state. In some cases, actually, it is seen as first to state. The church once again, began to be an essential part of the society. Unlike Russian Orthodox, or Christianity as a whole, Hinduism does not strive to convert people. Nor does it attempt to be part of any political movement. By its nature, Christianity declares that it is the only way for salvation. Hinduism, on the other hand, is able to accept any religion and treat it respectfully. Nonetheless, it became a tool for Hindus to regain their sovereignty and identity.

Although Hinduism did not undergo colossal termination of its followers as Russian Orthodox Church did, nonetheless, it did suffer suppression throughout centuries. First, it was the Muslim invasion, which strived to convert India to Islam. Then, Christianity came with the same focus in mind, to convert the "unspiritual," "demon worshiping," Hindus (Encarta). The last external force that tried to rule India, were the British. Just like Russians, Hindus were in a need of nationalism. While still under the British rule, in the nineteenth century, Hindu leaders tried to reform Hinduism. A figure who was successful at doing so was Vivekânanda. Other two important figures who helped in revitalization of Hinduism were Dayanada Sarasvati and Arya Samaj (Encarta).

While Sarasvati used Hinduism as a response to challenges of Christianity, Samaj revitalized Hinduism. Further rise of Hindu nationalism fell upon the twentieth century. It became politically and socially expressed. In the second quarter of the twentieth century, Gandhi preached the non-violent and civil disobedience on a large scale. This became known as Satyagraha. It made the traditional values of Hinduism relevant and important to the people. Gandhi gave modern Hinduism the defining features it now has, by uplifting the tradition to a level of political awareness (Encarta). When Hinduism was revitalized, it helped the people to break away from the British rule and establish independence. It helped people to reestablish connection with their past and regain their identity as a nation. Similarly, the Russian Orthodox Church helped Russians to regain their identity as well.

By drawing the two parallels, it can be seen that religion plays an important role in establishing self awareness of a society. It also helps to pull through the tough times in a country's history and can help rebuild people's belief in them. Most individuals, who consider themselves Russian Orthodox, do not follow the numerous ritual practices of the church. Due to the repression of the church during the Soviet rule, many people lost the essential teaching of the rites of passage of the Orthodox Church. Therefore, many people believe in other phenomena such as astrology, reincarnation, and other pseudo-religious teachings. However, when it pertains to true Christian traditions, an individual's life can be divided into three stages: birth, life (as a Christian), and death.

Most Orthodox believers in Russia baptize their children when they are roughly two weeks old. The ritual of baptism is the first essential step in the life of an individual on becoming a Christian. It is a symbol of overpowering the original sin, which entered the world through the first man, Adam (Bible). The act of baptism is very important in Christian tradition. The ritual itself follows several steps. During baptism, the child (or an adult, depending on the situation), is dressed in a white garment, which represents purity. First, the Father (priest) reads a conjuration over the child in order to cast away the Devil in the name of Jesus Christ. Then, the sign of the cross is made over the child. It carries the same power as the name of Jesus Christ. Orthodox Christians use the sign of the cross in many instances to bring on the power of Christ.

During the baptism, a physical cross is put on the person. This represents a passage from the Bible where Jesus speaks that a person must bear his cross. Then, a person is submerged under water three times: in the name of the Father, the Son, and the Holy Spirit. After the child is baptized, the Father walks around the tub with a lit candle. If it is an adult, then the person walks around the tub himself, holding a candle. The significance is that the flame represents joy of the new soul in the body of Christ. After baptism, a person is anointed with chrism on different parts of the body: the knees, the upper parts of the feet, the reverse side of the palms, the temples, the earlobes, and the forehead. When this is done, the gifts of the Holy Spirit return to the person. The anointing is also carried out after baptism throughout the life of an individual.

Once the person has been baptized, it is a promise to God to serve Him as written in the Bible. However, no one is perfect, and people make mistakes during their lives. Therefore, certain rituals take place in order to help an individual return on the right path. One of the most important ones is confession. The confession exists not to embarrass a person, or to learn of his private life, but to help him understand where he went wrong and fix it. Confessions are private and confidential. Usually, a person is not required to tell the whole story behind his particular sin. It is important that he understands the wrong doing and brings it to God in front of a witness, the Father (Catechesis: 2005).

In order for a person to stay connected with his faith, the church has many rituals, prayers, and sacraments one can follow. However, not everyone follows every single ritual every waking moment of their lives. Most Russian Orthodox Christians do not attend church on regular basis, or stay for the full length of the liturgy. Some people attend regularly and try to follow the Christian teaching; others come once a week, or on major holidays. The main reason most people come to church is to gain peace, strength, and ask God for health (for themselves or their loved ones). The rituals, symbols, iconography, and the singing all create a feeling of holiness and the presence of God in the church. The physical objects represent the spiritual aspects of the divine. Perhaps the two most essential parts of the church are the icons and the singing. Iconography plays an important role in the life of the church, as well as an individual.

A common misconception about icons is that it is idolatry. This is far from the truth. The meaning of an icon lies not only in the representation of an archetype. They represent those people who have proven with their lives their sainthood. According to Neo-Platonic theories, the icon is a mystery, a vehicle of divine power, grace, and means of God's knowledge. It is an essential part of the liturgy worship. Icon unites the celestial and terrestrial Church. Despite being an important part of the liturgy, the icons play a role in sacraments. Thus, the baptism and the confessions take place in the presence of the icons. As Orthodox Christians believe in the God of the Living, they also believe that those who are represented on the icons, although dead physically, are alive in a different realm. Therefore, they can help a person by praying to God on the celestial level. This can help and solve the misunderstanding that people pray to icons. Rather, they ask the Saints to pray with them.

This can be seen as the constructive power of the icon. However, where the icons are supposed to help people connect with the divine, they can also play a destructive role. Because many people come to church when needed, rather than for the spiritual aspect, they tend to forget the true meaning of the icons. Instead, people can misrepresent the meaning of the icon, and instead of asking a saint to join him or her in a prayer, they directly ask a saint to help them out. This can be viewed as a destructive side of the icons. However, it is not because of the icon itself, but rather due to people's spiritual ignorance.

Another essential part of the worship in Russian Orthodox is the singing. Unlike the Catholic, Russian Orthodox singing is not accompanied by a musical instrument. Rather, it focuses on the emotional aspect of the musical element. The verbal elements of the liturgy are sung. This creates an emotional mood to the ideas being expressed. Depending on a service, the mood of the singing can go from a sad, emotional quality, and gradually build up to an uplifting musical element. In some instance, it becomes a chant through which prayers are recited. Perhaps the singing and the chanting in the Russian Orthodox can, in a way, relate to the chanting of mantras in Hinduism.

Mantras are hymns that are chanted or sung by the devotee. It is similar to the Orthodox tradition in that it uses the speech in a form of singing, or chanting, to achieve a certain spiritual mood. However, it differs in a way that the chant tries to evoke the power that is related to a specific word. According to Grammarian teaching, repetition of a word or a phrase can stir up the referent of the word and whatever spiritual power may be attached to it..

One of the major Hindu ways of life is the caste system. It is a system of social stratification. In this scheme, classes are defined by endogamous hereditary groups. Of these groups, the Brahmin take the highest place, followed by Kshatriyas, Vaishya, and Shudras. The levels of the system are believed to be determined by Veda. The castes are ordered by their degree of access to Veda. However, the doorway to Veda is the caste, and without the knowledge how to behave, the caste can be lost. Therefore, the crucial information the Vedas provide is what not to do in order to preserve the caste. Even though this is practiced in the social level, it also spreads across the political spectrum.

Same as the Russian Orthodox, Hinduism has its own rites of passage. They consist of the following rites: Jatakarma-birth, Upanayana-initiation (sacred-thread ceremony), Vivaha-marriage, and Antyeshti-funeral (The Heart of Hinduism). The marriage, perhaps, is one of the most elaborate ceremonies as it involves two families, uniting them in numerous rituals. According to Hindu beliefs, the marriage that takes place is a continuation from the previous births of the two people who are joining once again. It is also believed that the two families must develop bondage to fulfill their responsibilities toward their parents and ancestors. The responsibility is the procreation, love for their children, and thus fulfilling the God's creation.

Even though Hinduism believes that the two people are joining from previous birth, families from the male and the female sides make efforts to find the best match for their children.

Once a potential bride or groom is found, the family asks their child what they feel about their match. If the boy or the girl agrees (it is common for Hindus to call the unmarried people boy and girl), the family searches for a person who can act as a confidant to feel out their side. Once everything is arranged, the two families meet. This serves two purposes: the families can see if they like each other, and the potential bride and groom can evaluate one another as well. This is more of a social event. The first ritual comes in during the engagement.

Using astrological signs, a priest from both sides sets the date of the engagement. On the set day, the girl's family goes to the boy's family. For the special moment, everyone sits on the floor, as they would in any other religious ceremony. The girl's eldest brother marks the groom's to be forehead with red powder. He then presents a gift, a gold ring, a gold chain, or some other offering. The boy takes the offering, and in turn, his family presents the girl with gifts. Usually it is cosmetics. The present signifies the boy's parents' permission for the girl to learn proper use of cosmetics. The ceremony is accompanied by the chanting of the priests and some singing of the women. Five days before marriage, religious ceremonies take place in both homes. One of the most important events is the managalagâna. It is carried out by the ladies of the community. Music, dances, skits, and distribution of sweets are taking place on this event. It may continue for the five days.

One very important occasion is the reception. A maternal uncle is invited on the girl's side. On the day of the reception, the girl wears nath (nose ring), golden tika (forehead ornament), and let and bicwas (silver toe rings). The nath signifies that the girl is a virgin. This is given in a testimony of her uncle. The actual marriage ceremony is the marriage dinner. The ceremony itself takes place in the vivaha mandapa. After that, guests take their seats at the table. Here, another important ceremony takes place. Money is given to cooks or servants. The tray that is used for this is carried by the girl's brothers. Then, the giving of clothes takes place. This is a symbol that shows the newly accepted girl into the family. She is now fully accepted into her new family and is promised to be treated like a daughter.

Religion plays an important role in social relationships. It also is essential in helping maintain a healthy society. Religion is a pillar of society. Governments may come and go, but if people's spirituality is strong, their spirit will not be broken during hard times. By observing and maintaining the rituals that have been passed down through generations, a society develops its national identity. As history shows, this identity cannot be broken or taken away as long as the institution of religion remains strong. In order for that to happen, people must make every effort to preserve their beliefs on the individual level. Only when people's faith and traditions are strong, their identity will not be lost.

RELIGION IN SOCIETY COMPARED TO THAT OF SCIENCE

The function of religion in society, as it is generally (mis)understood, is that it provides answers to questions of our existence and how to conduct our lives in relationship to oneself as well as others. Another function of religion is that it prepares oneself for the supposed life hereafter. Many theists in modern society believe that, as another function of religion, the Bible has been a vital reference for the construction of our contemporary moral code and "law of the land." If common law were governed by religious dogma such as the Bible, then we would still be practicing slavery, stoning people to death, etc. The basis for our moral behaviour as a species is not influenced by any organized religion. If anything, I would say that our morality has evolved in spite of the Bible. This has been done through a constantly shifting Zeitgeist over history. We see this especially in issues such as sexism, racism, and slavery, all of which the Bible has at one point condoned. Through time, religious moderates have come to cherry pick certain parts of the Bible that happen to coincide morally with the Zeitgeist.

The parts of the Bible that jive with modern belief are merely a matter of happenstance. Humanity from every civilization throughout time has had some sense of morality, and they clearly have had no access to the Bible. It may have been legislation only through secular means that has allowed us to return to the Bible with the ability to cherry pick what we have come to understand as moral or immoral. There can also be a Darwinian explanation. But whatever has given us our contemporary moral outlook; it certainly is not the Bible. Furthermore, despite popular views that this nation was founded on Christian principles, I would argue that Thomas Jefferson, by today's standards, would be considered an agnostic, if not an atheist. To talk of immaterial existences, is to talk of nothings. To say that the human soul, angels, God, are immaterial, is to say they are nothings, or that there is no God, no angels, no soul. I cannot reason otherwise. - Thomas Jefferson

Durkheim viewed religion as linked with a deep-seated division within all human experiences. This division, as Durkheim described, fell upon two ideas: The profane and the sacred. The profane refers to the realm of routine experience and ordinary, everyday life. The sacred, on the other hand, is the realm of human experience "outside" that of the mundane, whose existence is non-empirical. The sacred seems to demand a sort of unwarranted respect, as it is often seen as taboo to question someone's faith. However, Durkheim's postulated division seems to have gone into overdrive, as religion has gained an impenetrable cloak to criticism; whereas science seems to be chastised mercilessly for its doings - from the outset of teaching evolution in schools to current stem cell research.

The faithful direct their focus toward monuments, hymns, and ritualistic activities to make sense of things. This kind of behaviour, for many, is relied upon for support and guidance in turbulent times, whether internal or external. President George W. Bush rushed to Virginia to speak at a large convocation the day after the college shooting and tried to set the tone for what could be said about them. "It's impossible to make sense of such violence and suffering," he said. Refrain from asking ask "why," and do not even try to understand. It makes no sense according to Bush. Instead, his message was this:

These sources of strength are also in the faith that sustains so many of us. Across the town of Blacksburg and in towns all across America, houses of worship from every faith have opened their doors and have lifted you up in prayer. People who have never met you are praying for you; they're praying for your friends who have fallen and who are injured. There's a power in these prayers, real power. In times like this, we can find comfort in the grace and guidance of a loving God. - George W. Bush.

Religious Rights under the Ottoman Empire

The new Ottoman government that arose from the ashes of Byzantine civilization was neither primitive nor barbaric. Islam not only recognised Jesus as a great prophet, but tolerated Christians as another People of the Book. As such, the Church was not extinguished nor was its canonical and hierarchical organisation significantly disrupted. Its administration continued to function. One of the first things that Mehmet the Conqueror did was to allow the Church to elect a new patriarch, Gennadius Scholarius. The Hagia Sophia and the Parthenon, which had been Christian churches for nearly a millennium were, admittedly, converted into mosques, yet countless other churches, both in Constantinople and elsewhere, remained in Christian hands.

Moreover, it is striking that the patriarch's and the hierarchy's position was considerably strengthened and their power increased. They were endowed with civil as well as ecclesiastical power over all Christians in Ottoman territories. Because Islamic law makes no distinction between nationality and religion, all Christians, regardless of their language or nationality, were considered a single millet, or nation. The patriarch, as the highest ranking hierarch, was thus invested with civil and religious authority and made ethnarch, head of the entire Christian Orthodox population. Practically, this meant that all Orthodox Churches within Ottoman territory were under the control of Constantinople. Thus, the authority and jurisdictional frontiers of the patriarch were enormously enlarged.

However, these rights and privileges, including freedom of worship and religious organisation, were often established in principle but seldom corresponded to reality. The legal privileges of the patriarch and the Church depended, in fact, on the whim and mercy of the Sultan and the Sublime Porte, while all Christians were viewed as little more than second-class citizens. Moreover, Turkish corruption and brutality were not a myth. That it was the "infidel" Christian who experienced this more than anyone else is not in doubt. Nor were pogroms of Christians in these centuries unknown. Devastating, too, for the Church was the fact that it could not bear witness to Christ. Missionary work among Moslems was dangerous and indeed impossible, whereas conversion to Islam was entirely legal and permissible. Converts to Islam who returned to Orthodoxy were put to death as apostates. No new churches could be built and even the ringing of church bells was prohibited. Education of the clergy and the Christian population either ceased altogether or was reduced to the most rudimentary elements.

Corruption

The Orthodox Church found itself subject to the Turkish system of corruption. The patriarchal throne was frequently sold to the highest bidder, while new patriarchal investiture was accompanied by heavy payment to the government. In order to recoup their losses, patriarchs and bishops taxed the local parishes and their clergy. Nor was the patriarchal throne ever secure. Few patriarchs between the fifteenth and the nineteenth centuries died a natural death while in office. The forced abdications, exiles, hangings, drowning, and poisonings of patriarchs are well documented. But if the patriarch's position was precarious so was the hierarchy's. The hanging of patriarch Gregory V from the gate of the patriarchate on Easter Sunday 1821 was accompanied by the execution of two metropolitans and twelve bishops.

Devshirmeh

Devshirmeh was the system of the collection of young boys from conquered Christian lands by the Ottoman sultans as a form of regular taxation in order to build a loyal army (formerly largely composed of war captives) and the class of (military) administrators called the "Janissaries", or other servants such as tellak in hamams. The word devirme means "collecting, gathering" in Ottoman Turkish. Boys delivered to the Ottomans in this way were called ghilmán or acemi oglanlar ("novice boys").

Western Schism

The Western Schism, or Papal Schism, was a prolonged period of crisis in Latin Christendom from 1378 to 1416, when there were two or more claimants to the See of Rome and there was conflict concerning the rightful holder of the papacy. The conflict was political, rather than doctrinal, in nature. In 1309, Pope Clement V, due to political considerations, moved to Avignon in southern France and exercised his pontificate there. For sixty-nine years popes resided in Avignon rather than Rome. This was not only an obvious source of not only confusion but of political animosity as the prestige and influence of city of Rome waned without a resident pontiff.

Though Pope Gregory XI, a Frenchman, returned to Rome in 1378, the strife between Italian and French factions intensified, especially following his subsequent death. In 1378 the conclave, elected an Italian from Naples, Pope Urban VI; his intransigence in office soon alienated the French cardinals, who withdrew to a conclave of their own, asserting the previous election was invalid since its decision had been made under the duress of a riotous mob. They elected one of their own, Robert of Geneva, who took the name Pope Clement VII. By 1379, he was back in the palace of popes in Avignon, while Urban VI remained in Rome.

For nearly forty years, there were two papal curias and two sets of cardinals, each electing a new pope for Rome or Avignon when death created a vacancy. Each pope lobbied for support among kings and princes who played them off against each other, changing allegiance according to political advantage. In 1409, a council was convened at Pisa to resolve the issue. The council declared both existing popes to be schismatic (Gregory XII from Rome, Benedict XIII from Avignon) and appointed a new one, Alexander V.

But the existing popes refused to resign and thus there were three papal claimants. Another council was convened in 1414, the Council of Constance. In March 1415 the Pisan pope, John XXIII, fled from Constance in disguise; he was brought back a prisoner and deposed in May. The Roman pope, Gregory XII, resigned voluntarily in July. The Avignon pope, Benedict XIII, did not refuse to come to Constance; nor would he consider resignation. The council finally deposed him in July 1417. The council in Constance, having finally cleared the field of popes and antipopes, elected Pope Martin V as pope in November.

Church and the Italian Renaissance (1399–1599)

The Renaissance was a period of great cultural change and achievement, marked in Italy by a classical orientation and an increase of wealth through mercantile trade. The City of Rome, the Papacy, and the Papal States were all affected by the Renaissance. On the one hand, it was a time of great artistic patronage and architectural magnificence, where the Church pardoned such artists as Michelangelo, Brunelleschi, Bramante, Raphael, Fra Angelico, Donatello, and da Vinci. On the other hand, wealthy Italian families often secured episcopal offices, including the papacy, for their own members, some of whom were known for immorality, such as Alexander VI and Sixtus IV.

In addition to being the head of the Church, the Pope became one of Italy's most important secular rulers, and pontiffs such as Julius II often waged campaigns to protect and expand their temporal domains. Furthermore, the popes, in a spirit of refined competition with other Italian lords, spent lavishly both on private luxuries but also on public works, repairing or building churches, bridges, and a magnificent system of aqueducts in Rome that still function today. It was during this time that St. Peter's Basilica, perhaps the most recognised Christian church, was built on the site of the old Constantinian basilica. It was also a time of increased contact with Greek culture, opening up new avenues of learning, especially in the fields of philosophy, poetry, classics, rhetoric, and political science, fostering a spirit of humanism–all of which would influence the Church.

Muslim History

Muslim history began in Arabia with Muhammad's first recitations of the Quran in the 7th century. Islam's historical development has affected political, economic, and military trends both inside and outside the Islamic world. The concept of an Islamic world is useful in looking at different periods of human history; similarly useful is an understanding of the identification with a quasi-political community of believers, or ummah, on the part of Islam's practitioners down the centuries. Within a century of Muhammad's recitations of the Quran, an Islamic state stretched from the Atlantic Ocean in the west to Central Asia in the east. This new polity soon broke into a civil war known to Islamic historians as the First Fitna, and was later affected by a Second Fitna.

Through its history, there would be rival dynasties claiming the caliphate, or leadership of the Muslim world, and many Islamic states and empires offered only token obedience to a caliph unable to unify the Islamic world. The subsequent empires of the Umayyads, Abbasids, the Fatimids, the Mughals, the Safavids, and Ottomans were among the largest and most powerful in the world. The peoples of the Islamic world gave rise to many centers of culture and science and produced notable scientists, astronomers, mathematicians, doctors, nurses and philosophers during the Golden Age of Islam. Technology flourished; there was much investment in economic infrastructure, such as irrigation systems and canals; stress on the importance of reading the Quran produced a comparatively high level of literacy in the general populace.

In the 18th and 19th centuries A.D., Islamic regions fell under the sway of European imperial powers. Following World War I, the remnants of the Ottoman Empire were parcelled out as European protectorates. Since then, there has been no major widely-accepted claim to the caliphate (which had been last claimed by the Ottomans). Although affected by various ideologies, such as communism, during much of the twentieth century, Islamic identity and Islam's salience on political questions have arguably increased during the late twentieth century and early twenty-first century. Rapid growth, western interests in Islamic regions, international conflicts and globalization influenced Islam's importance in shaping the world of the twenty-first century.

There are several Muslim versions of early Islamic history as written by the Sunni, Shi'a, and Ibadi sects. Nineteenth century Western scholars tended to privilege the Sunni versions; the Sunni are the largest branch of Islam, and their books and scholars were easily available. Over the last hundred years, Western scholars have become much more willing to question the orthodox view and to advance new theories and new narratives.

According to the traditionalist view, the Quran began with revelations on Muhammad's divine revelations in AD 610. The verses of the Quran were written down and memorized during his life. Mecca was conquered by the Muslims in the year AD 630. In 628 the Meccan tribe of Quraish and the Muslim community in Medina had signed a truce called the Treaty of Hudaybiyya beginning a ten-year period of peace, which was broken when the Quraish and their allies, the tribe of Bakr, attacked the tribe of Khuza'ah, who were allies of the Muslims. Muhammad died in June 632. The Battle of Yamama was fought in December of the same year, between the forces of Rashidun Caliph Abu Bakr and Musailima.

The gains of the Ummayad Empire were consolidated upon when the Abbasid dynasty rose to power in 750, with the conquest of the Mediterranean islands including the Balearics and Sicily. The new ruling party had been instated on the wave of dissatisfaction propagated against the Ummayads, cultured mainly by the Abbasid revolutionary, Abu Muslim. Under the Abbasids, Islamic civilization flourished. Most notable was the development of Arabic prose and poetry, termed by The Cambridge History of Islam as its "golden age." This was also the case for commerce and industry (considered a Muslim Agricultural Revolution), and the arts and sciences (considered a Muslim Scientific Revolution), which prospered, especially under the rule of Abbasid caliphs al-Mansur (ruled 754 — 775), Harun al-Rashid (ruled 786 — 809), al-Ma'mun (ruled 809 — 813), and their immediate successors.

Baghdad was made the new capital of the caliphate (moved from the previous capital, Damascus) due to the importance placed by the Abbasids upon eastern affairs in Persia and Transoxania. It was at this time however, that the caliphate showed signs of fracture and we witness the uprising of regional dynasties. Although the Ummayad family had been killed by the revolting Abbasids, one family member, Abd ar-Rahman I, was able to flee to Spain and establish an independent caliphate there in 756. In the Maghreb region, Harun al-Rashid appointed the Arab Aghlabids as virtually autonomous rulers, although they continued to recognise the authority of the central caliphate. Aghlabid rule was short lived, as they were deposed by the Shiite Fatimid dynasty in 909. By around 960, the Fatimids had conquered Abbasid Egypt, building a new capital there in 973 called "al-Qahirah" (meaning "the planet of victory", known today as Cairo).

Similar was the case in Persia, where the Turkic

Ghaznavids managed to snatch power from the Abbasids. Whatever temporal power of the Abbasids remained had eventually been consumed by the Seljuq Turks (a Muslim Turkish clan which had migrated into mainland Persia), in 1055. During this time, expansion continued, sometimes by military warfare, sometimes by peaceful proselytism. The first stage in the conquest of India began just before the year 1000. By some 200 (from 1193 — 1209) years later, the area up to the Ganges river had been conquered. In sub-Saharan West Africa, it was just after the year 1000 that Islam was established. Muslim rulers are known to have been in Kanem starting from sometime between 1081 to 1097, with reports of a Muslim prince at the head of Gao as early as 1009. The Islamic kingdoms associated with Mali reached prominence later, in the 13th century.

During the Abbasid reign, Baghdad became one of the greatest cultural centers of the world. The Abbasids were said to be descendents of Abbas the uncle of Muhammad claiming that they were the 'messiah' or saviours of the people under the Ummayad rule. Abbasid caliphs Harun al-Rashid and Al-Mamun were great patrons of arts and sciences, and enabled these domains to flourish. Islamic philosophy also developed as the Shariah was codified, and the four Madhabs were established and built. This era also saw the rise of classical Sufism. The greatest achievement, however, was completion of the canonical collections of Hadith of Sahih Bukhari and others.

The Fatimids entered Egypt in the late 900s, conquering the Ikhshidid dynasty and founding a new capital at al-Qâhira (Cairo) in 969. The name was a reference to the planet Mars, "The Subduer", which was prominent in the sky at the moment that city construction started. Caïro was intended as a royal enclosure for the Fatimid caliph and his army, though the actual administrative and economic capital of Egypt was in cities such as Fustat until 1169. After Egypt, the Fatimids continued to conquer the surrounding areas until they ruled from Tunisia to Syria and even crossed over into Sicily and southern Italy.

Under the Fatimids, Egypt became the center of an empire that included at its peak North Africa, Sicily, Palestine, Lebanon, Syria, the Red Sea coast of Africa, Yemen and the Hejaz. Egypt flourished, and the Fatimids developed an extensive trade network in both the Mediterranean and the Indian Ocean. Their trade and diplomatic ties extended all the way to China and its Song Dynasty, which eventually determined the economic course of Egypt during the High Middle Ages.

Unlike other governments in the area, Fatimid advancement in state offices was based more on merit than on heredity. Members of other branches of Islam, like the Sunnis, were just as likely to be appointed to government posts as Shiites. Tolerance was extended even to non-Muslims such as Christians and Jews, who occupied high levels in government based on ability. There were, however, exceptions to this general attitude of tolerance, most notably Al-Hakim bi-Amr Allah. The Fatimid palace was two parts. it used to be in the Khan el-Khalili area at Bin El-Quasryn street.

The Abbasids soon became caught within a three-way rivalry of Arabs, Persians and the immigrant Turks. In addition, the cost of running a large empire became too great. The political unity of Islam began to disintegrate. The Emirates, still recognizing the theoretical leadership of the caliphs, drifted into independence, and a brief revival of control was ended with the establishment of rival caliphates. Eventually the Abbasids ruled as puppets for the Buwayhid emirs. During this time, great advancements were made in the areas of astronomy, poetry, philosophy science and mathematics. The Arabs first began their conquest of southern Spain or al-Andalus in 710 and created a province under the Caliphate which extended as far as the north of the peninsula. After the Abbasids came to power, some Ummayads fled to Muslim Spain and established themselves in Córdoba. By the end of the 10th century, the ruler Abd al-Rahman III (912-61) took over the title of Caliph.

The Crusaders

Beginning in the 8th century C.E. the Christian kingdoms of Spain had begun the Reconquista aimed at retaking Al-Andalus from the Moors. In 1095, Pope Urban II, inspired by the perceived holy wars in Spain and implored by the eastern Roman emperor to help defend Christianity in the East, called for the First Crusade from Western Europe which captured Edessa, Antioch, Tripoli and Jerusalem.

The Christian Kingdom of Jerusalem emerged and for a time controlled many holy sites of Islam. Saladin, however, restored unity within the Umma by defeating the Fatimids, and was then able to put an end to the Kingdom of Jerusalem in 1187 C.E. Other crusades were launched with at least the nominal intent to recapture the holy city and other holy lands, but hardly more was ever accomplished than the errant looting and occupation of Christian Constantinople, leaving the Eastern Roman, or Byzantine Empire severely weakened and ripe for later conquest. However, the crusaders did manage to weaken Muslim territories preventing them from further expansion into Christendom.

The Mamluks

In 1250 C.E., the shortlived Ayyubid dynasty (established by Saladin) was overthrown by slave regiments, and a new dynasty—the Mamluks—was born. The Mamluks soon expanded into Palestine, expelled the remaining Crusader states and repelled the Mongol attempt to invade Syria. Thus they united Syria and Egypt for the longest period of time between the Abbasid and Ottoman empires (1250-1517).

The 20th Century

The modern age brought radical technological and organizational changes to Europe and Islamic countries found themselves less modern when compared to many western nations. Europe's state-based government and rampant colonization allowed the West to dominate the globe economically and forced Islamic countries to question change.

Demise of the Ottoman Empire

By the end of the 19th century, the Ottoman Empire had declined due to internal conflict and the failure to keep pace with European technological and economic development. Their decision to back Germany in World War I meant they shared the Central Powers' defeat in that war, which led directly to the overthrow of the Ottomans by Turkish nationalists led by Kemal Atatürk. Following World War I, its remnants were parceled out as European protectorates or spheres of influence. Ottoman successor states include today's Albania, Bosnia and Herzegovina, Bulgaria, Egypt, Greece, Iraq, Lebanon, Montenegro, Romania, Saudi Arabia, Serbia, Syria, Jordan, Turkey, other Balkan states, North Africa and the north shore of the Black sea. Many Muslim countries sought to adopt European political organization and nationalism began to emerge in the Muslim world.

Countries like Egypt, Syria, and Turkey organized their governments with definable policies and sought to develop national pride amongst their citizens. Other places, like Iraq, were not as successful due to a lack of unity and an inability to resolve age-old prejudices between Muslim sects and against non-Muslims. Some Muslim countries, such as Turkey and Egypt, sought to separate Islam from the secular government. In other cases, such as Saudi Arabia, the new government brought out new religious expression in the reemergence of the puritanical form of Sunni Islam known to its detractors as Wahhabism which found its way into the Saudi royal family.

The partition of India refers to the creation in August 1947 of the two sovereign states of India and Pakistan. The two nations were formed out of the former British Raj, including treaty states, when Britain granted independence to the area. In particular, the term refers to the partition of Bengal and Punjab, the two main provinces of what would be Pakistan. In 1947, after the partition of India, Pakistan became the largest Islamic Country in the world (by population) and the tenth largest post-WWII state in the modern world. In 1971, after a bloody war of independence the Bengal part of Pakistan became an independent state called Bangladesh. Today, Pakistan is the second largest Islamic country in the world following Indonesia. Pakistan is presently the only nuclear power of the Muslim world.

RELIGION AND THE UNITED NATIONS

Given the record of religious fanaticism, it is understandable that the United Nations has been hesitant to invite religion into its negotiations. However, the UN can no longer afford to ignore the immeasurable good that religions have done and continue to do in the world, or the salubrious, far-reaching contributions that they can make to the establishment of a peaceful, prosperous and sustainable global order. Indeed, the United Nations will only succeed in establishing such a global order to the extent that it taps into the power and vision of religion. To do so will require accepting religion not merely as a vehicle for the delivery and execution of development initiatives, but as an active partner in the conceptualization, design, implementation and evaluation of global policies and programs.

The historically justified wall separating the United Nations and religions must fall to the imperatives of a world struggling toward unity and justice. The real onus, however, is on the religions themselves. Religious followers and, more important, religious leaders must show that they are worthy partners in the great mission of building a sustainable world civilization and to do so will require that religious leaders work conscientiously and untiringly to exorcise religious bigotry and superstition from within their faith traditions. It will necessitate that they embrace freedom of conscience for all people, including their own followers, and renounce claims to religious exclusivity and finality. It should not be imagined that the acceptance of religion as a partner within the United Nations will be anything but gradual or that religious hostilities will be eliminated any time soon. But the desperate needs of the human family make further delay in addressing the role of religion unacceptable.

Possible Next Steps

For its part, the United Nations might begin the process of substantively involving religion in deliberations on humankind's future by hosting an initial gathering of religious leaders convoked, perhaps, by the Secretary-General. As a first priority, the leaders might call for a convention on freedom of religion and belief to be drafted and ratified, as expeditiously as possible, by the governments of the world, with the assistance of religious communities. Such an action by the world's religious leaders, which would signal their willingness to accept freedom of conscience for all peoples, would significantly reduce tensions in the world.

The gathering might also discuss the foundation within the United Nations System of a permanent religious forum, patterned initially perhaps on the UN's recently founded Permanent Forum on Indigenous Issues. The creation of this body would be an important initial step toward fully integrating religion into the UN's work of establishing a peaceful world order. For their part, religious leaders will need to show that they are worthy of participation in such a forum. Only those religious leaders who make it clear to their followers that prejudice, bigotry and violence have no place in the life of a religious person should be invited to participate in the work of this body.

The Promised Reign of Peace and Justice

It is evident that the longer the United Nations delays the meaningful involvement of religion in its work, the longer humanity will suffer the ravages of injustice and disunity. It is equally clear that until the religions of the world renounce fanaticism and work whole-heartedly to eliminate it from within their own ranks, peace and prosperity will prove chimerical. Indeed, the responsibility for the plight of humanity rests, in large part, with the world's religious leaders. It is they who must raise their voices to end the hatred, exclusivity, oppression of conscience, violations of human rights, denial of equality, opposition to science, and glorification of materialism, violence and terrorism, which are perpetrated in the name of religious truth. Moreover, it is the followers of all religions who must transform their own lives and take up the mantle of sacrifice for and service to the wellbeing of others, and thus contribute to the realization of the long-promised reign of peace and justice on earth.

4

Clash of Civilizations

That some barbed cartoons of the Prophet Mohammed could generate turmoil in so many countries tells us some rather important things about the contemporary world. Among other issues, it points up the intense sensitivity of many Muslims about representation and derision of the prophet in the Western press (and the ridiculing of Muslim religious beliefs that is taken to go with it) and the evident power of determined agitators to generate the kind of anger that leads immediately to violence. But stereotyped representations of this kind do another sort of damage as well, by making huge groups of people in the world to look peculiarly narrow and unreal.

The portrayal of the prophet with a bomb in the form of a hat is obviously a figment of imagination and cannot be judged literally, and the relevance of that representation cannot be dissociated from the way the followers of the prophet may be seen. What we ought to take very seriously is the way Islamic identity, in this sort of depiction, is assumed to drown, if only implicitly, all other affiliations, priorities, and pursuits that a Muslim person may have. A person belongs to many different groups, of which a religious affiliation is only one.

To see, for example, a mathematician who happens to be a Muslim by religion mainly in terms of Islamic identity would be to hide more than it reveals. Even today, when a modern mathematician at, say, MIT or Princeton invokes an "algorithm" to solve a difficult computational problem, he or she helps to commemorate the contributions of the ninth-century Muslim mathematician Al-Khwarizmi, from whose name the term algorithm is derived (the term "algebra" comes from the title of his Arabic mathematical treatise "Al Jabr wa-al-Muqabilah"). To concentrate only on Al-Khwarizmi's Islamic identity over his identity as a mathematician would be extremely misleading, and yet he clearly was also a Muslim. Similarly, to give an automatic priority to the Islamic identity of a Muslim person in order to understand his or her role in the civil society, or in the literary world, or in creative work in arts and science, can result in profound misunderstanding.

The increasing tendency to overlook the many identities that any human being has and to try to classify individuals according to a single allegedly pre-eminent religious identity is an intellectual confusion that can animate dangerous divisiveness. An Islamist instigator of violence against infidels may want Muslims to forget that they have any identity other than being Islamic. What is surprising is that those who would like to quell that violence promote, in effect, the same intellectual disorientation by seeing Muslims primarily as members of an Islamic world. The world is made much more incendiary by the advocacy and popularity of single-dimensional categorization of human beings, which combines haziness of vision with increased scope for the exploitation of that haze by the champions of violence.

A remarkable use of imagined singularity can be found in Samuel Huntington's influential 1998 book *The Clash of Civilizations and the Remaking of the World Order*. The difficulty with Huntington's approach begins with his system of unique categorization, well before the issue of a clash—or not—is even raised. Indeed, the thesis of a civilizational clash is conceptually parasitic on the commanding power of a unique categorization along so-called civilizational lines, which closely follow religious divisions to which singular attention is paid. Huntington contrasts Western civilization with "Islamic civilization," "Hindu civilization," "Buddhist civilization," and so on. The alleged confrontations of religious differences are incorporated into a sharply carpentered vision of hardened divisiveness.

In fact, of course, the people of the world can be classified according to many other partitions, each of which has some—often far-reaching—relevance in our lives: nationalities, locations, classes, occupations, social status, languages, politics, and many others. While religious categories have received much airing in recent years, they cannot be presumed to obliterate other distinctions, and even less can they be seen as the only relevant system of classifying people across the globe. In partitioning the population of the world into those belonging to "the Islamic world," "the Western world," "the Hindu world," "the Buddhist world," the divisive power of classificatory priority is implicitly used to place people firmly inside a unique set of rigid boxes. Other divisions (say, between the rich and the poor, between members of different classes and occupations, between people of different politics, between distinct nationalities and residential locations, between language groups, etc.) are all submerged by this allegedly primal way of seeing the differences between people.

The difficulty with the clash of civilizations thesis begins with the presumption of the unique relevance of a singular classification. Indeed, the question "Do civilizations clash?" is founded on the presumption that humanity can be preeminently classified into distinct and discrete civilizations, and that the relations between different human beings can somehow be seen, without serious loss of understanding, in terms of relations between different civilizations. This reductionist view is typically combined, I am afraid, with a rather foggy perception of world history that overlooks, first, the extent of internal diversities within these civilizational categories, and second, the reach and influence of interactions—intellectual as well as material—that go right across the regional borders of so-called civilizations.

And its power to befuddle can trap not only those who would like to support the thesis of a clash (varying from

Western chauvinists to Islamic fundamentalists), but also those who would like to dispute it and yet try to respond within the straitjacket of its prespecified terms of reference. The limitations of such civilization-based thinking can prove just as treacherous for programs of "dialogue among civilizations" (much in vogue these days) as they are for theories of a clash of civilizations. The noble and elevating search for amity among people seen as amity between civilizations speedily reduces many-sided human beings to one dimension each and muzzles the variety of involvements that have provided rich and diverse grounds for crossborder interactions over many centuries, including the arts, literature, science, mathematics, games, trade, politics, and other arenas of shared human interest.

Well-meaning attempts at pursuing global peace can have very counterproductive consequences when these attempts are founded on a fundamentally illusory understanding of the world of human beings. Increasing reliance on religion-based classification of the people of the world also tends to make the Western response to global terrorism and conflict peculiarly hamhanded. Respect for "other people" is shown by praising their religious books, rather than by taking note of the many-sided involvements and achievements, in nonreligious as well as religious fields, of different people in a globally interactive world. In confronting what is called "Islamic terrorism" in the muddled vocabulary of contemporary global politics, the intellectual force of Western policy is aimed quite substantially at trying to define—or redefine—Islam.

To focus just on the grand religious classification is not only to miss other significant concerns and ideas that move people. It also has the effect of generally magnifying the voice of religious authority. The Muslim clerics, for example, are then treated as the ex officio spokesmen for the so-called Islamic world, even though a great many people who happen to be Muslim by religion have profound differences with what is proposed by one mullah or another. Despite our diverse diversities, the world is suddenly seen not as a collection of people, but as a federation of religions and civilizations. In

Britain, a confounded view of what a multiethnic society must do has led to encouraging the development of state-financed Muslim schools, Hindu schools, Sikh schools, etc., to supplement pre-existing state-supported Christian schools. Under this system, young children are placed in the domain of singular affiliations well before they have the ability to reason about different systems of identification that may compete for their attention.

Earlier on, state-run denominational schools in Northern Ireland had fed the political distancing of Catholics and Protestants along one line of divisive categorization assigned at infancy. Now the same predetermination of "discovered" identities is now being allowed and, in effect encouraged, to sow even more alienation among a different part of the British population. Religious or civilizational classification can be a source of belligerent distortion as well. It can, for example, take the form of crude beliefs well exemplified by U.S. Lt. Gen. William Boykin's blaring—and by now well-known—remark describing his battle against Muslims with disarming coarseness: "I knew that my God was bigger than his," and that the Christian God "was a real God, and [the Muslim's] was an idol." The idiocy of such bigotry is easy to diagnose, so there is comparatively limited danger in the uncouth hurling of such unguided missiles.

There is, in contrast, a much more serious problem in the use in Western public policy of intellectual "guided missiles" that present a superficially nobler vision to woo Muslim activists away from opposition through the apparently benign strategy of defining Islam appropriately. They try to wrench Islamic terrorists from violence by insisting that Islam is a religion of peace, and that a "true Muslim" must be a tolerant individual ("so come off it and be peaceful"). The rejection of a confrontational view of Islam is certainly appropriate and extremely important at this time, but we must ask whether it is necessary or useful, or even possible, to try to define in largely political terms what a "true Muslim" must be like.

A person's religion need not be his or her all-encompassing and exclusive identity. Islam, as a religion, does not obliterate responsible choice for Muslims in many spheres of life. Indeed, it is possible for one Muslim to take a confrontational view and another to be thoroughly tolerant of heterodoxy without either of them ceasing to be a Muslim for that reason alone. The response to Islamic fundamentalism and to the terrorism linked with it also becomes particularly confused when there is a general failure to distinguish between Islamic history and the history of Muslim people. Muslims, like all other people in the world, have many different pursuits, and not all their priorities and values need be placed within their singular identity of being Islamic.

It is, of course, not surprising at all that the champions of Islamic fundamentalism would like to suppress all other identities of Muslims in favor of being only Islamic. But it is extremely odd that those who want to overcome the tensions and conflicts linked with Islamic fundamentalism also seem unable to see Muslim people in any form other than their being just Islamic. People see themselves—and have reason to see themselves—in many different ways. For example, a Bangladeshi Muslim is not only a Muslim but also a Bengali and a Bangladeshi, typically quite proud of the Bengali language, literature, and music, not to mention the other identities he or she may have connected with class, gender, occupation, politics, aesthetic taste, and so on. Bangladesh's separation from Pakistan was not based on religion at all, since a Muslim identity was shared by the bulk of the population in the two wings of undivided Pakistan.

The separatist issues related to language, literature, and politics. Similarly, there is no empirical reason at all why champions of the Muslim past, or for that matter of the Arab heritage, have to concentrate specifically on religious beliefs only and not also on science and mathematics, to which Arab and Muslim societies have contributed so much, and which can also be part of a Muslim or an Arab identity. Despite the importance of this heritage, crude classifications have tended to put science and mathematics in the basket of "Western science," leaving other people to mine their pride in religious depths. If the disaffected Arab activist today can take pride only in the purity of Islam, rather than in the many-sided richness of Arab history, the unique prioritization of religion, shared by warriors on both sides, plays a major part in incarcerating people within the enclosure of a singular identity.

Even the frantic Western search for "the moderate Muslim" confounds moderation in political beliefs with moderateness of religious faith. A person can have strong religious faith—Islamic or any other—along with tolerant politics. Emperor Saladin, who fought valiantly for Islam in the Crusades in the 12th century, could offer, without any contradiction, an honored place in his Egyptian royal court to Maimonides as that distinguished Jewish philosopher fled an intolerant Europe. When, at the turn of the 16th century, the heretic Giordano Bruno was burned at the stake in Campo dei Fiori in Rome, the Great Mughal emperor Akbar (who was born a Muslim and died a Muslim) had just finished, in Agra, his large project of legally codifying minority rights, including religious freedom for all.

The point that needs particular attention is that while Akbar was free to pursue his liberal politics without ceasing to be a Muslim, that liberality was in no way ordained—nor of course prohibited—by Islam. Another Mughal emperor, Aurangzeb, could deny minority rights and persecute non-Muslims without, for that reason, failing to be a Muslim, in exactly the same way that Akbar did not terminate being a Muslim because of his tolerantly pluralist politics.

The insistence, if only implicitly, on a choice less singularity of human identity not only diminishes us all, it also makes the world much more flammable. The alternative to the divisiveness of one preeminent categorization is not any unreal claim that we are all much the same. Rather, the main hope of harmony in our troubled world lies in the plurality of our identities, which cut across each other and work against sharp divisions around one single hardened line of vehement division that allegedly cannot be resisted. Our shared humanity gets savagely challenged when our differences are narrowed into one devised system of uniquely powerful categorization.

Perhaps the worst impairment comes from the neglect—and denial—of the roles of reasoning and choice, which follow from the recognition of our plural identities. The illusion of unique identity is much more divisive than the universe of plural and diverse classifications that characterize the world in which we actually live. The descriptive weakness of choice less singularity has the effect of momentously impoverishing the power and reach of our social and political reasoning. The illusion of destiny exacts a remarkably heavy price.

RELIGION AS A FORCE FOR GOOD AND EVIL

Religion is a unique force in society. It promotes both good and evil. Historically, it has helped to abolish slavery. It has promoted racial integration, equal rights for women, and equal rights for gays and lesbians. It has motivated individuals to create massive support services for the poor, the sick, the hurting, and the broken. Conversely, it has been used to justify human slavery; racial segregation; oppression of women; discrimination against homosexuals; other conflicts, oppression, and discrimination; and mass murder terrorism, and genocide."

"Religion drives some to dedicate their lives to help the poor and needy. (e.g. Gandhi, Albert Schweitzer, Mother Teresa) It drives others to exterminate as many "heretics" as they can....Religion has the capability to generate unselfish love in some people, and vicious, raw hatred in others." Unfortunately, a heresy as seen by one faith group is another denomination's or religion's orthodoxy. And so the hatred continues.

Expressions of Religious Hatred in Recent Decades

Christianity's main rule of human behaviour, the Golden Rule, tells its followers to treat other people as they would wish to be treated. This is referred to as an "Ethic of Reciprocity." Similar passages are found in almost all other world religions. Yet, even a casual examination of today's newspaper will show that religious hatred is often a motivation for intolerance, hatred, mass crimes against humanity, terrorism, and genocide. In the past 15 years, such behaviour has been observed in Afghanistan, Bosnia, Cyprus, India, Iran, Iraq, Kosovo, Macedonia, Northern Ireland, Nigeria, Pakistan, Philippines, Sri Lanka, Sudan, etc.

Even the United States is not free of religious hatred. In recent decades, we have noted reports of many isolated events displaying religiously inspired hatred. Some were:

- A lynching of person because they are a Wiccan — a follower of the religion of Wicca.
- A longing by a teleminister to return to olden times when we stoned religious minorities to death.
- A call by a Baptist minister for the U.S. army to napalm all Wiccans.
- Multiple calls for genocide to wipe out all Muslims or Jews.
- An attempted mass stoning in Arkansas of demonstrators advocating greater religious freedom and tolerance.
- Continuing attacks on churches, mosques, synagogues and other religious buildings.

Two of the Causes of Hatred

Religion can generate strong personal commitment and passion, expressed as caring, love, respect, and support for others. It can motivate believers to dedicate their lives to the alleviation of suffering and need. However, it can also motivate people to reject and hate both followers of other religions, and followers of no religion. This can escalate into actions of oppression, and worse.

We suggest that a much of the hatred are caused by two factors:

1. Truth claims: According to David Barrett, et al., there are 270 large religious traditions, and many smaller ones, in the world. Many people believe that:

Their own religious tradition is unique. It is divinely inspired revealed truth. The author(s) of their holy book(s) were guided directly by God to write religious text that is free of error. Some consider their faith's holy text to be the unique Word of God. We refer to this type of religion as a "top-down' faith: one that consists of divinely inspired truth that God has revealed to humanity.

Other religions were created by humans without any direct inspiration from God. Their holy books are very human documents, mistaken in parts, and limited by the scientific knowledge and the cultural outlook of the authors. Their God or pantheons of deities were created by humans. We refer to this type of religion as "bottom-up" faith: a belief system created by humans and projected onto God.

Religiously-based conflict is facilitated when believers from different religions come in contact with each other, each believing that:

They alone have the complete "truth."
All others are in various degrees of error, and
Their group represents God on Earth.

A major reduction in religiously motivated conflict might occur if people:

Recognized that their religious beliefs are largely determined by where they were born. If they were raised in Saudi Arabia, they would almost inevitably be Muslim. If the stork was blown off course and delivered them to a family in Alabama, they would probably be Evangelical Christian; if Brazil: Roman Catholic. If Iceland, perhaps Unitarian. And so on.

Their holy books are very human documents, mistaken in parts, and limited by the scientific knowledge and the cultural outlook of the authors. Their God or pantheons of deities were created by humans. We refer to this type of religion as "bottom-up" faith: a belief system created by humans and projected onto God. Realized that since their religion is only one of hundreds in the world, and that since religions teach very different beliefs, that the chances of their faith group holding the full truth is slim.

US VS. THEM PHENOMENON

All major religions teach an Ethic of Reciprocity. One example is the Golden Rule in Judaism and Christianity — to do onto others as you would wish them to do onto you. In practice, the Golden Rule fails because many people limit the application to their fellow believers only. We suggest that a substantial reduction in religiously motivated conflict occur if people were taught to consider the entire human race as their neighbors — all equally worthy of respect and caring. For Christians and Muslims, the Good Samaritan parable in Luke 10:30-37 might be a useful teaching aid.

The Connection between Religion and Anger

John S. Spong, a retired bishop of the Episcopal Church, USA distributed an essay titled "Understanding Religious Anger" to his subscribers during 2006-AUG. He has noted that it is common for religious people to express anger towards individuals of other denominations or faiths. He described two verbal attacks that he personally experienced: one happened while lining up at a university graduation ceremony; the other when a heckler interrupted him giving a speech.

He wrote:

"When one looks at the history of religious persecution, which has included such things as excommunication, torture, and the burning of heretics at the stake, there is ample evidence of hostility associated with Christianity. When one adds to that the Crusades designed 'to kill the infidels,' a history of anti-Semitism, and the wars between Catholics and Protestants, the picture of religion as a source of anger in human society, victimizing people in every generation, becomes clear."

He suggests that most of the anger expressed during the debate on women suffrage early in the 20th century, and on equal rights for homosexuals and bisexuals today has originated in the Christian churches. He links religious rage to the "frightened human psyche" that "needs the certainty of religion, no matter how narrowly defined, in order to feel secure."

He asks:

"Has religion in general and Christianity in particular degenerated to the level that it has become little more than a veil under which anger can be legitimatised? What happened to that biblical proclamation that the disciples of Jesus are to be known by their love? How does religious anger fit in with the Fourth Gospel's interpretation of Jesus' purpose to be that of bringing life more abundantly?"

"Perhaps the time has come to recognize that Christianity was never meant to be about religion; it is to be about life. The achievement of personal security is the goal of religion. The ability to live with integrity in the midst of the insecurity of life is the goal of Christianity. Religion seeks to control life with guilt. Christianity seeks to free people to be all that they can be. There is a vast difference. Perhaps it will take the death of religion to open us once again to the meaning of Christianity, even 'Religion less Christianity.' For the purpose of Jesus was not to make us religious but to make us fully human."

RAGE AGAINST THEISM

Stupidity beyond Belief

It almost seems as if religions are competing to see whose followers will believe the most outrageously ridiculous story.

It seems as if the religious hierarchies are testing their followers, seeing how far they can push the absurdity of their claims and still be believed. What they have shown is that it is not possible to concoct a story that is too ludicrous to be believed. Humans are basically so stupid that they are capable of believing absolutely anything and everything, no matter how ludicrous, absurd, incredible, irrational, illogical, contradictory and inconsistent. Among humans collectively there is no such thing as beyond belief.

Tell people that you can see and have conversations with their dead relatives and you will be believed. Tell people that there is an alien spaceship hiding behind the Hale-bop comet and you will be believed. Tell them that you have been kidnapped by aliens and subjected to probing and guess what, people will believe you. Tell people that you are a son of a god and you will be believed. Tell people that they are immortal and that if they follow your instructions they will get to spend eternity in heaven and they will believe you. Tell people that if they kill and die in the name of Allah they will go to a paradise where they will be eternally serviced by 72 perpetual virgins and they will believe you. You can then get them to fly jets into highrise buildings. You can even tell people that one plus one plus one, equals one and they will believe you. Mankind has a history of totally ludicrous beliefs. Mankind's stupidity makes religion possible.

Irrational Behaviour

People with irrational beliefs are far more prone to irrational behaviour. Religions are primitive superstitions based on ancient myths. Belief in primitive superstitions is irrational and leads to irrational behaviour. Flying passenger jets into the World Trade Center but one example. Practicing a 'go forth and mutiply' doctrine in the midst of an over population crisis, is another, but with far more dire consequences. Religions promote irrational, false beliefs that lead to irrational behaviour.

In 1215 the Fourth Lateran Council of the Vatican proclaimed the doctrine of transubstantiation. This truly bizarre doctrine claims that the host wafer miraculously turns into the body of Jesus during the mass. Soon rumors spread that Jews were stealing the sacred wafers and stabbing or driving nails through them, to crucify Jesus again. Reports said that the pierced wafers bled, cried out, or emitted spirits. On this charge, Jews were burned at the stake in 1243 in Belitz, Germany — the first of many killings that continued into the 1800s. To avenge the tortured wafers, the German knight Rindfliesch led a brigade in 1298 that exterminated 146 defenseless Jewish communities in six months.

During the Inquisitions the Catholic Church sentenced hundreds of thousands of innocent woman to death, (often by burning) for the bizarre crime of having had sex with the devil. During the Crusades millions of people were slaughtered for not being christians. Today a billion christians view the Crusades with pride. In 1980 a pig caused hundreds of Indians to kill one another. The animal walked through a Muslim holy ground at Moradabad, near New Delhi. Muslims, who think pigs are an embodiment of Satan, blamed Hindus for the defilement. They went on a murder rampage, stabbing and clubbing Hindus, who retaliated in kind. The pig riot spread to a dozen cities and left more than 200 dead.

Still in the Dark Ages

Here in the twenty first century, hundreds of exorcisms rituals are still performed daily. This barbaric ritual stems from the Dark Ages when people believed that illness was caused by demons and evil spirits. People who display the symptoms associated with possession are obviously suffering from severe psychotic episodes and should be handled with kid gloves by trained psychiatrists and not subjected to bizarre rituals based on primitive superstitions.

Religious psychosis

This world is one big madhouse in which billions of delusional people pray to thousands of imaginary gods. Religious beliefs are so totally absurd, that to actually believe them your have to be either insane or stupid. Insanity or stupidity, both scare me. Over 80% of humans are religious.

- No wonder this world is such a mess.
- No wonder humans are doing such a terrible job of managing this world.
- No wonder this planet is mismanaged beyond belief.
- No wonder we are heading headlong into environmental catastrophe.
- No wonder there are over three dozens wars currently being fought.
- No wonder there are over 100 million laid land mines in the world.
- No wonder trillions of dollars are spent on weapons while millions of children starve.

RELIGION AND WAR

There is this misperception that religions are about peace. Humans are so stupid that one only has to repeat something over and over again and the majority will end up believing it, even in the face of overwhelming contradictory evidence. For instance it is repeated ad nauseam that religions (even the Abrahamic religions) are about peace. Nothing could be further from the truth. One has only to occasionally read a newspaper or watch the news on TV to realize that. The evidence proves the exact opposite. G.W. Bush repeatedly describes Islam as a religion of peace. Even a man with an IQ as low as Bush's knows this is utter bullshit.

Right now the two largest religions in the world are effectively at war and that war is intensifying every day and is threatening to escalate into an all out global war with devastating consequences for all mankind including those of us who do not belong to any of them.

Religion's Crimes against Humanity

Daily we read about the awful atrocities committed in the name of religion. In the Middle East, in India, Pakistan,

Sri Lanka, in Indonesia, the Philippines, Northern Ireland, England, Nigeria, the USA, Afghanistan, Iran, Algeria, Sudan, Saudi Arabia, Bosnia, Chechnya, Mexico, etc. From the Sept. 11 massacre to the murder of doctors who perform abortions and violent riots over cartoons, religion is the prime motivating factor behind these insane deeds. History is littered with religious crimes, the inquisitions, the crusades, slavery, colonialism, countless wars and massacres. Those who can make you believe absurdities can make you commit atrocities - Voltaire

Far from promoting peace, religions do the opposite, they promote conflict. As long as there are different religions, as long as there are different denominations within religions, there will never be peace on earth.

How religions stimulate intolerance, hate, bigotry and violent conflict. There will never be world peace if religious leaders don't stop insisting that their particular brand of religion is the one and only true religion, the only path to salvation. For peace to have a chance, religious leaders would have to publicly recognize that other religions have equally legitimate claims to the truth, in other words they will have to admit that their religion might be the false one. Of course this will never happen because religions require absolute belief, absolute faith, in order to receive the level of commitment that they desire. The level of commitment, the level of devotion that high priests demand cannot be achieved among followers if there is the slightest doubt about the truth of their particular religion. They cannot allow for any uncertainties, any doubts about the truth and validity of their religion. People are not going to base their whole lives around, devote their lives to, blindly obey, worship, indoctrinate their children, donate money, pay a tithe, become preachers, priests, monks, nuns and missionaries etc. for a system that they are not absolutely convinced is true.

All claim exclusive truth, all, except maybe one, must be lying. There are lots of different religions, many claiming absolute truth, claiming to be the only path to truth, claiming mutual exclusivity, yet only one if any, can be right. Religions are threatened by other religions because the mere existence of other religions casts doubts about the truth of any one religion. The mere fact that there are many religions means that it is probable that any particular religion is wrong. Religions will always refuse to recognize that other religions have equally legitimate claims to the truth, because this would mean that they have to admit the converse, i.e. that all religions including themselves have an equal probability of being false. Claims of exclusive truth are vital in religious marketing, but imply that other religions are false, that they are based on lies, that they worship false gods. This leads to intolerance, animosity, violence and wars.

Religious Competition

The main causes of conflict in the world today are the fierce competition between religions, and between denominations within religions, for followers, for the minds and money of the public, for power and influence. Religion is a multi billion dollar business, religions hold enormous political clout. Religious hierarchies love power. It takes ambition to become a pope, archbishop, bishop, rabbi, ayatollah, imam, mullah, high priest or guru. Ambitious people always want more, more status, more power and influence, more money. Religious leaders not only want to hold on to their followers but they want to increase their number of followers. As long as there are different religions on this planet, there will be competition between them for followers, resulting in conflict and wars.

Divisive

You shall have no other gods before me. (First of the Ten Commandments) Religions are divisive, each claiming to be the only true religion, therefore claiming that other religions are false and untrue. This stimulates intolerance, hate, bigotry, an us and them, laager mentality, which often leads to violent conflict. "If you're not a born-again Christian, you're a failure as a human being." Jerry Falwell

"We should invade their countries, kill their leaders and convert them to Christianity." Ann Coulter Demonize

It is a common tactic of religions to demonize other competing religions, this stimulates intolerance and hate, leading to violent conflict, resulting in destruction, suffering and death. "The God of Islam is not the same God. He's not the son of God of the Christian or Judeo-Christian faith. It's a different God, and I believe it is a very evil and wicked religion." - Rev. Franklin Graham (son of Billy Graham) *(This idiot is of course too stupid to realize that this is a tactic admission that there are other gods)*

"First, set fire to the Jews' synagogues and schools. Bury and cover with dirt whatever will not burn, so that no man will ever again see a stone or cinder of them. This is to be done in honour of our Lord of Christendom . . ." Martin Luther

"The Westminster Confession of Faith, which was ratified by the Scottish Parliament in 1649 (Charles I Parl. 2 Act 16) and which became the subordinate standard of the Reformation Church of Scotland, identifies the Pope of Rome as "that Antichrist, that man of sin, and son of perdition, that exalteth himself, in the Church, against Christ and all that is called God". Mr Macleod

"To label people as death-deserving enemies because of disagreements about real world politics is bad enough. To do the same for disagreements about a delusional world inhabited by archangels, demons and imaginary friends is ludicrously tragic." Richard Dawkins

God's Chosen People

Claims that members of a particular religion or race are special in the eyes of their god leads to arrogance, to feelings of superiority, that others are of less value, less worthy, that their lives are cheaper. This makes it much easier to slaughter them.

Global Conflict

Vicious competition between the three main monotheistic religions, Judaism, Christianity and Islam has resulted in animosity and intolerance with each claiming to be the only true representative, the only path to the one true god. None of the religious conflicts have been as long lasting, intense and destructive as the Christian/Islam conflict. Today there is a very real danger of a global conflict between these two largest religions on earth with Judaism acting as the catalyst. Christianity and Islam both have their roots in ancient Judaism. Right from their inception there has been constant conflict, strife and violent confrontation, fueled by the intense rivalry between these closely related religions. Millions of lives have been lost.

The September 11 attack on the World Trade Center in New York has triggered a sharp rise in tension between Christianity and Islam and there now exists the very real possibility that this will escalate into an all out global confrontation. Religion could plunge the whole planet into war, with disastrous consequences for mankind. For as long as they have existed there has been animosity and strife between religions. As long as religions claim to be mutually exclusive, as long as they claim to be the one and only true religion, as long as they claim that the other religions, the other gods, the other worshipping rituals are false, as long as they continue to demonize each other, there will never be peace on earth.

More Twisted Morality

The Terri Schiavo saga is a typical example of how twisted, irrational dogmatic Christian morality can get. The whole hysteria over whether to keep Terri Schiavo on life support or not, was centred on whether she was conscious or not, i.e. in a vegetative state. The issue being that if she showed the slightest sign of consciousness she should be keep 'alive' but if it was shown that she truly was in a 'vegetative state' then the life support should be discontinued. In a display of stupidity so typical of fundamentalists they have got everything the wrong way round. It seems not the slightest attempt was made to image what it must be like to be conscious yet not able to move a muscle.

This inability at empathy results in not realising what a truly horrific nightmare it is to suffer from what doctors refer to as 'locked in syndrome'. It has to be the most horrific thing that can possibly happen to someone. Put yourself in that nightmare situation; imagine the absolute unbearable horror of not being able to move a single muscle. And it can sometimes go on for more than a decade. The whole issue was back to front. If the slightest sign of consciousness was shown then the machine should have been switched off. If she really was in a 'vegetative state' it would be neither here nor there if she was kept on life-support. If her parents could afford it and it was a source of comfort to them then by all means keep her on life support, but if there was the slightest possibility that she may have been conscious then her hell should have been ended and the machines turned off.

Heaven and Hell

The Christian right that fought to keep her on life support and prolong her so called life are the ones who supposedly believe in heaven. Unless they are sadistic, psychopathic bastards, why would they want to prolong her hell and delay her heavenly bliss? Surely if her parents and the fundamentalists really believed in heaven, really believed that she would experience infinite bliss after death, they would gladly have allowed her to die.

God's Will and Lack of Logic

It's the fundamentalists that harp on about 'God's Will'. So why didn't they leave it to God and disconnect the life support machines. Surely the logic of the 'God's Will' doctrine would demand that the machines that artificially kept her alive should have been disconnected and her fate left 'in God's hands'. Surely man shouldn't interfere with God's Will and artificially keep her alive with his machines. Let God's Will be done. Of course fundamentalists don't get logic, otherwise they wouldn't be fundamentalists.

Euthanasia

In a secular civilised nation, the option would not have been two weeks of starvation it would be an injection of morphine over in ten minutes.

In May 2002 the European Court decided that Diane Pretty should die a slow and agonizing death. This absurd conclusion was reached not through rational reason but by the irrational influence of religion. Twisted religious morality forces thousands of people to die slow painful deaths, it denies them the most fundamental human right of all, the right to one's self. The right to one's owns life, the right to decide when one's life should end, the right not to live in agony.

Stem Cells and Therapeutic Cloning

The twisted morality that would prevent science from researching cures for degenerative diseases, and head and spinal injuries, a perverse morality where a clump of cells assumes more importance than a fully developed, conscious, intelligent human being. So for the sake of a bunch of cells people should spend the rest of their lives in a wheelchair, incontinent and hooked to a respirator or die slow agonizing deaths. Children must watch as a parent slowly loses his/her mind. All this based on ignorance, on the primitive, obviously erroneous, superstition of soul. The real motive for this Luddite backwardness is that fundamentalism is threatened by the power of science, science makes their faith healing scams insignificant. Real scientific miracles totally overshadow their false miracles. Science is more powerful than their god, this is why they try and restrict science in every way, this is why they try to ban the teaching of evolution in schools. They fear the power of science; they fear that science will one day be able to help the paralyzed walk.

If these ignorant hypocrites manage to delay this research by say ten years, so it takes ten years longer to find the cure for spinal cord injuries that would mean that millions of paraplegics and quadriplegics would spend ten years longer in wheelchairs. If they delay a cure for Alzheimer's disease, millions will die in the most horrific way imaginable. And this is supposed to be about morality. No its not about morality, its about power. Fundamentalists are threatened by science, because science has proven to be much more powerful than their god, in fact science has proved the falseness of their beliefs, science has shown creationism to be false. Catholics believe birth control is 'immoral', and they base this on the primitive superstition of ancient scriptures. In fact uncontrolled breeding on an already overcrowded planet is immoral. It is greedy and arrogant to assume you have a god given right to spread more of your genes than anyone else. This planet is overpopulated and all those with more than two children are to blame. Famine and poverty are results of overbreeding. Catholic so-called morality leads to famine and poverty and all the suffering that goes along with it and will ultimately lead to a total environmental collapse.

HOLY HORRORS

A pig caused hundreds of Indians to kill one another in 1980. The animal walked through a Muslim holy ground at Moradabad, near New Delhi. Muslims, who think pigs are an embodiment of Satan, blamed Hindus for the defilement. They went on a murder rampage, stabbing and clubbing Hindus, who retaliated in kind. The pig riot spread to a dozen cities and left more than 200 dead. This swinish episode tells a universal tale. It typifies religious behaviour that has been recurring for centuries.

Ronald Reagan often called religion the world's mightiest force for good, "the bedrock of moral order." George Bush said it gives people "the character they need to get through life." This view is held by millions. But the truism isn't true. The record of human experience shows that where religion is strong, it causes cruelty. Intense beliefs produce intense hostility. Only when faith loses its force can a society hope to become humane.

The history of religion is a horror story. If anyone doubts it, just review this chronicle of religion's gore during the last 1,000 years or so:

- The First Crusade was launched in 1095 with the battle cry "Deus Vult" (God wills it), a mandate to destroy infidels in the Holy Land. Gathering crusaders in Germany first fell upon "the infidel among us," Jews in the Rhine valley, thousands of whom were dragged from their homes or hiding places and hacked to death or burned alive. Then the religious legions plundered their way 2,000 miles to Jerusalem, where they killed virtually every inhabitant, "purifying" the symbolic city. Cleric Raymond of Aguilers wrote: "In the temple of Solomon, one rode in blood up to the knees and even to the horses' bridles, by the just and marvelous judgment of God."
- Human sacrifice blossomed in the Mayan theocracy of Central America between the 11th and 16th centuries. To appease a feathered-serpent god, maidens were drowned in sacred wells and other victims either had their hearts cut out, were shot with arrows, or were beheaded. Elsewhere, sacrifice was sporadic. In Peru, pre-Inca tribes killed children in temples called "houses of the moon." In Tibet, Bon shamans performed ritual killings. In Borneo builders of pile houses drove the first pile through the body of a maiden to pacify the earth goddess. In India, Dravidian people offered lives to village goddesses, and followers of Kali sacrificed a male child every Friday evening.
- In the Third Crusade, after Richard the Lion-Hearted captured Acre in 1191, he ordered 3,000 captives — many of them women and children — taken outside the city and slaughtered. Some were disemboweled in a search for swallowed gems. Bishops intoned blessings. Infidel lives were of no consequence. As Saint Bernard of Clairvaux declared in launching the Second Crusade: "The Christian glories in the death of a pagan, because thereby Christ himself is glorified."

- The Assassins were a sect of Ismaili Shi'ite Muslims whose faith required the stealthy murder of religious opponents. From the 11th to 13th centuries, they killed numerous leaders in modern-day Iran, Iraq and Syria. They finally were wiped out by conquering Mongols — but their vile name survives.
- Throughout Europe, beginning in the 1100s, tales spread that Jews were abducting Christian children, sacrificing them, and using their blood in rituals. Hundreds of massacres stemmed from this "blood libel." Some of the supposed sacrifice victims — Little Saint Hugh of Lincoln, the holy child of LaGuardia, Simon of Trent — were beatified or commemorated with shrines that became sites of pilgrimages and miracles.
- In 1209, Pope Innocent III launched an armed crusade against Albigenses Christians in southern France. When the besieged city of Beziers fell, soldiers reportedly asked their papal adviser how to distinguish the faithful from the infidel among the captives. He commanded: "Kill them all. God will know his own." Nearly 20,000 were slaughtered — many first blinded, mutilated, dragged behind horses, or used for target practice.
- The Fourth Lateran Council in 1215 proclaimed the doctrine of transubstantiation: that the host wafer miraculously turns into the body of Jesus during the mass. Soon rumors spread that Jews were stealing the sacred wafers and stabbing or driving nails through them to crucify Jesus again. Reports said that the pierced host bled, cried out, or emitted spirits. On this charge, Jews were burned at the stake in 1243 in Belitz, Germany — the first of many killings that continued into the 1800s. To avenge the tortured host, the German knight Rindfliesch led a brigade in 1298 that exterminated 146 defenseless Jewish communities in six months.
- In the 1200s the Incas built their empire in Peru, a society dominated by priests reading daily magical signs and offering sacrifices to appease many gods. At major

ceremonies up to 200 children were burned as offerings. Special "chosen women"—comely virgins without blemish—were strangled.

- Also during the 1200s, the hunt for Albigensian heretics led to establishment of the Inquisition, which spread over Europe. Pope Innocent IV authorized torture. Under interrogation by Dominican priests, screaming victims were stretched, burned, pierced and broken on fiendish pain machines to make them confess to disbelief and to identify fellow transgressors. Inquisitor Robert le Bourge sent 183 people to the stake in a single week.
- In Spain, where many Jews and Moors had converted to escape persecution, inquisitors sought those harboring their old faith. At least 2,000 Spanish backsliders were burned. Executions in other countries included the burning of scientists such as mathematician-philosopher Giordano Bruno, who espoused Copernicus's theory that the planets orbit the sun.
- When the Black Death swept Europe in 1348-1349, rumors alleged that it was caused by Jews poisoning wells. Hysterical mobs slaughtered thousands of Jews in several countries. In Speyer, Germany, the burned bodies were piled into giant wine casks and sent floating downs the Rhine. In northern Germany Jews were walled up alive in their homes to suffocate or starve. The Flagellants, an army of penitents who whipped themselves bloody, stormed the Jewish quarter of Frankfurt in a gruesome massacre. The prince of Thuringia announced that he had burned his Jews for the honor of God.
- The Aztecs began their elaborate theocracy in the 1300s and brought human sacrifice to a golden era. About 20,000 people were killed yearly to appease gods — especially the sun god, who needed daily "nourishment" of blood. Hearts of sacrifice victims were cut out, and some bodies were eaten ceremoniously. Other victims were drowned, beheaded, burned or dropped from heights. In a rite to the rain god, shrieking children were killed at several sites

so that their tears might induce rain. In a rite to the maize goddess, a virgin danced for 24 hours, then was killed and skinned; her skin was worn by a priest in further dancing. One account says that at King Ahuitzotl's coronation, 80,000 prisoners were butchered to please the gods.

- In the 1400s, the Inquisition shifted its focus to witchcraft. Priests tortured untold thousands of women into confessing that they were witches who flew through the sky and engaged in sex with the devil — then they were burned or hanged for their confessions. Witch hysteria raged for three centuries in a dozen nations. Estimates of the number executed vary from 100,000 to 2 million. Whole villages were exterminated. In the first half of the 17th century, about 5,000 "witches" were put to death in the French province of Alsace, and 900 were burned in the Bavarian city of Bamberg. The witch craze was religious madness at its worst.
- The "Protestant Inquisition" is a term applied to the severities of John Calvin in Geneva and Queen Elizabeth I in England during the 1500s. Calvin's followers burned 58 "heretics," including theologian Michael Servetus, who doubted the Trinity. Elizabeth I outlawed Catholicism and executed about 200 Catholics.
- Protestant Huguenots grew into an aggressive minority in France in the 1500s — until repeated Catholic reprisals smashed them. On Saint Bartholomew's Day in 1572, Catherine de Medicis secretly authorized Catholic dukes to send their soldiers into Huguenot neighborhoods and slaughter families. This massacre touched off a six-week bloodbath in which Catholics murdered about 10,000 Huguenots. Other persecutions continued for two centuries, until the French Revolution. One group of Huguenots escaped to Florida; in 1565 a Spanish brigade discovered their colony, denounced their heresy, and killed them all.

- Members of India's Thuggee sect strangled people as sacrifices to appease the bloodthirsty goddess Kali, a practice beginning in the 1500s. The number of victims has been estimated to be as high as 2 million. Thugs were claiming about 20,000 lives a year in the 1800s until British rulers stamped them out. At a trial in 1840, one Thug was accused of killing 931 people. Today, some Hindu priests still sacrifice goats to Kali.
- The Anabaptists, communal "rebaptizers," were slaughtered by both Catholic and Protestant authorities. In Munster, Germany, Anabaptists took control of the city, drove out the clergymen, and proclaimed a New Zion. The bishop of Munster began an armed siege. While the townspeople starved, the Anabaptist leader proclaimed him king and executed dissenters. When Munster finally fell, the chief Anabaptists were tortured to death with red-hot pincers and their bodies hung in iron cages from a church steeple.
- Oliver Cromwell was deemed a moderate because he massacred only Catholics and Anglicans, not other Protestants. This Puritan general commanded Bible-carrying soldiers, whom he roused to religious fervor. After decimating an Anglican army, Cromwell said, "God made them as stubble to our swords." He demanded the beheading of the defeated King Charles I, and made himself the holy dictator of England during the 1650s. When his army crushed the hated Irish Catholics, he ordered the execution of the surrendered defenders of Drogheda and their priests, calling it "a righteous judgment of God upon these barbarous wretches."
- Ukrainian Bogdan Chmielnicki was a Cossack Cromwell. He wore the banner of Eastern Orthodoxy in a holy war against Jews and Polish Catholics. More than 100,000 were killed in this 17th-century bloodbath, and the Ukraine was split away from Poland to become part of the Orthodox Russian Empire.

- The Thirty Years' War produced the largest religious death toll of all time. It began in 1618 when Protestant leaders threw two Catholic emissaries out of a Prague window into a dung heap. War flared between Catholic and Protestant princedoms, drawing in supportive religious armies from Germany, Spain, England, Holland, Denmark, Sweden, France and Italy. Sweden's Protestant soldiers sang Martin Luther's "Ein 'Feste Burg" in battle. Three decades of combat turned central Europe into a wasteland of misery. One estimate states that Germany's population dropped from 18 million to 4 million. In the end nothing was settled, and too few people remained to rebuild cities, plant fields, or conduct education.
- When Puritans settled in Massachusetts in the 1600s, they created a religious police state where doctrinal deviation could lead to flogging, pillorying, hanging, cutting off ears, or boring through the tongue with a hot iron. Preaching Quaker beliefs was a capital offense. Four stubborn Quakers defied this law and were hanged. In the 1690s fear of witches seized the colony. Twenty alleged witches were killed and 150 others imprisoned.
- In 1723 the bishop of Gdansk, Poland, demanded that all Jews be expelled from the city. The town council declined, but the bishop's exhortations roused a mob that invaded the ghetto and beat the residents to death.
- Islamic jihads (holy wars), mandated by the Koran, killed millions over 12 centuries. In early years, Muslim armies spread the faith rapidly: east to India and west to Morocco. Then splintering sects branded other Muslims as infidels and declared jihads against them. The Kharijis battled Sunni rulers. The Azariqis decreed death to all "sinners" and their families. In 1804 a Sudanese holy man, Usman dan Fodio, waged a bloody jihad that broke the religious sway of the Sultan of Gobir. In the 1850s another Sudanese mystic, 'Umar al-Hajj, led a barbaric jihad to convert pagan African tribes — with massacres, beheadings and a mass execution of 300 hostages. In the 1880s a third Sudanese

holy man, Muhammad Ahmed, commanded a jihad that destroyed a 10,000-man Egyptian army and wiped out defenders of Khartoum led by British general Charles "Chinese" Gordon.

- In 1801 Orthodox priests in Bucharest, Romania, revived the story that Jews sacrificed Christians and drank their blood. Enraged parishioners stormed the ghetto and cut the throats of 128 Jews.
- When the Baha'i faith began in Persia in 1844, the Islamic regime sought to exterminate it. The Baha'i founder was imprisoned and executed in 1850. Two years later, the religious government massacred 20,000 Baha'is. Streets of Tehran were soaked with blood. The new Baha'i leader, Baha'ullah, was tortured and exiled in foreign Muslim prisons for the rest of his life.
- Human sacrifices were still occurring in Buddhist Burma in the 1850s. When the capital was moved to Mandalay, 56 "spotless" men were buried beneath the new city walls to sanctify and protect the city. When two of the burial spots were later found empty, royal astrologers decreed that 500 men, women, boys, and girls must be killed and buried at once, or the capital must be abandoned. About 100 were actually buried before British governors stopped the ceremonies.
- In 1857 both Muslim and Hindu taboos triggered the Sepoy Mutiny in India. British rulers had given their native soldiers new paper cartridges that had to be bitten open. The cartridges were greased with animal tallow. This enraged Muslims, to whom pigs are unclean, and Hindus, to whom cows are sacred. Troops of both faiths went into a crazed mutiny, killing Europeans wantonly. At Kanpur, hundreds of European women and children were massacred after being promised safe passage.
- Late in the 19th century, with rebellion stirring in Russia, the czars attempted to divert public attention by helping anti-Semitic groups rouse Orthodox Christian hatred for

Jews. Three waves of pogroms ensued — in the 1880s, from 1903 to 1906, and during the Russian Revolution. Each wave was increasingly murderous. During the final period, 530 communities were attacked and 60,000 Jews were killed.

- In the early 1900s, Muslim Turks waged genocide against Christian Armenians, and Christian Greeks and Balkans warred against the Islamic Ottoman Empire.
- When India finally won independence from Britain in 1947, the "great soul" of Mahatma Gandhi wasn't able to prevent Hindus and Muslims from turning on one another in a killing frenzy that took perhaps 1 million lives. Even Gandhi was killed by a Hindu who thought him too pro-Muslim.
- In the 1950s and 1960s, combat between Christians, animists and Muslims in Sudan killed more than 500,000.
- In Jonestown, Guyana, in 1978, followers of the Rev. Jim Jones killed a visiting congressman and three newsmen, and then administered cyanide to themselves and their children in a 900-person suicide that shocked the world.
- Islamic religious law decrees that thieves shall have their hands or feet chopped off, and unmarried lovers shall be killed. In the Sudan in 1983 and 1984, 66 thieves were axed in public. A moderate Muslim leader, Mahmoud Mohammed Taha, was hanged for heresy in 1985 because he opposed these amputations. In Saudi Arabia a teenage princess and her lover were executed in public in 1977. In Pakistan in 1987, a 25-year-old carpenter's daughter was sentenced to be stoned to death for engaging in unmarried sex. In the United Arab Emirates in 1984, a cook and a maid were sentenced to stoning for adultery—but, as a show of mercy, the execution was postponed until after the maid's baby was born.
- In 1983 in Darkley, Northern Ireland, Catholic terrorists with automatic weapons burst into a Protestant church on a Sunday morning and opened fire, killing three

worshipers and wounding seven. It was just one of hundreds of Catholic-Protestant ambushes that have taken 2,600 lives in Ulster since age-old religious hostility turned violent again in 1969.

- Hindu-Muslim bloodshed erupts randomly throughout India. More than 3,000 were killed in Assam province in 1983. In May 1984 Muslims hung dirty sandals on a Hindu leader's portrait as a religious insult. This act triggered a week of arson riots that left 216 dead, 756 wounded, 13,000 homeless, and 4,100 in jail.
- Religious tribalism—segregation of sects into hostile camps—has ravaged Lebanon continuously since 1975. News reports of the civil war tell of "Maronite Christian snipers," "Sunni Muslim suicide bombers," "Druze machine gunners," "Shi'ite Muslim mortar fire," and "Alawite Muslim shootings." Today 130,000 people are dead and a once-lovely nation is laid waste.
- In Nigeria in 1982, religious fanatic followers of Mallam Marwa killed and mutilated several hundred people as heretics and infidels. They drank the blood of some of the victims. When the militia arrived to quell the violence, the cultists sprinkled themselves with blessed powder that they thought would make them impervious to police bullets. It didn't.
- Today's Shi'ite theocracy in Iran—"the government of God on earth"—decreed that Baha'i believers who won't convert shall be killed. About 200 stubborn Baha'is were executed in the early 1980s, including women and teenagers. Up to 40,000 Baha'is fled the country. Sex taboos in Iran are so severe that: (1) any woman who shows a lock of hair is jailed; (2) Western magazines being shipped into the country first go to censors who laboriously black out all women's photos except for faces; (3) women aren't allowed to ski with men, but have a separate slope where they may ski in shrouds.
- The lovely island nation of Sri Lanka has been turned

hellish by ambushes and massacres between Buddhist Sinhalese and Hindu Tamils.

- In 1983 a revered Muslim leader, Mufti Sheikh Sa'ad e-Din el'Alami of Jerusalem, issued a fatwa (an order of divine deliverance) promising an eternal place in paradise to any Muslim assassin who would kill President Hafiz al-Assad of Syria.
- Sikhs want to create a separate theocracy, Khalistan (Land of the Pure), in the Punjab region of India. Many heed the late extremist preacher Jarnail Bhindranwale, who taught his followers that they have a "religious duty to send opponents to hell." Throughout the 1980s they sporadically murdered Hindus to accomplish this goal. In 1984, after Sikh guards riddled Prime Minister Indira Gandhi with 50 bullets, Hindus went on a rampage that killed 5,000 Sikhs in three days. Mobs dragged Sikhs from homes, stores, buses and trains, chopping and pounding them to death. Some were burned alive; boys were castrated.
- In 1984 Shi'ite fanatics who killed and tortured Americans on a hijacked Kuwaiti airliner at Tehran Airport said they did it "for the pleasure of God."

Obviously, people who think religion is a force for good are looking only at Dr. Jekyll and ignoring Mr. Hyde. They don't see the superstitious savagery pervading both history and current events. During the past three centuries, religion gradually lost its power over life in Europe and America, and church horrors ended in the West. But the poison lingered. The Nazi Holocaust was rooted in centuries of religious hate. Historian Dagobert Runes said the long era of church persecution killed three and a half million Jews — and Hitler's Final Solution was a secular continuation.

Meanwhile, faith remains potent in the Third World, where it still produces familiar results. It's fashionable among thinking people to say that religion isn't the real cause of today's strife in Lebanon, Sri Lanka, Northern Ireland, India and Iran — that sects merely provide labels for combatants. Not so. Religion keeps the groups in hostile camps. Without it, divisions would blur with passing generations; children would adapt to new times, mingle, intermarry, and forget ancient wounds. But religion keeps them alien to one another.

5

Religion

An Aid and Hindrance to Development

ISLAM AND CHRISTIANITY

There is little disagreement among social scientists that the integration of state and religion, which usually results in a theocracy or semitheocracy, is a serious hindrance to socio-economic development and progress. This is clearly evident in the experiences of many Islamic societies where religious states have hindered democratization and overall development of society. Such a hindrance has not been endemic among Muslims or Islamic societies. Stagnation of the Western civilization for a long period of time (between the fifth and thirteenth centuries) too was due to a similar characteristic, though not the same, that is, integration of church and state power. Joseph Stayer believes that the Church contained some characteristics of a state. Church was a permanent institution, and organized as a judicial system. At the time of secularization in 16th and 17th centuries these responsibilities were transferred to a secular state. Despite a common perception, however, development in the West was not due to the separation of the church and state; on the contrary, it was certain changes in society—primarily the emergence of capitalism— that resulted in this separation. What caused the emergence of capitalism? Many social scientists believe that rationalism was the main factor behind capitalist development in the West.

While these factors opened the path to capitalism, progress, modernity, and industrialization in the Christian West, the continuation of the predominance of religiosity of power in the Islamic East (the Ottoman Empire and the Safavid state) kept it lagging behind. Was this contrast in the course of development between the two due to some essential differences between Christianity and Islam, rendering the former open to but the latter incompatible with rationalism and modernity? As Lapidus argues, while there is consensus over the role of rationalism in capitalist development, there is no commonly accepted explanation as to what caused the prevalence of rationalism in the first place. With a focus on the case of Iran as a predominantly Muslim society, this chapter attempts to challenge religious determinism in general and Islamic determinism in particular. This chapter does not deal specifically with underdevelopment but rather with the question of why socioeconomic development has differed in the (Christian) West and the (Islamic) East, and why the integration of religion and state has been so persistent in the Islamic world but not in the Christian (Western) world.

Rather than seeing the role of Islam in socio-economic development as essentially different from that of Christianity, this study emphasizes the role of broader societal and historical differences rooted in the objective and material conditions of the societies in where Islam or Christianity were born or fostered. This chapter will argue that rather than Christianity or Islam per se, it is the variation in societal, historical and ecological conditions that led to the persistence of integration of religion and state and underdevelopment in Iran. The integration of religion and state in the historical process of Irans development is one of the most important factors contributing to the slowness of the trend of development in modern time in this country. This has been a product of the subsistence mode of production governing Iran. In order to analyze the role of religion in the development or underdevelopment of Iranian society and its comparison with the West, a number of assumptions or questions should be addressed first. Is there a causal relationship between Christianity and development in the West, and a likewise relationship between Islam and underdevelopment in Iran as has been assumed by some scholars?

The second question is whether the role of Christianity in the state power of Western societies is identical to the role of Islam in the state power of Islamic Societies. In other words, is there a difference between Islam and Christianity as far as integration of religion and state is concerned? A brief explanation of these questions is offered in the forthcoming section. By integration of religion and state, or a religious state, I mean a theocratic society. In a theocratic society, social regulations that ought to be based on rational, relative, changeable and collective agreements are based on religious principles; hence they are absolute, unchangeable, and autocratic. In such a society, the government gains its legitimacy not from peoples consent but from Gods will.

In a society in which a religious government rules, freedom of expression is limited and human creativity is repressed. The integration of religion and state leads to a more centralized and a more absolutist power, and this in turn leads to the creation of obstacles to rationalism, secularization, and pluralism, i.e. the three fundamental elements of modern civilization in the West. The medieval mind was dominated by the Church, literally, emotionally and intellectually. In this situation every decision made and behaviour is defined by revelation; faith, tradition, and ecclesiastical authority offered the answers and gave the orders.

POST-CONFLICT COEXISTENCE WORK

An unprecedented level of paradoxical religious movement characterizes the contemporary era. On the one hand, there is a greater number of people than ever before who are expressing either a secular perspective on life or a view of their own religion that is completely independent of traditional religious authority, dogma and law. In fact, there is more and more experimentation in some quarters on the basic meaning systems of traditional religion. This is particularly due to the unprecedented level of involvement of women in public religious life, but primarily due to the interesting interaction of the liberal state and free religious inquiry and experimentation. This is also due to the generalized modern experimentation with sexual roles and lifestyles. Furthermore, the unprecedented mixture of people of all faiths in many parts of the globe, but especially in large cosmopolitan centers, has also given birth to great creativity in religious life.

At the same time we are witnessing an unparalleled invigoration of extreme enthusiasm for old patterns of belief and practice on the part of many others. One is a function of the other, and a reaction to the other. Whereas the former depends on the liberal state, the latter is often expressed in active opposition to state authorities, secular authorities, and the basic institutions of global secular culture. This has set many religious people on a collision course with the rest of society, and in some cases, is creating serious levels of destructive conflict and violence. On the other hand, this religious revivalism is shaking up complacent cultural institutions of the modern state, and it is forcing most people to rethink their moral and political assumptions as citizens of their state, as well as citizens of global society.

This extraordinary level of religious activity takes place in the post-Cold war era. The post-Cold War era is also characterized by two countervailing trends. One trend is unprecedented economic integration and cultural homogenization, especially at the hands of materialist culture associated with the Western forms of investment, media, advertising and entertainment. But the other trend is unprecedented cultural/religious fractionalization. People the world over are rebelling against this materialist homogenization, searching out the roots of their identity, exploring the uniqueness of their background and its original systems of meaning. The pattern of intense integration, referred to above, is also felt in the liberal religious sphere in terms of multifaith communication and cooperation that has never seen its equal in human history. This too is transforming modern life and creating a common global culture. Thus, while the fractionating character of religious revivalism is more noticeable, and sometimes more violent, there is a quiet revolution of integration taking place as well.

It is not an age of a new world order, but an age of great social, cultural and psychological uncertainty in the context of an overwhelming and almost overpowering economic integration of the world. It is in eras of great uncertainty that we see some human beings gravitate to traditional religious systems in search of stability and identity. But how this search is undertaken, and how it integrates or disintegrates with the world at large, depends very much on the socio-economic, psychological and political situation of the individual and the individual group. The most important implication of this is that we see very different possible futures emerging from the human interaction with traditional religion at this point in time. There are patterns at work that indicate that religion is one of the most salient phenomena that will cause massive violence in this century. But there are other indicators from our current experience that suggest that religion will play a critical role in constructing a global community of shared moral commitments and vision.

Religion's visionary capacity and its inculcation of altruistic values has already given birth to extraordinary leaders, such as Gandhi, King, the Dalai Lama, Bishop Tutu, who, in turn, have had a dramatic effect on pushing the global community toward ever greater commitments to human rights and compassion for human and nonhuman life, regardless of race or citizenship. In other words, religion has helped set the stage for a fully functioning global moral community that may take a very long time to fully materialize, but that is unquestionably closer to fruition than a century ago. There have always been exclusive religious visions of a peaceful world. Never before in history, however, have so many leaders and adherents been inspired to work for a truly inclusive vision that is multicultural and multireligious. The contraindications to this trend are painfully apparent in the murders and tortures, and the religiously donated financial support for brutal regimes that have been abundant in recent history. At the same time there is an unmistakable level of global commitment to shared values that is being upheld and defended every day by literally hundreds of government and nongovernment agencies globally who adhere to and legally uphold the international agreements of the United Nations.

There is no doubt that, difficult as it is to imagine, the brutal abuses in places such as Bosnia, Kosovo, Tibet, and Burma, would be even worse than they have been if it were not for this global consensus. Admittedly, the latter still lacks the teeth of enforcement, and we stand deeply frustrated at the tragic failures. But from the long view of history, there is a remarkable shift toward moral consensus. Religious leaders, visionaries and activists played no small role in this, especially since World War II. What overwhelms our consciousness as of the Fall of 2001is the power of religious terrorists to kill an unprecedented number of civilians, especially due to willingness to commit suicide for the sake of otherworldly gains. In point of fact, suicide is the most difficult of all security breaches because it puts into question every human being one sees and what he may be carrying around, literally or figuratively.

In addition to the Al Qaida network, we should not forget that Timothy McVeigh was also deeply influenced by a paranoid and bizarre form of Christian identity. Furthermore, religious murder used to take much longer to carry out due to poor technology, but the sum total of its effects historically, in terms of the great religious wars and crusades, is well known for its massive atrocities. Our subject is how to deal with these paradoxical contributions of religion to the social order (or disorder) in the post-conflict setting when there is at least some collective efforts underway to promote coexistence between enemy groups. Radical religion as a destabilizing and destructive force in human history is well known, and forms a considerable obstacle to such effort in the past. From the earliest stages of monotheism this destructive side was manifest. Biblically based monotheisms—Judaism, Christianity, and Islam—insist on the sacred nature of the Hebrew Bible, and in that book genocide of select "idolatrous" nations is not only permitted, it is commanded. Whether or not genocides upon entry into the land of Canaan ever actually took place is hard to know, but the textual precedent for mass murder gave permission since that time for centuries of massacres of polytheistic natives across the world.

This is the sad result of successful Christian conquest of Europe, Africa and the Americas. Theology was always there at the critical moment to justify the slaughter. It goes without saying that millions of believers abhorred this, but, by and large, the organized hierarchy of religion was either silent or complicitous. From the Crusades to turn-of-the-century American decisions to Christianize the Phillipines, the results were always the same, the deaths of hundreds of thousands accompanied by cynical theological constructs. Islam's success was built on violent conquest as well, and the conquests continued well after Mohammed's death. The results were less bloody comparatively but quite intolerant by standards today of civil rights, especially for polytheists. And there were occasional periods of extremism at the hands of radicals such as the Almohides and Almoravides which were quite riddled with the deaths of innocent non-believers. Enslavement of polytheists and destruction of their own religions became standard, and some of this continues to this day, in Sudan for example.

Eastern and indigenous religions have had similar problems and byproducts. Indigenous religions in and stemming from Africa were often predicated on the use of occult powers to destroy one's enemies, while wars and violence built on Buddhist or Taoist principles have been well known from Japan to Sri Lanka, especially in the twentieth century. Religion had an important role to play in under girding the neofascist and racist political movements in South Africa, Bosnia, and Rwanda. In each case the complicity of leading religious figures or institutions was critical to the success of the oppression. Furthermore, at any number of times in the last twenty-five years, Israelis and Arabs came closer together, inching toward solutions, only to have religious extremists assassinate major leaders, including Sadat and Rabin, and slaughter hundreds in the most brutal fashion, thus creating impossible political circumstances that stalemated all efforts. The majority of Jews now killed by Arabs in this war are being killed by heavily funded religious extremists, whereas the backbone of the settler presence in the West Bank continues to be the religious settlers and their ideological supporters in the government.

Only the truly intolerant secularist would divorce this horrific evidence of religion's folly, on the other hand, from the equally compelling evidence that the creative imagination of religious geniuses from Amos and Isaiah to Jesus, Rumi, and Gautama Siddharta, have saved millions of people from their own worst impulses. In so doing they made a more peaceful world than what might have been. This is in addition to religion's inspiration providing the world, blessing the world, with political geniuses such as Gandhi, King, and the Dalai Lama, who undoubtedly saved hundreds of thousands, if not millions of lives, by steering their constituencies to nonviolent resistance and constructive forms of pursuing justice and peace. The interesting question is what are the cognitive and emotional underpinnings of great religious souls? What beliefs, practices, and mental disciplines animate their extraordinary courage and creativity? And how can this be put to use in coexistence work?

These are very large questions addressed elsewhere, but, in short, it comes down a series of beliefs and practices that become second nature, habits of the mind and heart that generate extraordinary paradigms of interpersonal behaviour that can be of benefit to religious and nonreligious actors alike. These beliefs tend to include: the connection or interrelatedness of all sentient life, the sacredness of each and every human being, and the possibility of human change and evolution for the better, or repentance. Practices tend to include a series of mental assumptions and concentrations that lead to a habitual embrace of compassion, peace, justice, mourning as a sacred task, forgiveness, and apology. Finally, the extraordinary religious peacemakers understand the power and importance of story, mythic structure, and, above all, ritual as a transformative act. Despite the presence of such extraordinary religious figures both in history and today, the fact is that we face some unprecedented circumstances of so many millions of religious people bumping up against competitors in a crowded and confusing world.

The question then becomes how to take the best of religious beliefs and practices and apply them to unprecedented levels of interaction. Here is where the intellectual class across the world, the ones who for centuries have been at the forefront of often courageous interreligious exploration, have done such a great disservice. They have emphasized the skills that they have—and not others—and overlooked the importance of skills that they sometimes lack. They have emphasized ideas, words, abstract discussions of theology or even comparative studies of myth, but not the single most important ingredient of coexistence: relationships and the emotional bond that is the bedrock of all moral interactions. What is needed globally is not just discussion and dialogue but relationship building, only one part of which is intellectual discussion and dialogue. It is the level of relationship that matters, not the level of dialogue. Relationship depends upon gestures of honor, shared understandings of civility, hospitality, generosity, expressions of regret, and shared defense against needless suffering. And that is just a brief list of characteristics of relationship building.

All of these characteristics of relationship building can be and must be justified by religious sources, especially because extremists will bring their own sources to deny the possibility or permissibility of relationship based on respect and equality. There is a critical role to be played in the generation of these relationships by model leaders on all sides. But, on the other hand, no peace process should be tyrannized and suffocated by backward leaders, religious or otherwise. Creative conflict resolution, including religiously informed conflict resolution, must work with but also circumvent encrusted leadership that is part of the problem.

There is one trait that is more important than all the rest for peacemaking, and that is humility, and the silence and listening to the soul of the other, that emerge from the discipline of humility. I am reminded of the enthusiasm that Buddhist teachers receive when they come to Israel, and how odd it is that these 'polytheists' would receive such a warm welcome, especially from Israeli youth. Young people always help us perceive what is missing in a culture, what its great weaknesses are. A young person has not yet had to buy into his/her culture and socio-economic prison, and therefore becomes an important barometer of tragic flaws. It is no surprise to me that these Buddhist teachers, who practice silence, laugh at themselves in ways unthinkable to monotheistic hierarchies, and speak, above all, and repeatedly, about humility and compassion to all living things, are the leaders that would attract young disaffected Israelis in search of spiritual solace. This is what is missing in life for many people of this region, both Jewish and Arab.

These young people are happy to respect and accept the more unfamiliar and strange aspects of Eastern spirituality because the underlying gentleness, humanity, and non-combativeness of these great teachers, such as the Dalai Lama, are qualities that they so rarely see in an environment that has made a tension-ridden state of no-war and no-peace into a cultural centerpiece. One cannot blame the inhabitants of

Israel and the Palestinian lands for evolving a culture of stress and argumentation. No one can pass judgment on how others cope with interminable violence. But one can, indeed one must diagnose what is wrong on a deep cultural, psychological and spiritual level, note how many are rebelling against this, and recommend future alternatives. It seems clear that, from a religious if not cultural viewpoint, humility, silence, and the wisdom of compassionate listening, have ample precedent in monotheistic literature, both as recommended moral behaviour, and as deep religious experience.

Throughout Biblical and Qura'nic literature humility is a *sine qua non* of the human being's position before God. It is a quintessential act of faith. In Judaism it is even portrayed as a Divine attribute to be emulated, and for all Abrahamic traditions the great prophet of the Bible, Moses, is described as the humblest of all men. As far as silence is concerned, Judaism and Islam are rather loquacious, in comparison to Buddhism, for example. Prayer is communal and loud; study is the same. But, in truth, Tibetan Buddhism has some pretty lively and loud elements to it that has struck a number of Jewish observers as strikingly similar to old Jewish forms of study and debate. It is the balance of silence and speech, of talking and listening that is intriguing in Buddhism. It is also the case that the Biblical prophetic tradition is a tradition that is characterized by as much silent listening as it is by long speeches. After all, where do the classical monotheistic prophets and heroes receive their wisdom if not through silent listening in desert and wilderness?

The monotheistic cultural tendencies of recent times could use a corrective from A. conflict resolution theory and practice and B. global religious traditions about humility, silence and listening. In this case, at least, there is a happy coalescence of at least some religious traditions and the most avant garde conflict resolution practice. The best peacemakers that watched work—the best social change makers in general—are people who understand silence, who value the "power" of orchestrating the evolution of human relationships without dominating those relationships or encounters. Such peacemakers are not afraid of and even welcome open discussion, but they do not relish argumentation for its own sake. They do not see every conversation as a win/lose phenomenon, and they do not mistake overall progress and success in their endeavors with the need to "win" in every encounter and conversation, even in their peace efforts. This requires great personal discipline, a very long view of time and "outcomes", and a strong degree of personal inner peace. It also requires a deeply felt patience, a basic trust of humanity and the world, viewed over time, and a love of imperfect human beings as such.

Many people I know who love peace have not internalized these values sufficiently, and thus become bad peacemakers despite their best intentions. The task of evoking and inculcating these values and worldviews is something that could benefit from a fusion of spiritual values and training in conflict resolution. The character of the peacemaker is a major concern in religious literature, and it should be the same for conflict resolution theory and practice. Till now far too much of the emphasis of conflict resolution has been on process, replicable processes for use in all contexts, as if peacemaking were a General Motors car to be disassembled and assembled in all parts of the world and all circumstances. But this becomes impossible and even barbaric, culturally speaking far better to offer ways to evoke the peacemaker herself from each culture and religion. Furthermore, eliciting the peacemaker is important and vital, but more emphasis should be placed on the moral character of the peacemaker.

A peacemaking personality has been the goal of many religious traditions. It is also a more elastic phenomenon. If you can trust in the personality of a peacemaker, you can trust her to adjust herself with humility to new and different situations, particularly involving alien or enemy others. Let us go further with the necessary characteristics of encounter.

The Compassionate Listening Project, founded by Leah Green, represents a conscious institutionalization of listening as peacemaking, together with another crucial psychological/ ethical capacity, compassion. Compassion is a basic Divine attribute in all monotheistic traditions, and there is much to build upon in terms of merging this value with techniques of peacemaking. Leah, and many others, such as Paula Green, have combined the capacity of "active listening" with compassion. Active listening distinguishes itself as a proactive process of probing, but subtle, questions which indicate to the other much more than respectful silence.

The complete silence of strangers, even the respectful kind is often viewed with suspicion: 'Do they really hold me in disdain?' 'Are they really seething with hatred behind the urbane smile and false courtesies?' etc. But compassionate, active listening is the kind of listening that leaves no doubts about the position of the listener. The listener may not agree with everything she hears. The listener may even oppose, when asked, the violent choices of the group. But she has demonstrated that she has not just been silent before the suffering—or the joy—of the other, but that she has heard, understood, and indeed felt it. Finally, humility necessarily interlaces—as many emotive/ethical gestures do—with the bestowal of dignity and honor, mentioned above. Human beings, particularly those who have suffered indignity and injury, crave the dignity of being heard and understood, almost as much as they need air to breathe and water to drink.

In our rush to economic and geographic negotiations of conflict we constantly forget this basic need. Leah's group has specialized in bringing groups to Israel to listen compassionately to the entire spectrum of Jewish and Palestinian political and religious life. This has proved to be transformative for many participants and should be studied further. Active listening is part of a much larger set of new and innovative paths of peacemaking that emphasize gestures, rituals, narrative, and relationships, all of which are under girded by the moral discipline of humility combined with compassion, active demonstrations of respect, and honor. And it truly is a discipline that requires years of practice.

Some further examples of this new work include shared study of sacred texts in Jerusalem, across enemy lines, with the act of study becoming the actual gesture of respect and reconciliation, but also the basis of relationship building, shared mourning, and constructive argumentation. Rebuilding destroyed religious sites has been an important part of reconciliation in Bosnia. The restoration of devastated or abused cemeteries has proven to be of immense value, as has been the visitation of sites of massacres, with the accompanying acknowledgment by word and deed of the pain of the other. In fact, much of the successful Christian-Jewish reconciliation work of the last thirty years has occurred at these very sites. Just recently in Jerusalem, just two days after Islamic extremist suicide bombers destroyed the lives of dozens of Israeli teenagers, there were shared celebrations of Ramadan and Chanukah by those superior religious souls of the region who hold on, sometimes by a thread, to relationships and humanization of the other.

The United States, Cambodia and India have seen marching used in an opposite way as it has been in Ireland. Both for war and peace, marching is a sacred act. But the point is that it is a vital and ongoing means of reconciliation, from Maha Gosananda's walks to Gandhi's marches, to marches retracing the path of slaves in Richmond, Virginia, and black and white congressman of the United States government retracing the Freedom Marchers' treacherous journeys through the South. All of these marches have been deeply spiritual events, rituals of immense power and transformation for those who participated in or witnessed them. Prayers became critical to some efforts to frame tough negotiations in Latin America, a way to make a moral space and presence in the midst of hard bargaining, a way to make an oasis of vision in the midst of the predictable and necessary tale of grievances and injuries. Increasingly, secular educational institutes, such as the Adam Institute in Israel, have seen the value of overlaying their education for democracy and human rights with cultural and religious foundations that will appeal to the spiritual side of the youth who they are educating. These are just a few examples.

A full documentation, a true telling of this global story, awaits the generosity of foundations and governments many of whom still need to see the wisdom of this new path. I want to conclude with one example that is close to my heart, and that is an effort on the part of sheikhs and rabbis in Israel and Palestine to create a religious peace treaty, a symbol of peace and, more recently, a token ceasefire. An Islamic concept, referred to as *hudna*, has had a history in the Middle East that allows for the possibility of coexistence. This is a hotly debated topic, because religious ceasefire has the implication of a temporary cessation of hostilities, not true peace. Those of use who have worked on this have believed that the power of religious symbol as a force for even temporary cessation of violence and hate would be enough to generate other symbolic gestures, and further progress on the hardcore issues. It would give a momentum to religion as a source of healing rather than hatred, which could be built upon by further efforts.

Most importantly it would give a voice to those religious leaders who have been threatened and silenced by the well-financed radicals supported by oppressive leaders around the Middle East. The leaders are important, but the goal of their involvement should be to circumvent their intransigence and ultimately make their presence less important, historically speaking.

Despite the knee-jerk skepticism of many, we have now come to a situation in which key Arab businessmen, members of the Israeli Parliament, the Palestinian Legislative Council, the Attorney General of Israel, and the President of Israel, have publicly expressed interest in cultural and religious symbols of reconciliation, and, specifically, interest in *hudna*. This is rather startling considering that this is taking place in the midst of the Intifada and in the immediate aftermath of September 11, 2001. We have argued that such gestures have no business attempting to replace security cooperation and counter-terrorism measures, but that counter-terrorism measures have no business trying to substitute for a means to change the one thing that perpetuates all wars, fear and hatred. That requires trust, forgiveness, and many other treasures of the human mind that only the path of ritual and culture can truly provide.

Here are a series of suggestions, which I will elaborate upon one at a time:

1. Recognize the paradox of religious hate and love, violence and pro-social values, and face the implications.
2. Contain damage of prejudices and hatred emanating out of the texts and traditions of organized religion, as well as from religious leaders and representatives.
3. Understand the paradoxes of hermeneutical variation with time and place. Understand the war within each tradition traditionally and in the contemporary setting.
4. Find the peacemakers and strengthen within and between communities.
5. Build alliances of new hermeneutics.
6. Focus on deeds more than dialogue or make dialogue contingent upon or interactive with a regime of righteous bilateral deeds.
7. Understand and utilize the interaction of economics, psychology, power relations, and military reality that interacts with religious trends, in order to coordinate more effectively secular and religious efforts of peace, security, and development.
8. Face and focus on the tremendous psychological power of religion to stimulate mood swings and utilize for reconciliation gestures of acknowledgment, apology and repentance, but be prepared to combat the compelling contagion of righteous hatred.

9. Explore and utilize the power of symbols to divide, unite and reconcile.

The most important step to take is to abandon naïve beliefs about religion that register it mentally as either a categorical positive or negative in terms of coexistence. There may be political interests at work in either demonizing or lionizing religion, such as President Bush's attempts rhetorically to see Islam in only good terms. But for strategists of coexistence it is critical to examine and understand how each religion involved in the conflict promotes countervailing values. One of the most important reasons that this is so important is that the adversary groups are generally speaking very familiar with the worst and best in their religions, cleverly using both to strengthen us/them dynamics of conflict and violence wherein one's own group is the righteous victims and the others are only abusers. They will know when you are soft-pedaling religion, and when you are covering up their own religious leaders' contributions to the conflict. This will not help matters. It is imperative to acknowledge fully both contributions to the war, the positive and the negative, and it is important to appeal engage religion in a way that will be believable to inherently skeptical audiences.

How does one contain the damage done by organized religions in the context of war? By stimulating and generating a public repudiation of the activities of some in the war, especially if and when they used particular symbols, traditions, or texts, in the course of justifying or perpetrating any atrocities. Each use of religion for atrocity must be responded to hermeneutically in exactly a parallel fashion. The same goes for religious leaders or representatives who were active during the war must be encouraged, and, if possible, compelled to repudiate those same uses of religion during the war. They must reject and, if possible, disown actual religious perpetrators, especially those who committed atrocities in the name of religion. If these leaders cannot or will not repudiate prior religious hermeneutics then it is important to encourage alternative leaderships and courageous individuals who will engage in that repudiation.

This is most successfully accomplished where there are third party strategies to stimulate these reactions bilaterally and simultaneously or consecutively. These reactions should be accompanied by acknowledgments of the pain inflicted and apologies. This may take years but the efforts must begin as soon as possible and begin at a small scale. If one understands in a deep way the hermeneutical variation of traditions and the war within communities over their values choices, one is in a much better position to strengthen those who are engaged in battles for the pro-social side of a religious tradition. It is important to know the substance of the debate as well as the players, because conflict resolution or coexistence third parties will then be in a better position to design appealing peace strategies that gel nicely with the each community's way of framing their choices morally and spiritually.

Strengthening the peacemakers means helping them financially and spiritually. It means giving whatever they need to persist. They should be the ones, for the most part, to explain their needs and what will make them more effective. But it is also the case that sometimes peacemakers are so fringe that they are not necessarily adept at social influence. We must also keep in mind that in every corporate religious group there are those peacemakers who leave the group and struggle from the outside and those who work from within. Mechanisms of support for religious peacemakers should always be so structured by third parties as to be ready for inclusion. This is particularly problematic historically for peacemakers who tend to be as exclusive as any other in-bred groups. It is the job of third parties to not allow left/right, or peace/violence divisions to become encrusted in religious communities. There should a highly elastic and creative process of ever widening communication and creativity.

In the long run this will create more and more possibilities of interreligious alliances of new hermeneutics, new interpretations and symbols of coexistence. The more varied each group's religious actors are the more they will find their counterparts on the other side. Liberals will find liberals and conservatives will find conservatives, and out of a broadened coalition of those committed to coexistence will come a slow and steady defeat of those committed to violence. Focus on deeds more than dialogue, or make dialogue contingent upon or interactive with a regime of righteous bilateral deeds. Dialogue is overrated. It may make a good platform for leaders to demonstrate their political importance, but it just as often generates skepticism, especially when it is engaged too soon. It is the rage of the masses that this critical dynamic of religion and war, and that rage is not turned off like a spigot.

It is true that leaders are critical symbols of social change, and fostering their relationship with each other is crucial. But we must not overrate its contribution. The masses of people understand, in their wisdom, the evidence of reconciliation, acknowledgment and repentance, in the realm of deeds rather than in the rhetoric of political manipulation. Efforts at religious coexistence work can be hampered by bureaucratic division of efforts and poorly integrated thinking about the nature of conflict. Just as deeds are crucial to true religious trust, so is development and poverty relief at the heart of serious conflict resolution. These two insights can and should be integrated in the form of creative programs and joint activities that the warring communities design with the help of others. So too, religious healing and psychological recovery need to work hand in hand. Each must understand the peculiar approaches of the other, and attempt a cooperative or parallel set of processes. The same is the case with security concerns. Issues of public safety, crime and justice, should be framed where possible in terms of religious values.

This does not mean surrender the public order to religious authority. At the end of the day, there is no peace when one religious community or another controls the military or judiciary or the public space as such. Most religious adherents around the world have come to understand that religion is at its best when it does not control the temporal space. Democracy and human rights ultimately depend upon this. That having been said, there is not reason that the liberal forms of social order—judiciary, police, and democracy—should not be hermeneutically framed in religious ways. Enough adherents around the world are actively engaged in this framing process—often in very deep ways—so that this alliance of civil society need not be seen as the enemy of religion. This must be aggressively funded the world over. We are not engaged in a civilizational struggle today, or a war of religions, but rather a war within religions and civilizations over the future of civil liberties, particularly the freedom of women. It is my impression that most religious adherents want human rights and democracy, but do not want it if is perceived to be a means of crushing their identity or civilization. We need to work harder at making the case for a culture and religion friendly liberal social order. And we need the international corporations and representatives of capitalism to become an asset not a liability in this struggle.

Face and focus on the tremendous psychological power of religion to stimulate mood swings and utilize for reconciliation gestures of acknowledgment, apology and repentance, but be prepared to combat the compelling contagion of righteous hatred. The greatest danger that we face from religion today is its tremendous power to stimulate rage in massive numbers of people. Irresponsible clerics cannot resist the opportunity to capitalize on this power to actively fight world orders with which they see themselves, at the present time, unable to coexist. In a poverty of vision, these clerics have not reached yet the conclusions that millions of other clergy have discovered about the modern world, namely, that it is possible for religion to flourish even with Coca Cola, MTV, and absolute freedom of choice by women and men. But the free floating rage of millions of people is the single greatest danger of human history.

It waits, like a ripe fruit, for power hungry individuals and institutions to take advantage of that rage. And then the sociopaths, the fascistic leaders and terrorists come along as the great release of the rage. This is as true in the twentieth century, under the aegis of fascism and communism, as it is today under the aegis of fundamentalism. It is our job to undermine that rage aggressively with compassion, acknowledgment, anti-poverty plans, and inherent respect for cultural and religious diversity. If there is global religious rage then a global Marshall plan is necessary to undermine its roots. This is the ultimate way to undermine the violent potential of religion, and give voice to the majority in each religious tradition who tend to abhor the abduction of their religion by rage.

6

Debate
Religion the New Social Evil

In a poll conducted by the Joseph Rowntree Foundation in the United Kingdom, faith — defined here not as limited to extremism but rather in the broadest possible terms — was considered to be tantamount to "intolerance, irrational behaviour and the basis for justifying persecution". Many of those polled not only believed that faith was divisive but also that it brought about irrational educational and other policies. As an Orthodox Jew respectful to all faiths, including those who do not believe in any organised religion or in any religion at all, I was a bit taken aback by all of this. When I was growing up, religion was perceived to be the light guiding the path of the individual in his or her quest to attain a well-rounded and beneficial existence. Now it is being seen as some form of moral lassitude.

Yet it did occur to me that, amid the hubris and commercialism of modern-day religion and in particular the conduct of many of the leaders of the various faiths, there lies a compelling argument against organised religion. Setting aside the fact that many of the ongoing wars or conflicts, prejudices and even criminal activities are finding a home in religion, what many have forgotten is that the underlying *sine qua non* to faith is trust. Unlike science, where tangible evidence is at hand, a belief system or religion — to a greater or lesser degree—relies on people having faith in something they cannot see or touch. This means that their assessment will, in the main, be guided by those things they can get a handle on—such as the behaviour of a religious group, rabbi, imam or priest—and it is here where many organised religions are coming up woefully short.

In terms of actual wars, which are not the debate we're primarily concerned with here, religion often plays a part in occasioning the conflict and, in many instances, the intransigence in ending it. This can be due to an interpretation visited by some religious leaders or groups on the principles of their faith—hardly justifiable when humanity looks at the death toll that this occasions. This lends credence to those who want to see an end to organised religion. Yet most British people who were polled were not concerned with conflict. They were thinking more along the lines of the ways in which religions and their followers affect them on a day-to-day basis.

For example, Terry Sanderson, in his column for the *Guardian*, asks why the British government continues to praise religion to the skies when half of those surveyed do not believe in God. His article deals with the way the government goes about its business without giving consideration to the fact that half of the population isn't interested in religion. Why should they still have to complete documents relating to religious issues? If this surprises the more religious among us, then consideration must be given to the fact that many prejudices find a home in religion and a good example being the issue of gay and lesbian rights. There is no question that many of the major religions do discriminate against members of this community.

In my case I make no bones about calling this an irrational hatred with no place in modern society. Yet in religion, including my own, it encounters hatred and resentment where people should know better. We have even looked at the gay Iranian teenager who is facing the death penalty for having sex with another gay boy. Hardly surprising, then, that these communities see organised religion as their natural enemy. The women of Saudi Arabia apparently legally belong to their men – this being the strictest interpretation of sharia law within the Muslim world.

Jewish women, in the Orthodox community, are required to sit apart from their men at shul and follow several other rituals peculiar to them. In this regard we view a woman's role as different rather than inferior. In the case of Muslim women, I have quoted the Pakistani women who believe that sharia law offers them a buffer from the chaos and violence of modernity. Having said that, many women the world over believe that religion is misogynistic and treats them as inferior. This in turn alienates a vast number of them from pursuing a religion – or rather an organised religion. Indeed, as mothers bringing up children, it may lead them and their offspring away from it.

Of course, another issue that would be of concern to many is the amount of crime being committed using the guise of religion. In this regard, Pope Benedict XVI was forced to confront the sexual-abuse scandal currently rocking the Catholic Church during his recent visit to the United States. As many Jews will recall, we recently had the example of one of our Orthodox rabbis who was bust chasing after a member of his congregation's wife. This does not sit well with those who are considering the merits or demerits of religion. Again I must state that religion is based in faith, not science. Trust plays a major role in people's decision whether to follow or abandon this path.

If we consider the prejudice, intolerance and disgusting behaviour of some members of the various religions, it is hardly surprising that people are turning their backs on organised religion. In China, it is not easy to follow Christianity despite the size of the community. This also puts pressure on Christians either to abandon their faith or to go underground. This entails great sacrifice on their part and begs the question: How much longer will people keep doing this while the religious hierarchy lets them down so abysmally?

In Paraguay, we have a former bishop leaving the Catholic Church in order to make inroads into the devastating poverty afflicting his countrymen. His decision was based on effectiveness rather than persecution. How much more will this contribute to a decrease of church numbers in years to come? Will people regard the church as a hindrance to achieving social and political reform and other goals? Belief is being perceived to be the preserve of the nutcases and local yokels. Of course the attacks on atheists by religious observers do not do the cause any favours either. Religion has to be sold as logically as science, even if the main element requires blind faith.

To rant and rave as described in the article by Sue Blackmore sends the message that you have lost the argument, so you'll batter your opponent into submission. My belief in my own faith remains unshaken, but I believe that religious leaders across the board need to take stock urgently. If they continue to believe that they can carry on regardless — insensitive to other people's views and concerns — then organised religion is going to come under ever-increasing pressure from the age of information. People are quickly informed about the conduct of those who are teaching love, tolerance and redemption, while their behaviour suggests otherwise.

AN OBSTACLE TO UNITY

When organized religions subscribe to doctrines of "privileged access to truth," disastrous eruptions of fanaticism result, paid for with the loss of a leadership role in world affairs. As a result, these religions stand paralyzed on the threshold of the future, barring, rather than opening, the door to peace and harmony. The Baha'i international governing council recently raised this issue before the world's religious leaders. But an objective discussion of this predicament is difficult because of traditional loyalties and followers who claim superiority for the founders of their faith. Many Christians view Jesus Christ as God incarnate, consider Moses inferior in some way and regard Muhammad an impostor. A majority of orthodox Jews see Moses as the human vehicle through which the law of God was transmitted to humanity and consider Jesus Christ to be a false prophet.

• Muslims consider both Moses and Jesus Christ to be valid prophets, but the majority rejects the Buddha and the founders of other major faiths. For them, Muhammad was the last prophet whom God will send, and revelation of the divine will have ended with the Quran. Discussions are further hindered by the view that various religious systems result from human striving after truth. In this conception, the founders of the great religions do not reveal God to us, but are rather philosophers or thinkers, human beings who may have progressed farther than others in the discovery of truth.

This notion excludes the basic unity of religion, since the various religious systems are seen as representing the opinions and beliefs of fallible human beings rather than infallible revelations of truth from a single source. In spite of these roadblocks, the world's population continues to seek religious guidance. Religion remains an essential and imperishable element of human consciousness, a power that reaches to humanity's very core. It is a historically civilizing force, and, as such, the oneness of humankind cannot be effectively advanced without an infusion of spirituality.

For religions to avert a calamitous worldwide confrontation, the risks of which grow daily, their leadership must renounce assertions of exclusive access to truth and whole-heartedly accept the validity of all principal religions. The understanding must be embraced that truth and spirituality are equally accessible to all of mankind, that God is one and that, beyond all cultural diversity of human interpretation, religion is likewise one. The Baha'i faith supports "revealed religion." God, the creator, has and will continue to intervene in human history by means of chosen messengers. These messengers, or manifestations of God, are the founders of the major religions, such as Abraham, Moses, Buddha, Zoroaster, Jesus and Muhammad. The spirit released by their coming, their teachings and the social systems established by their laws and precepts have enabled humankind to progress in its collective evolution.

These mighty systems have proceeded from one source and are the rays of one light. That they differ one from another is to be attributed to the varying requirements of the ages in which they were promulgated. There is only the continually evolving religion of God, with each individual religious system representing a stage in the evolution of the whole. Baha'u'llah attributed the differences in some teachings of the great religions not to any human fallibility, but to the different requirements of the ages in which the revelations occurred. He maintained that a great deal of human error was introduced into religion through the corruption of texts and the addition of extraneous ideas. Baha'is consider none of the founders superior to another.

Religious truth is relative, not absolute. Divine revelation is a continuous and progressive process, with all the great religions of the world divine in origin. Their basic principles are in complete harmony, their aims and purposes one and the same. Their teachings are facets of one truth, their functions complementary and their differences only in the nonessential aspects of their doctrines. Their missions represent successive stages in the spiritual evolution of human society. There is Judaism. There is Islam. There is Christianity. There is plenty of other lesser heard of religions too. Then within Christianity, there are subdivisions. There is Catholicism. There is Protestantism. Within Protestantism there are subdivisions. Then there are evangelicals. There are subdivisions within the evangelicals to. Within subdivisions of all religions there are sub-subdivisions. Then within the sub-sub divisions there are people who say they follow multiple religions.

God teaches love, kind and forgiveness among other values in life. Nowhere does God say that there is one right way to honor, praise and worship Him. So why do some people believe their religion is the one and only? The other day my friend was approached by someone who practices a different religion then she does. And she was pelted with questions and received accusations that she "would be much more useful to God" in the other religion. How does a perfect stranger make this statement? Only on the basis that their religion is the better, or "right" one.

It works the same way with religion. Imagine telling a person, "If you don't become part of (insert religion here) right now, you will not be saved and you will go to hell." Given that command, a non-believer will stay exactly where they are and give *you* the look of death, maybe shake their head, or even shout, "No!" because they think you are the craziest thing since You'll say, "What a shame. They're screwed." They'll walk away. You'll walk away. Whether it's a two-year-old or a seventy-year-old who still hasn't found God, the only way to get a message across is to lead by example. If a young child is using inappropriate words, then it's up to you to use more appropriate words, while not responding to the child's "not-so-nice" words. With someone who is searching for God or has no want for God, all we can do is live our lives the way God asks us to and pray that other people notice.

Trying to force something upon someone will do nothing except drive him or her further from God then they ever were before. Instead, with the right leading, you might find yourself being approached by someone else who might say, "I want what you have." I will admit it. I struggle understanding all of this. The bottom line is that in world today, religion is dividing us rather than uniting and serving the purpose it should. I personally don't have a problem with other religions so long as they truly believe in it, they are tolerant of other beliefs and that they don't use religion as an excuse to harm others. I ask others to join me in doing the same. Truly learn what other people are doing. It's probably not all that different from what you are doing. You might find a new friend in the process. Or better yet, you could change the life of another only by living your life in the word of God.

The Tragedy of Theology

In recent decades, medieval scholars have persistently advanced the thesis that the Dark and middle Ages were not actually dark—that the 1,000-year period stretching from the fall of Rome (roughly 500 AD) to the Renaissance (roughly 1500) was an era of significant intellectual and cultural advance. This trend has culminated in the claims of Rodney Stark's *The Victory of Reason: How Christianity Led to Freedom, Capitalism, and Western Success* (and similar claims presented in Thomas Woods's *How the Catholic Church Built Western Civilization*). That such a theory would be welcomed by the religious right is not surprising. However, what might surprise some—and what is certainly ominous—is that such major organs of the liberal press as *The New York Times* and *The Chronicle of Higher Education* (the leading publication for university professors and administrators) have treated Stark's book with significant respect. This essay will demonstrate that such respect is entirely undeserved.

The thesis of Stark's book is that the Catholic Church promoted a cultural commitment to reason that enabled the West to rise. Medieval Christianity was fundamentally, perhaps exclusively, responsible for the great progress wrought by Western Civilization in philosophy, the arts, science, technology, and freedom. As Stark states his claim:

> But if one digs deeper, it becomes clear that the truly fundamental basis for . . . the rise of the West was an extraordinary faith in reason.

The Victory of Reason explores a series of developments in which reason won the day, giving unique shape to Western culture and institutions. The most important of these victories occurred within Christianity...While the other world religions emphasized mystery and intuition, Christianity alone embraced reason and logic as the primary guide to religious truth...Encouraged by the Scholastics and embodied in the great medieval universities founded by the church, faith in the power of reason infused Western culture, stimulating the pursuit of science and the evolution of democratic theory and practice. The success of the West, including the rise of science, rested entirely on religious foundations, and the people who brought it about were devout Christians.

This book and others like it — along with their admiring treatment by the mainstream liberal press—are signs of the resurgence of Christianity in America. This is all the more frightening because the arguments are being delivered and embraced at an intellectual, not merely a grassroots, level. If such arguments were sound, their growing acceptance among contemporary intellectuals would present no problem; but, as will be shown, this pro-religion thesis, although convincing to some, is egregiously and provably mistaken. Stark, a professor of social sciences at Baylor University is absolutely correct in his rare identification that a commitment to reason was the fundamental cause of the spectacular progress achieved in the West and nowhere else. But he is profoundly mistaken in ascribing the basis of that commitment to Christianity.

Indeed, the West has risen much more slowly and incompletely than it otherwise might have, precisely because of its deep ambivalence to reason. Throughout the ages, and continuing to this day, there has existed in the West a chronic backsliding into irrationality that has often tragically exceeded its commitment to rationality. There is a profound dualism in Western thought: Its dedication to reason, though certainly outstripping that of other cultures, exists in desperate conflict with several versions of unreason, including faith. Expressed in terms of major figures, Jesus and his followers—not merely Aristotle and his—have been enormously influential in Western thinking. Christianity, emphatically including the medieval Church, more than any other single factor, is responsible for the irrationality of Western society. The commitment to rationality is fundamentally a legacy of ancient Greece—preeminently of Aristotle—and of subsequent periods when the Greek element was dominant, for example, the 18th-century Enlightenment.

Stark's errors are rampant and across-the-board. They span the fields of history and, above all, philosophy. Indeed, as will be shown, Stark's claims are historically false and philosophically impossible.

Stark claims that, "the era from the fall of Rome through the Middle Ages was a time of spectacular technological and intellectual progress that erupted when innovation was freed from the grip of Roman despotism." Similarly: "Christian commitment to reason and progress wasn't all talk; soon after the fall of Rome, it encouraged an era of extraordinary invention and innovation." He describes the development of water mills, dams, and windmills—and repeatedly discusses improvements in agriculture that significantly increased production of food. For example, he claims that "medieval Europe greatly increased its agricultural production by pumping water off potential cropland," and that "these incredible gains in agricultural productivity so reduced the need for farm labor and increased yields that they greatly facilitated the formation and feeding of towns and cities."

After other similar claims, Stark concludes: "Not only did Europeans eat far better during the Dark Ages than in Roman times but they were healthier, more energetic, and probably more intelligent." Projecting such unsubstantiated fantasies is Stark's error—which is identical to that of the anticapitalist Left—of ignoring the entire field of economic history. Economic history is highly relevant, as it provides men with whatever factual data can be ascertained regarding human living standards of the past. Critically, it is supported neither by arbitrary assertions nor by woozy evaluations but by actual evidence. One of the leading thinkers of recent decades in this field is the Dutch economist, Angus Maddison. According to Maddison's research, Europe suffered through *zero economic growth* in the centuries from 500 AD to 1500, the exact period that Stark describes. Maddison shows that for a millennium there was no rise in per capita income, which stood at an abysmally low $215 in 1500. Further, he estimates that in the year 1000, the average infant could expect to live to roughly the age of 24 years—and that a third would die in the first year of life.

These are global estimates, with Europe showing no appreciable difference from the rest. Not surprisingly, per capita living standards show no dramatic increases until the 18th-century Enlightenment—the beginning of the Industrial Revolution. While other economic historians argue that some economic growth did take place in the late middle Ages, they nevertheless recognize that the growth was of so minimal a degree that it hardly improved the horrifying destitution of the European masses. For example, the research of economist Graeme Snooks indicates that economic growth occurred in England in the six centuries between 1086 and 1688. "If the average person in 1086 had about one-sixth the income of the average person in 1688, he or she did not have much...English peasants in 1086 had little more than enough food to keep them alive, and sometimes not even that. Houses were crude, temporary structures. A peasant owned one set of clothes, best described as rags, and little else."

Remarkably, Stark lists in his bibliography several leading historians who concur with these findings. For example, the superb French historian Fernand Braudel, writing about the pre-18th-century era, states that: "Famine recurred so insistently for centuries on end that it became incorporated into man's biological regime and built into his daily life. . . ." Braudel points out, for instance, that although France was, by standards of the day, a relatively prosperous country, it is nevertheless believed to have suffered ten *general* famines during the 10th century; twenty-six in the 11th; two in the 12th—and these are estimates that do not even count the "hundreds and hundreds of *local* famines....." Even granting that there are severe difficulties inherent in estimating medieval living standards with any degree of precision, the conclusion must be that what was then considered relative prosperity was, by comparison to prior and later ages, utter destitution.

Further, European sewage and sanitation regressed back to primitivism during this era. Human waste products were often thrown out the window and into the street or simply dumped in local rivers. (By contrast, ancient Rome had been significantly more advanced: "major cities of the Empire installed drainage systems to which latrines were connected"—and the "wealthy enjoyed such luxuries as indoor plumbing . . . even the indigent had access to public baths.") With the streets strewn with garbage and running with urine and feces—and with the same horrifying conditions permeating the rivers and streams from which drinking water was drawn—vermin and germs multiplied, and disease of every kind, untreatable by the primitive medical knowledge of the day, proliferated. Between 1347 and 1350, for example, the bubonic plague—the infamous "Black Death"—spread by the fleas that infest rats, ravaged Western Europe, obliterating roughly 20 million people, fully one-third of the human population. Norman Cantor, the leading contemporary historian of the middle Ages, states: "The Black Death of 1348–49 was the greatest biomedical disaster in European and possibly in world history." A Florentine writer of the era referred to it simply as "the exterminating of humanity."

Finally, the early middle Ages witnessed a stupefying decline in levels of education and literacy from the Roman period. In the endemic warfare of the period, human beings lost the skill of writing and, largely, of reading. "In the time of Augustine's youth [4th century AD] . . . even a Christian got a reasonably good classical education. A few generations later, literacy was a rarity even among the ruling classes." For example, during the 8th century, Charlemagne maintained that even the clergy knew insufficient Latin to understand the Bible or to properly conduct Church services. A related disaster was that Classical learning was largely lost in the West. One reason was that, in the days of the Roman Empire, educated Romans studied the writings of Plato, Aristotle, and other thinkers in their original Greek, so there had been no need to translate these writings into Latin.

Although the conquering barbarians learned some Latin, Westerners no longer learned Greek. The loss of literacy in Greek was catastrophic for civilization, for it meant "the simultaneous loss of philosophy, mathematics, medicine, engineering, and science." Andrew Coulson, a researcher in the field of educational history, points out that whereas the Greeks were fascinated by the natural world, taking pioneering steps in such sciences as anatomy, biology, physics, and meteorology, the Christians replaced efforts to understand the world with an attempt to know God; observation-based study of nature was, accordingly, subordinated to faith-based study of scripture. A decline in learning consequently afflicted every cognitive subject. "What limited medical knowledge had been accumulated by Greek and Roman physicians was supplanted by utter mysticism." For example, St. Augustine believed that demons were responsible for diseases, a tragic regression from Hippocrates. Scientific work in general declined as interest in the physical world did.

"From the standpoint of mass education . . . the medieval era was indeed a dark age. Despite isolated pockets of learning concentrated around the monasteries of Europe, the overwhelming majority of the populace was uneducated and illiterate." Contributing to the educational debacle, in 529 the Christian emperor, Justinian I, ruling the Eastern Empire from Constantinople and holding that Greek philosophy was "inherently subversive of Christian belief," closed all the pagan schools of philosophy, including Plato's Academy, which, for 900 years, had specialized in the teachings of its founder. To fully enforce his ban, Justinian forbade any pagan to teach. (Boethius (480–525), a Christian and the last serious philosopher for 350 years, had been educated in the great pagan schools.) As a result, nobody in the West would have the opportunity to study the achievements of Greek culture for six interminable centuries. The eminent historian, Will Durant, observed: "Greek philosophy, after eleven centuries of history, had come to an end."

W. T. Jones, the 20th century's leading historian of philosophy, succinctly captured the essence of the decline, and of Christianity's causal role in promoting it, when he stated: "Because of the indifference and downright hostility of the Christians...almost the whole body of ancient literature and learning was lost....This destruction was so great and the rate of recovery was so slow that even by the ninth century Europe was still immeasurably behind the classical world in every department of life...This, then, was truly a 'dark' age." That some advances were made during this millennium is not to be doubted, and Stark recounts them in detail. But by the standards of the post-18th-century, secular West, such progress was relatively—and enormously—insignificant. In effect, the minor advances are red herrings, for they provided little or no relief from the endemic misery under which Western Europeans suffered for centuries. Stark's claim that the period was one of "extraordinary invention and innovation" is a grotesque exaggeration—at best.

An era of "extraordinary invention and innovation" would involve equally extraordinary technological advancement and thus significantly improve men's living standards. At the very least, Stark implies—and, in some cases, openly asserts—that this is what happened during the middle Ages. In fact, nothing of the kind occurred. Important claims made by Stark are egregiously in error. For example, he states: "The idea that Europe fell into the Dark Ages is a hoax originated by antireligious and bitterly anti-Catholic, eighteenth-century intellectuals who were determined to assert the cultural superiority of their own time and who boosted their claim by denigrating previous centuries as—in the words of Voltaire—a time when 'barbarism, superstition, [and] ignorance covered the face of the world.'" Unfortunately for the men of the period, Stark's claim that the European Dark Age of the 5th–9th centuries was "a hoax" is not remotely borne out by the facts. The tragic truth is that from the fall of Rome until the Medieval Renaissance of the 12th and 13th centuries—*a full six hundred years*—Western Europe suffered through a period of material penury and intellectual deprivation when compared to both the Classical age that preceded it and the Renaissance that followed it.

By contrast, the 18th and 19th centuries witnessed the full flowering of the Industrial and Technological Revolutions. These were centuries not of Saint Boniface converting the heathens, and of minor improvements to windmills and water mills that still left men starving—but of James Watt and the steam engine, Thomas Edison and the electric lighting system, Alexander Graham Bell and the telephone, the Wright brothers and aviation, Henry Ford, Andrew Carnegie, John D. Rockefeller, and industrial mass production of consumer goods—and, consequently, these were centuries of skyrocketing living standards and life expectancies. This was an era of tremendous intellectual and material advance. The 18th and 19th centuries were a period of "extraordinary invention and innovation." The 8th and 9th centuries were not. What was the basic cause of such a long period of stagnation, especially when contrasted with the enormous forward motion men have created in just the past 250 years? To answer this question, it is necessary to identify both the fundamental cause of human progress and the social condition its flourishing requires.

The Church vs. Reason

There are two principles that one must grasp in order to understand Stark's errors; both principles were identified by Ayn Rand. The first is that the rational mind is man's fundamental tool of survival and progress. The second is that, in order to function, the mind requires liberty; it must be fully unshackled, free to pursue any avenue of thought or research it deems important. The 18th-century Enlightenment, and the principles it inherited from the Renaissance and the Age of Reason, gave rise to the American Revolution, and vastly increased political-economic freedom throughout the Western world.

It must not be forgotten that the revolutionaries who created the American Republic were, in many cases, the leading minds of the American Enlightenment: Benjamin Franklin, Thomas Jefferson, Thomas Paine, James Madison. One result of such vastly increased liberty has been extraordinary intellectual advance, especially in theoretical and applied science, in technological development and industrialization, and in medical research—all of which has led to living standards and life expectancies vastly higher than during any prior historical epoch. When the Isaac Newtons, the Charles Darwins, the Thomas Edisons, the Ayn Rands, and the Jonas Salks do not have to kowtow to political or religious authority, and cannot be legally suppressed by church or state, they are free to create the new ideas, inventions, and innovations that greatly improve man's life on earth. Did such freedom exist during the middle Ages? If the mind was not free—if it was wholly or largely suppressed—then one must expect an era of stagnation, even regression. If the mind was, indeed, substantially repressed during this era, what was the Church's role in such suppression?

In fairness to the medieval Church, several points must be made at the outset. First, there were great thinkers during this period—Albertus Magnus and Thomas Aquinas are two illustrious examples. Second, these thinkers were all devout Catholics, indeed, generally members of the Catholic clergy. Third, the official position of sundry popes and high-ranking Church officials was, on occasion, to encourage education and intellectual advance (albeit with endless qualifications and restrictions). Fourth, as widely advertised, Catholic monasteries were, at times, a conduit of classical wisdom, as monks laboriously copied and saved the few surviving ancient manuscripts. Fifth, although heretics and other freethinkers were continually suppressed, it must be noted that a condemned heretic could, in every case, save his life right up to the last moment by recanting his illicit beliefs. It might be damning the medieval Church with faint praise, but it is nonetheless true that it was not a murderous institution on the same order of the regimes founded by the National Socialists or Communists.

Further, while the Church was an integral component of the *ancient regime*—the feudal system that brutally suppressed the serfs and commoners—if one is inclined to be generous, one might argue that, in the chaotic centuries following Rome's collapse, the tribal chiefs and warlords who rose to power and declared themselves aristocrats held a whip-driven primordial power not to be mitigated by an institution theoretically founded to save souls. In other words, it is at least possible that responsibility for the endless bloody warfare, and the brutal suppression of serfs and commoners, did not lie primarily at the doorstep of the Church. Nevertheless, institutions, like individual men, are often mixtures of good and evil. Despite such apologia, and on the most generous terms imaginable, the Catholic Church was, and remains, a force of incalculable evil.

The reason starts with the nature of orthodoxy and its pervasive hostility toward heresy. Orthodoxy, in this context, means the establishment of an official faith-based doctrine and the requirement, under threat of excommunication, even death, of uncritical conformity to it. *Webster's Collegiate Dictionary*, 9th edition, defines "heresy" as: "adherence to a religious opinion contrary to church dogma." Indeed, a heretic is a member of a religious denomination who disagrees with (or merely questions) some aspect of that denomination's doctrine. In short, a heretic is nothing more than an independent mind whose freethinking leads him into conflict with the prevailing religious sect. Over literally centuries of theological dispute, the Church hammered out its official position regarding hundreds of religious controversies—including those of the Trinity, the Eucharist, the problem of evil, and countless others. Predictably, given the logical impossibility of proving any faith-based, transcendent claim, there was endless intellectual disagreement with the official conclusions.

Many of those who rejected the orthodox findings were condemned as heretics. What is the history of the Church's dealings with those Catholic thinkers independent enough to dispute some aspect of its official doctrine? It is not pretty. Consider several examples that indicate the essence and extent of the suppression. The Arian Heresy is a representative place to start. Arius (256–336 AD), a presbyter of the Church in Alexandria, in order to protect monotheism, taught that Christ is not perfect and eternal like God the Father, but, rather, was created by God out of nothing. In short, if monotheism was true, as Arius certainly claimed it was, then Jesus could not be God. As Jones made the point: "He [Jesus] must have his own nature and an essence different from God's." The conflict between the Arians and those who upheld the Trinity—the belief that Jesus is God, but distinct from God the Father, but nevertheless that God is one—was a bitter struggle.

The Emperor Constantine called the Council of Nicea, a conference of Church bishops in 325, to arbitrate the dispute; it upheld the Trinitarian viewpoint and condemned Arius's theory. The Arians refused to accept theological defeat and, ultimately, thousands were killed in the century-long struggle that ensued. Philosophically, Arius was a distant epistemological descendant of the Greek proponents of rationality, seeking to make logical sense of the universe, including the nature of Jesus and God the Father. But those defending, and transforming into orthodoxy, the doctrine of the Trinity, upheld the faith-based notion that Christian belief did not have to be rationally intelligible. Therefore, "the Arian controversy points up important differences in method and approach, as well as in basic outlook, between the Greek and Christian mentalities...The solution that won out, and became orthodox, was a sign that, for better or worse, the Church had assigned reason a subordinate place in its scheme of things."

In the same century, the Donatist Heresy—the belief that the Church's sacraments are ineffective if performed by morally unworthy priests—was ruthlessly expunged. "The Donatists were proscribed [by the Church]; many were exiled; many others were killed or committed suicide." St. Augustine (354–430), who reluctantly supported the persecution, held that its net result was humane, as it daily brought men from the darkness of ignorance to "the living and true God." Jones observed that: "In this way the basis was laid and authority was provided for the institution of the Inquisition—for the cooperation of Church and state in the holy work of extirpating heresy and dissent and of saving souls against their wills."

The Manichean Heresy, which has for millennia stubbornly resisted all attempts to stamp it out, is an attempt to resolve the implacable problem of evil: How can evil exist in a universe created and governed by an all-good, all-powerful God? The Manichean belief, plausible on religious premises, is that God is all-good but not all-powerful? God, in effect, is a more powerful version of Batman: He fights evil relentlessly and effectively, but evil has undeniable power in the world. Although Manicheanism was suppressed by the Church late in the 5th century, it reemerged in a widespread form during the 12th and 13th centuries. The Albigensian or Catharist Heresy, as it was known during this specific renewal, was exterminated in a bloody war called by Pope Innocent III in 1208. The Pope's army of heretic hunters stormed the city of Beziers in 1209. Both loyal Catholics and Catharists of the city took refuge in the churches; the invaders burst in and slaughtered everyone—men, women, children, babies, invalids, priests.

In a story that may be apocryphal, the papal emissary, Arnald-Amalric, when informed that many sincere Catholics inhabited the city, responded: "Kill them all. God will recognize His own." There is no doubt that he wrote gleefully to the Pope after the massacre, proclaiming that "nearly twenty thousand of the citizens were put to death, regardless of age and sex. The workings of divine vengeance have been wondrous." The sect limped on in vastly diminished numbers for another century; the last Catharists were burned in Italy in 1330. The Catharist writings were burned, orthodoxy triumphed, and the Papal Inquisition was established in 1227. "Church and state agreed that impenitent heresy was treason, and should be punished with death." These were the bitter results of the crusade against the Albigensian Heresy. Not snidely, but in an utterly serious manner, Stark's critics should ask him: Is this what you mean by your claims of the medieval Church's support for reason?

Nor was proscription for heresy limited to those who challenged specific tenets of the faith. All original thinkers lived under threat of condemnation. For example, from Boethius in the 6th century to Abelard in the 12th—*a full 600 years*—there was merely one original thinker in philosophy: John Scotus Erigena (810–877). So, naturally, several of his conclusions were condemned in 855—and one of his books so successfully burned that not a single copy of it survived. Peter Abelard (1079–1142), the most brilliant European mind in centuries, was hounded for decades by the official watchdogs of Church dogma. In 1121, a Church council condemned Abelard's writing on the Trinity and compelled him to cast his book into a fire. In 1141, sixteen propositions from his books, including his definition of sin, were condemned. Shortly thereafter, Pope Innocent II imposed a sentence of perpetual silence on him, confining him to a monastery.

Abelard, a master of Aristotelian logic, infuriated Church authorities by his refusal to exclude any precept of faith from rational analysis. "What disturbed the Church more than any specific heresy in Abelard was his assumption that there were no mysteries in the faith, that all dogmas should be capable of rational explanation." One of Abelard's contemporaries, William of Conches (1080–1154), drew the Church's predictable ire by condemning those who attacked philosophy and science on the grounds that heartfelt faith was sufficient. The wayward scholar soon decided that resignation was preferable to excommunication. William "retracted his heresies . . .

abandoned philosophy as an enterprise in which profit was not commensurate with the risk, became tutor to Henry Plantagenet of England, and retired from history." In the terms of Ayn Rand's novel *Atlas Shrugged*, William of Conches went on strike.

Jean Roscelin (1050–1120), one of Abelard's teachers, was threatened with excommunication for challenging the Trinity by teaching that three cannot be one. He was hauled before an Episcopal council in 1092 and presented with a stark choice: retraction or excommunication. He chose retraction. Even Thomas Aquinas (1225–1274), the greatest philosophic genius since Aristotle, did not escape the Church's suppressive vigilance. In the Condemnation of 1277, just three years after this great man's death, the Bishop of Paris, Étienne Tempier, banned as heresies 219 propositions taught at the University of Paris, including several of Aquinas's. Further evidence could be adduced (e.g., the systematic repression of the pagans and the Jews, inevitably including the leading minds among them), but the above examples are sufficient to establish the point.

During the medieval period, the freethinking human mind, best exemplified by heretics and dissidents, lived under perennial threat of condemnation, proscription, book-burning, excommunication, decrees of perpetual silence, even execution. Stark's assertions to the contrary notwithstanding, the Church conducted relentless, pervasive, often lethal warfare against the independent mind. A reader will search Stark's book in vain for any reference to the Church's suppression of innovative thinkers. For example, the terms "heresy" and "heretics" are not listed in his Index. His brief mentions of these phenomena give no hint of the grim reality. As an illustration, discussing the theological work of Augustine and Thomas Aquinas, he states: "Of course, thousands of other theologians also tried to make their mark on doctrines.

Some succeeded, most were ignored, and some of them

were rejected as heretics." Observe his employment of the vague, misleading, utterly whitewashed term "rejected." One can conclude from his version of history that heretical theories were merely dismissed as intellectual errors by a community of scholars, without further consequences to their proponents. Even worse is the discussion of his (mistaken) view that Christianity was responsible for the abolition of slavery. In this context, he writes: "Here too can be seen the principles of theological progress at work, making it possible for theologians to propose new interpretations without engendering charges of heresy." But as already noted, a more accurate account of this period establishes that it was often exceedingly difficult for "new interpretations" to escape charges of heresy. Further, he also makes no mention of the suppression of pagans, Jews, or other dissidents or non-believers.

The truth is that the creative mind cannot function under such a reign of terror. Its holy quest for knowledge does not permit it to cease asking challenging questions, to second-guess truthful principles, to gaze over its shoulder for the Inquisition's haunting presence, or to impose selfcensorship because it is compelled to live in chronic dread of its freedom, even its life. If such are the social parameters imposed, then rational inquiry is curtailed, even stifled; man's survival instrument is abrogated, and many men will not survive in the inevitable Dark Age that ensues. That, under the Church's aegis, faith was supreme over reason is a clear historical fact. But which specific philosophic principles did medieval Catholicism uphold—and which did it eschew? Which ideas were responsible for the Dark Age? Who codified those ideas? And whose ideas smashed that code to pieces, paving the way for the superlative advances of the modern, secular West?

PHILOSOPHY

The fundamental error in Stark's account, the misconception underlying and giving rise to his mistaken interpretation of history, is his misunderstanding of the nature of reason. Stark holds that Catholicism is inherently rational, thereby capable of creating significant scientific and technological advance. In effect, his view is: Since the medieval era was a fountain of rational thought, it must have been a seething cauldron of scientific advance—and, consequently, claims of a "dark age" could only be prejudicial mythology hatched by religion's cultural enemies.

In the most important section of his book, Chapter One, "Blessings of a Rational Theology," he claims that medieval "theologians placed far greater faith in reason than most philosophers are willing to do today." It was Christian attempts to understand the nature of God that set "the precedent for a theology of deduction and inference. . . ." The basis of Western commitment to reason was set because "from very early days Christian theologians have assumed that the application of reason can yield an *increasingly accurate* understanding of God's will." To understand the profound error committed here, and to grasp the actual nature of reason, one must refer to the basics of philosophy.

Philosophy seeks to answer five major questions: What is the nature of reality? How—by what means—do men gain knowledge of it? What is the nature of man? What is good—and what is evil? What is the ideal society? Religion, as a particular kind of philosophy, is an attempt to answer these questions. Regarding reality, the essence of religion is belief in metaphysical dualism—that is, two worlds: the natural universe and a transcendent, more important world beyond it. Since there exist no observation-based means to access a "higher" world, it follows that, regarding important knowledge; faith in the infallible truths of a revealed text provides the foundation of cognition. Augustine's famous dictum that belief is the necessary basis of knowledge is representative of the religious approach. Writes one scholar: "The main use of reason by the mature Augustine is unquestionably to understand what is already believed." Man is a metaphysical biped: his soul being of the transcendent realm and his body being of this one.

A fallen creature beset with the sin of his ancestors, his earthly flesh is prone to lust and temptation, which his otherworldly soul must devoutly resist. The good is to place God first and foremost in one's pantheon of values, and to unquestionably obey His every command; the evil is to disobey. A proper society is theocratic—based on divine commandments as interpreted by the initiated spiritual elite: the clergy. Religion, as an attempt to answer all the important philosophical questions of human life, is a species of philosophy, which is its genus. It is a faith-based, not a reason-based philosophical system. Religion can be (roughly) defined as: a philosophical system, based in faith, not reason, upholding the existence and supremacy of a transcendent God, who requires unquestioning obedience from the sinful human subjects He created and governs.

Religion was the dominant, indeed, exclusive philosophical framework of the early middle Ages, from the 6th century until, roughly, the 12th. Augustine (354–430) was the period's principal influence and intellectual spokesman. His philosophy, though complex in some respects, is, in essential terms, quite simple: Knowledge requires acceptance of authority—God's first, then the Church's. Reason is, at best, a supplementary faculty, perhaps able to explicate what is antecedently believed, perhaps not. Only Adam possessed free will. His descendants are grotesquely, irremediably sinful, incapable of saving themselves; all deserve, and most will receive, only damnation; a select few alone will be saved by a rigid process of predestination. Sin is transmitted through sexual intercourse, which is evil and to be avoided except for purposes of procreation—and even then, not to be enjoyed. Though God's creation is inherently lawful, miracles—violations of nature's laws—occur repeatedly; numerous men have been raised from the dead.

Pride is a lethal sin, especially intellectual pride—commitment to the use of one's rational capacity to pry into the mysteries of God's universe. The Greek thinkers were condemned for their "efforts to discover the hidden laws of nature." Science was damned as the "lust of the eyes." Such a philosophical system is in profound conflict with the intellectual foundations of science. A precondition of science is the view that nature is fascinating, important, and superlatively valuable—a conviction logically congruent with the secular understanding that nature is reality. This view is incompatible with the Christian belief that this world is debased and deficient, while the ideal lies beyond man's earthly grasp. Science begins with observation of facts, not the infallible pronouncements of a revealed text. Further, science (especially its offshoots of applied science and technology) rests upon the premise that rational beings are (at least potentially) good, that man's earthly life is of value, that knowledge is both attainable and desirable, and that men are worthy of elevated living standards.

The idea that man should seek scientific advancement is incompatible with the assumption that men are creatures who are, in Augustine's pregnant utterance, "foul... crooked ...sordid...be spotted....and ulcerous," overwhelmingly (and understandably) condemned to perdition by an outraged deity. Stark conveniently ignores these points. Why did the medieval Church suppress freethinkers who dared to challenge orthodoxy? Because as a leading historic example of undiluted religion was necessarily an institution of undiluted authoritarianism. It saw itself as the intermediary between God and hopelessly fallen man, who could not aspire to rise without its intercession. Its orthodoxy was literally the word of God; any deviation spurned God's earthly agency, thereby the divinity itself—and was, consequently, profoundly intolerable. Where men possess no capacity to ameliorate their earthly lot—much less save themselves—and are utterly dependent on God's Church, any criticism of it is an assault on the deity and undermines the sole institution capable of bringing men redemption.

To tolerate independence of thought, given men's loathsome essence, is to tolerate inevitable spiritual sedition. For man to be saved from his ineradicably sinful nature, his mind must be shackled. Augustine, philosophically a Christian neoPlatonist, glorified the locus of the Platonic-Christian worldview: the metaphysical dualism, the supremacy of a transcendent world, the diminished stature of this one, the ignoble baseness of man's bodily existence. Such fundamentals lead necessarily to the elevation of theology (the study of God) as the ruling cognitive discipline, and the devaluation of science and secular philosophy (the study of nature and man's earthly life).

Herein lies the root cause of the tragedy that was the middle Ages—and of Stark's fundamental error in ascribing to Christian theology the West's commitment to rational thought. *Reason is an observation-based methodology*. It does not begin with beliefs already accepted on prejudicial grounds, and then proceed to "prove" their truth. Whether studying man, the inner workings of his mind, germs, rocks, insects, atoms, the far reaches of intergalactic space, or anything else, reason proceeds from sensory observation by a method of logical thought embodying Aristotle's famed Law of Non-Contradiction: No existent can be both x and non-x at the same time and in the same respect.

But there is, and can be, no sensory experience of a dimension beyond this one. More to the point, there is no evidence upon which to establish that the existence and activities of material bodies are wrought by an immaterial cause. (How could spirit or consciousness exist without bodily means, e.g., sense organs, nervous system, brain? How could such a non-bodily ghost create, control or remotely impact bodily beings?) Theologians and religionists in general, start with a fantasy premise and then proceed to apply rigorous formal logic to tease out its implications. Stark himself points out that "theology consists of formal reasoning about God." This is admirably exact. Theologians, beginning with a wished-for creation of their own minds, analyze that creation's characteristics by rigorous application of the principles of formal—that is, deductive—logic.

But the method of reason, properly understood, is emphatically not the employment of formal logic to explicate the consequences entailed by arbitrary premises. Reasoning consists, first and foremost, in observation and induction there from. Deductive logic provides knowledge only when applied to premises rooted ultimately in observational fact. In the history of philosophy, the term "rationalism" has two distinct meanings. In one sense, it signifies an unbreached commitment to reasoned thought in contrast to any irrationalist rejection of the mind. In this sense, Aristotle and Ayn Rand are preeminent rationalists, opposed to any form of unreason, including faith. In a narrower sense, however, rationalism contrasts with empiricism as regards the false dichotomy between commitment to so-called "pure" reason (i.e., reason detached from perceptual reality) and an exclusive reliance on sense experience (i.e., observation without inference there from).

Rationalism, in this sense, is a commitment to reason construed as logical deduction from non-observational starting points, and a distrust of sense experience (e.g., the method of Descartes). Empiricism, according to this mistaken dichotomy, is a belief that sense experience provides factual knowledge, but any inference beyond observation is a mere manipulation of words or verbal symbols (e.g., the approach of Hume). Both Aristotle and Ayn Rand reject such a false dichotomy between reason and sense experience; neither are rationalists in this narrow sense. Theology is the purest expression of rationalism in the sense of proceeding by logical deduction from premises ungrounded in observable fact—deduction without reference to reality. The so-called "thinking" involved here is purely formal, observationally baseless, devoid of facts, cut off from reality. Thomas Aquinas, for example, was history's foremost expert regarding the field of "angelology."

No one could match his "knowledge" of angels, and he devoted far more of his massive *Summa Theologica* to them than to physics. Here is the tragedy of theology in its distilled essence: The employment of high-powered human intellect, of genius, of profoundly rigorous logical deduction—studying nothing. In the Middle Ages, the great minds capable of transforming the world did not study the world; and so, for most of a millennium, as human beings screamed in agony—decaying from starvation, eaten by leprosy and plague, dying in droves in their twenties—the men of the mind, who could have provided their earthly salvation, abandoned them for otherworldly fantasies. Again, these fundamental philosophical points bear heavily against Stark's argument, yet he simply ignores them.

Religion as a field, *at its best,* is rationalism—deduction from fantasy premises—not genuine rationality. (At its worst, it repudiates even this attenuated connection to logic in favor of adherence to unadulterated faith.) Stark himself provides a perfect example of this fallacious method. Although it is well known to scholars that Jesus had at least one brother, James, a leader of the Jerusalem church after Christ's death, Stark asserts, as an illustrious example of Christian "reasoning," that "Thomas Aquinas analyzed the doctrine of Christ's virgin birth to deduce that Mary did not bear other children." In other words, the religious approach to "truth" is to ignore facts if they clash with logical deductions from bizarre, faith-based premises. Thus even such a monumental genius as Thomas Aquinas—an Aristotelian, a thinker holding great respect for facts and observation, and the greatest Christian philosopher of history—was not immune to the cognitive infection of religious methodology.

By the very nature of its metaphysics, religion is incapable of upholding reason. Religion is compatible only with rationalistic deductions from faith-based premises. And, in the middle ages, if one's deductions clashed with orthodoxy, one ran the risk of punishment for heresy. Religion and rationality are primordial antipodes. (There is a field of natural religion that employs observation in the attempt to prove God; but it derives its original beliefs from faith, makes gratuitous leaps into the transcendent world, is easily refuted by rational philosophers, and, consequently, its validity is hotly debated even by theologians.) Rationality includes—indeed, begins with—an inviolable respect for facts. But as Jones points out, the identification of facts, so important to Aristotle and modern secularists, was considered of little value by men of the medieval era.

To them, the requirements of salvation were of vastly greater import than the facts of nature. "About things that did not touch one's faith—about the properties of sapphires or the cure for leprosy, for instance—it did not matter a great deal whether or not one went wrong." The greatest philosopher in history, the man whose method preeminently embodied observation-based rationality, was Aristotle. Despite his errors, Aristotle's extraordinary achievements significantly advanced man's understanding of nature, his method for grasping its properties, and thus his ability to engage in science. It is impossible to recognize the egregious falsity of Stark's claim that medieval Catholicism, not Greek culture, was preeminently responsible for the West's commitment to reason, without considering the work and influence of Aristotle.

To Aristotle, reality was fundamentally composed of formed matter, what he called "ousiai" or primary beings (i.e., entities); reality was, therefore, neither a congeries of discrete sense impressions nor a higher spiritual dimension but the realm of nature. Such entities (and all other existents) are what they are (the Law of Identity), and are not what they are not (the Law of Non-Contradiction). Natural change (or process) is rationally analyzed in terms of matter reformed, cf things becoming what they always had the capacity to become. While not properly applicable to inanimate objects, Aristotle's principle of things striving to actualize their potential is profoundly fruitful for the understanding of living beings. Study of virtually any subject, from plants to politics, begins with careful observation of a wide range of relevant facts.

"He was impressed by the fact that although facts alone do not give understanding . . . facts are nevertheless far more certain than any theory." Human beings, by realizing their potential for rational thought and conduct, could aspire to, and achieve, excellence, including in the all-important moral sphere. Men could, therefore, be proud—deservedly so—and generally happy over the course of a lifetime. In contrast to the medieval, Aristotle's thinking was thoroughly grounded in observation, in naturalism, in rationality—not in rationalistic deduction from arbitrary premises. If modern terms can be applied non-anachronistically to the ancients, his worldview is predominantly, virtually exclusively, *secular*. His interests are nature, life, and man—not supernature, next life, and god. His extraordinary intellectual curiosity and energy led him to investigate every field known to men of his time—logic, ethics, esthetics, metaphysics, physics, biology, meteorology, and more—and to pioneer man's understanding in many of them.

Throughout the vast corpus of his writing, his work exhibited "the passionate search for passionless truth." The noted contemporary Aristotle scholar, Jonathan Barnes, makes the point this way: "He [Aristotle] bestrode antiquity like an intellectual colossus. No man before him had contributed so much to learning. No man after him might aspire to rival his achievements." He is the crowning high-point of Greek commitment to the study of nature and science. Much of pre-Aristotelian Greek philosophy—Thales, Anaximenes, Heraclitus, Democritus—was an attempt to understand the difficult questions inherent in the teeming multiplicity of nature: the related problems of change (e.g., How can a baby grow into a man yet remain the same person?) and of the one in many (e.g., How can a plant, an insect, a fish, and a man be the same kind of thing: a living organism?).

Aristotle, the seminal logician, brought as much passionate rationality to this work as any of his predecessors—but, in his zeal for observation, he dispensed with their rationalism. As one example, in the *History of Animals*, Aristotle gives an account of an embryo chicken's development based on careful observation. Quoting Jones: "Aristotle's method was a healthy corrective to the over rationalism of his philosophical predecessors. . . ." How much more so to that of his philosophical successors in the medieval period? Although hardly a medieval scholar, this writer does not know of any scientist of the Middle Ages prior to Albertus Magnus in the 13th century—a period of greater than 600 years—who adopted Aristotle's painstaking approach to studying nature.

Like other medieval thinkers, Albert quoted previous texts, religious or secular, as unquestioned authorities. Additionally, however, he was a first-rate observer of nature, who sailed the North Sea to accumulate specimens for research, and who contributed significantly to both the resurgence of Aristotle studies and the development of medieval science. "Albert both helped to introduce Aristotle's philosophy of science to the medieval world and challenged prevailing conceptions of nature. In response to the older Augustinian tradition, Albert criticized the notion that ideas in the mind of God ...exist independently and provide the formal natures of sensible objects...As a result, we are not compelled to rely upon knowledge of God for knowledge of things. . . . Nature itself can reveal this order to us. With Albert, nature, which had too often been rendered mute by medieval intellectuals, would find its own voice. Once discovered and suddenly made articulate, its voice would gradually liberate science (and the arts) from theology."

Prior to Albert, for at least 500 years, the dominant "scientific" figure of medieval Europe had been Isidore of Seville (560–636), whose book, the *Etymologies*, "a hodge-podge . . . mass of information and misinformation . . . was a primary authority for the whole of the early Middle Ages." Isidore, in keeping with the religious spirit of his era, regarded claims about the supernatural realm to be of vastly greater importance and certainty than those about nature. Consequently, he uncritically repeated groundless fables regarding the material world, and placed no importance on sensory observation. Nevertheless, he was, for centuries, quoted as a leading authority on science and, as Jones observes, "twelfth-century science had advanced little beyond Isidore of Seville."

Stark knows, of course, but makes little mention that the preponderance of Aristotle's writings were lost in the West during the Dark Age of the 5th–9th centuries—and that, not accidentally, the Medieval Renaissance of the 12th and 13th centuries largely coincides with the recovery of the full Aristotelian corpus from the great Islamic centers of learning in Spain. It is an historical truism that the significant intellectual advances wrought by Albert, his brilliant student, Thomas Aquinas, and their peers of the early Scholastic period, were under the monumental influence of Aristotle. Even today, the profoundly beneficent influence of Aristotle is not fully appreciated. It was not merely (or even primarily) Aristotle's writings that were lost to the Dark and early middle Ages; it was his spirit, his approach, his orientation, his cognitive love affair with this world.

If one studies the writings of Aristotle—and the history of them being lost and, centuries later, rediscovered by Western man—one sees clearly the enormously positive and reciprocal causal relationship between the recovery of Aristotle's works and the Medieval Renaissance. After interminable centuries of reason serving as a handmaiden of faith—and of secular philosophy and science lying dormant—the men of the 12th and 13th centuries were hungry for greater knowledge of nature and the practical advances such knowledge brings in its train. And who, in the entire history of mankind up until that era, had as extensive a knowledge of nature as Aristotle?

Early in the 12th century, after La Reconquista wrested large portions of Spain from the Muslims and delivered them once again to Catholic dominion, Archbishop Raymund I of Toledo supported Christian, Muslim, and Jewish scholars translating into Latin previously lost Greek masterpieces, including those of Aristotle. And knowledge of those masterpieces—preeminently of Aristotle's—inspired, in some cases inflamed, the leading thinkers of the period with an even greater passion for the truths of nature. In sum, Western Europeans rediscovered Aristotle's writings when they were desperately eager for the wisdom and cognitive method those work contained. It is no exaggeration to claim that when Aristotle's method of observation-based rationality, in concert with his innumerable specific theories and insights, was culturally prevalent, great advances followed; when absent or suppressed, there ensued only ages miserably dark.

In a staggering reversal of this truth, however, Stark claims that Western commitment to reason and science was a function of medieval Christianity and of Augustine—and that Aristotle and the Greeks were a hindering influence. For example, he writes: "St. Augustine *reasoned* that astrology is false because to believe that one's fate is predestined in the stars stands in opposition to God's gift of free will." Based on such "reasoning" (i.e., on such non-observational, rationalistic deductions from a faith-based premise), Stark claims that science came to the fore in medieval Europe.

Stark, allegedly a supporter of logic, gives little or no credit to Aristotle for the Greek thinker's revolutionary founding of virtually the entire field of logic. Nor does Stark make any reference to the superlative scientific achievements of Aristotle, Archimedes, Hippocrates or the like. Instead, he makes such claims as: "The antiscientific elements of Greek thought were withstood by Augustine . . ." and "It was in explicit opposition to Aristotle and other classical writers that the Scholastics advanced toward science." Stark states that, the Greeks were unscientific (even antiscientific because "their empiricism was quite a theoretical, and their theorizing was non empirical." He claims that Aristotle did not permit facts to curtail his theorizing. In *On the Heavens*, the Greek philosopher taught that the velocity with which objects drop toward the earth is directly proportional to their weight; that a rock of ten pounds, for example, will fall twice as fast as one of five. Stark observes wryly that "a trip to any of the nearby cliffs would have allowed him to falsify this proposition."

But it can be similarly pointed out to Stark that a trip to the Moody/Jones Libraries on the Baylor University campus would have allowed him access to the full *Works of Aristotle* and sufficient data to disprove his theory. For one thing, On the Heavens is probably early Aristotle, when he was still much under the influence of Plato and, consequently, more other-worldly, less empirical, and less scientific in his thinking. Although current specialists in Aristotle generally reject many claims of Werner Jaeger, a leading 20th-century Aristotle scholar, they generally affirm his overall insight that The Philosopher evolved from an early Platonic, quasi-religious mode of thought to the great scientist/naturalistic philosopher of his mature years.

Even so, in *On the Heavens*, Aristotle often criticizes his predecessors, including Plato, precisely for non-empirical, rationalistic theorizing—and insists that theoretical reasoning always be consonant with sensory observation. For example, he says: "The reason [his predecessors go wrong] is that their ultimate principles are wrongly assumed; they had certain predetermined views, and were resolved to bring everything into line with them. . . . As though some principles did not require to be judged from their results and particularly from their final issue. And that issue . . . in the knowledge of nature is the phenomena always and properly given by perception." More fundamentally, Aristotle's groundbreaking work in biology alone refutes Stark's overall thesis. For Aristotle was, on the one hand, a careful, incisive observer of biological fact. Sir David Ross, the preeminent English-language Aristotle scholar of the 20th century, points out as one example that Aristotle "recognized . . . the mammalian character of the cetaceans—a fact which was overlooked by all other writers till the sixteenth century."

Similarly, David Lindberg, a leading contemporary expert regarding the history of science, writes that Aristotle "described the placenta of the dogfish . . . in terms that were not confirmed until the 19th century." Aristotle did not merely exceed prior thinkers in his devotion to observational fact regarding animal species—he was also "the first to undertake the problem of their classification." He discussed more than five hundred species in his *History of Animals*; "the structure and behaviour of many are described in considerable detail, often on the basis of skillful dissection." But, above all, Aristotle sought to explain the causes of animals being as they are. He was not content to merely observe, dissect, and describe the parts and functioning of animals; he strove to identify the first principles that explained the reasons they are what they are. Professor Allan Gotthelf of the Department of History and Philosophy of Science at the University of Pittsburgh, and one of the foremost contemporary scholars of Aristotle's biology, made the point this way:

> By any reasonable criteria of what counts as a scientific enterprise—the aim of understanding what things are and why they are as they are, of achieving that understanding through a discovery of causes, of seeking those causes through a careful and systematic examination of the full range of relevant data, of basing one's conclusions only on the rational assessment of the evidence, and of organizing it all into a systematic whole, a set of theories with broad explanatory power going back to first principles . . . Aristotle was a great scientist, and among the greatest. It was not without reason that, a full two millennia subsequently, a biologist of no less stature than Charles Darwin could say: "Linnaeus and Cuvier have been my two gods, though in very different ways, but they were mere schoolboys to old Aristotle."In a similar vein, Ernst Mayr, one of the most distinguished 20th-century biologists, wrote:

> No one prior to Darwin has made a greater contribution to our understanding of the living world than Aristotle. . . . Aristotle's outstanding characteristic was that he searched for causes. He was not satisfied merely to ask how-questions, but was amazingly modern by asking also why-questions. Why does an organism grow from a fertilized egg to the perfect adult form? . . .

Stark could easily have identified that, today, early in the 21st century, Aristotle is widely and properly recognized as one of the seminal biologists of history—a thinker who, in

Lindberg's terms, "contributed monumentally to developments in the biological sciences." If a contemporary scholar wishes to denigrate Aristotle's scientific accomplishments, he should at least familiarize himself with the relevant sources. For example, Stark could have (and should have) read the readily available work of Jonathan Barnes, who, in the midst of discussing Aristotle's accomplishments in zoology and biology, observed that "his [Aristotle's] studies on animals laid the foundation of the biological sciences; and they were not superseded until more than two thousand years after his death."

Overall, Stark's view that science rests on a theoretical framework of Augustine and Christian theology, and that its development was hindered by Aristotle and the Greeks, represents a fantastic jumble of errors. That science is not and cannot be grounded in the rationalistic, faith-based deductions of religion has already been established. The fallacious nature of Stark's attempt to sever science from its roots in Greek, especially Aristotelian, thought has been exposed as well. The Scholastics, the thinkers of the 13th century and for centuries following, were Christian *Aristo-telians.* To the everlasting credit of many Catholic scholars of the period, they were fascinated by what "The Philosopher" had written. His works were studied avidly during the medieval renaissance of this period.

Thankfully for the modern world, the Scholastics did, indeed, at least initially, "advance toward science." Albertus Magnus and Thomas Aquinas were monumentally important in this regard. But it was the Aristotelian element of the mixture—his naturalism, his secularism, his observation-based rationality—that was responsible for the new surge of interest in nature. The Scholastics, however, were also *Christian* Aristotelians, and as the centuries wore on, true to Christian methodology, they turned Aristotle's works into authoritative texts, as if based in faith or rationalistic dogma. As a result, these Christian Aristotelians did oppose the beginnings of modern science. But it was the Christian component of the mixture that eschewed the latest empirical findings, clinging to Aristotle's specific conclusions as they clung to beliefs that burning bushes spoke and virgins gave birth.

In terms of the respective epistemologies involved, it was the Christian element that relied heavily on authorities—generally refusing to challenge either Holy Scripture or writings of the Church Fathers. Observe, for example, the verdict imposed on Galileo by the Papal Inquisition, which condemned him because he "held and believed a doctrine which was false and contrary to Holy Scripture." The Inquisition punished Galileo for believing that "one may hold and defend ...an opinion after it has been declared and defined contrary to Holy Scripture." This latter was, from the Inquisition's perspective, Galileo's darkest transgression. Aristotle's method, on the other hand, was reality-oriented, not text-based—observational and fact-driven, not centered around faith in authorities—and he consequently did not hesitate to challenge earlier authorities, including his respected mentor, Plato.

The truth is that the Scholastics did not move toward science in opposition to Aristotle, as Stark claims. Rather, they impeded science in spite of Aristotle. They opposed Galileo in the same way—and via the same method—that, centuries later, Fundamentalists opposed Darwin. As Galileo—though locked in a cultural death struggle with such mentalities—accurately hinted: Aristotle himself, with his overriding respect for evidence, would never have rejected the observational findings revealed by the telescope. But 17th-century Scholastics, clasping Aristotelian content in the death grip of a Christian method, would and did. It is difficult to imagine a book more profoundly mistaken, in so many areas of intellectual inquiry, than Stark's *The Victory of Reason*. Other than his identification—shared with others, especially Ayn Rand—that commitment to reason was the fundamental cause of Western achievements, every major point in the book is egregiously mistaken. To the prospect that this work should be culturally influential, or that the Western world should experience a long-term religious revival, the only rational response is: God forbid.

RELIGIOUS FANATICS

The threat from religious fundamentalists is not merely coming from the Islamic world, it is also emanating from the United States and Israel. The strongest supporters of the Bush administration in the United States are Christian fundamentalists who believe in the biblical prophecy that Jerusalem needs to come completely under Israeli occupation for the second coming of Christ. This religious fundamentalist belief is helping to fuel the conflict in the Middle East, while international media attention is distracted towards the Islamic fundamentalist threat to world peace. This was the message from three speakers at a forum on religious fundamentalism yesterday. Professor Denis Brutus from the University of Pittsburgh in the United States warned that what is happening in that country today is a very dangerous attack on the freedom of the peoples of the world.

"There is in the U.S. a very powerful religious force that has a special preoccupation," he explained. "They use the Bible, the Old Testament, to say that the end of the world is coming. Armageddon (in northern Israel) is where the final battle will take place and the rapture will take all believers up to heaven."

"What is worrying," continued the professor, "is that Jerusalem is at the centre of (this belief) and (the fundamentalists believe) it should be completely under Israeli governance. This segment of the U.S. population is urging Bush to support the Israeli government and the army to conquer the whole territory."

Brutus pointed out that this Christian fundamentalist segment of the U.S. population has become so powerful today because "they stole the (2000) elections" for Bush and they have got a president in the White House with an IOU (I owe you). Sherif Herata, an 80-year-old activist from Egypt agreed with the professor's assessment and even went a step further claiming that it is "Christian-Jewish fundamentalism" that is fuelling the neoliberal global capitalist model. He argued that

Islamic fundamentalism could be seen as the other side of this neoliberal capitalist globalisation where people who are suffering from poverty and misery think, that through religion, they can solve every problem.

"Religious fundamentalism is the most dangerous evil we have today," said Herata. But he argues that religion gives people a message of hope and a desire to live in a better world. "When they can't understand the forces that are pushing changes happening around them — such as the activities of multinational companies, use of foreign military might — they get confused. They have lost faith in the political parties to help them out, so they turn to what is familiar to them — their religion, which they understand traditionally." But rather than seeing the religious fundamentalists as enemies, activists need to win over their rank-and-file to fight global neoliberal capitalism. "It is totally defamatory to say (religious) fundamentalists are all Arabs and Muslims," thundered Raji Sourani, director of the Palestine Centre for Human Rights, to loud cheers.

"Fundamentalism is a real disease we need to uproot as civilised people of this world," he added. Pointing out that when people talk about Israel they talk about the only state in the world whose existence is justified by "a promise by God". "If this is not fundamentalism, then what can it be?" he asked the audience some 5,000, which proved overwhelmingly sympathetic to the Palestinian situation. In a moving and emotional speech, interrupted a number of times by applause, Sourani who lives in the occupied territories, went on to argue that it is Israeli Jewish religious fundamentalism that is standing in the way of the implementation of international human rights law in Palestine. And since the September 11 attacks in the United States, Islamic fundamentalism has been used to paint Israeli occupiers as victims and Palestinians as terrorists. "We have a real battle with not the church in the U.S., but Christian-Zionists there, and we need to hear more and more voices from around the world in support of the Palestinian people," Sourani said.

THE PROBLEM OF EVIL IN WORLD RELIGIONS

The problem of evil is a touchstone of any religion and from our direct confrontation with evil results suffering and thus endless questions about the meaning of life. That is why all religions have to give a proper answer regarding the origin, nature and end of evil. There are three major religious alternatives in explaining evil, stated by the pantheistic, dualistic and monotheistic religions. Pantheistic religions regard evil as ultimately unreal. Human suffering is a product of spiritual ignorance gathered in previous lives and distributed in the present one according to the dictates of karma. In the dualistic religions, good and evil are two eternal and rival principles. Neither has created the other one and each acts according to its own nature. In the monotheistic religions, evil has a personal identity. Its source is a being that has fallen from an initial good status as a result of misusing freedom of will. Let us analyze these perspectives and see to what extent they are compatible with one another.

Evil in Hinduism

As mentioned, Hinduism is a complex mixture of religious trends. Concerning the relation between Ultimate Reality and evil, there are at least three major perspectives, given by:

1. The Vedas;
2. The Upanishads and the whole corpus of pantheistic writings;
3. The Epics and Puranas

Evil in the Vedas

In the hymns addressed to Varuna evil is a matter of humans not fulfilling his laws or not performing the ritual properly. Often it has a moral significance, in that people are evilminded or commit adultery (*Rig Veda* 4,5; 10,10). Those who commit evil deeds must repent before Varuna (*Rig Veda* 5, 85) and try to repair their evil deeds through ritual sacrifices. In other hymns, as those addressed to Indra, evil is personified by demons. Thus the fight against evil is a perpetual combat between personalized good and evil forces.

Evil in the Upanishads

The Upanishads ground a pantheistic perspective on Ultimate Reality and introduce karma as the explanation of evil in the world. Ignorance launches karma into action and karma brings suffering. As the manifestations and dissolutions of the world have no beginning and no end, so is karma, meaning that suffering is a part of the eternal cosmic cycle. Suffering in the present life is the natural consequence of past lives' ignorance and it has to be endured without questioning.

Evil in Samkhya-Yoga

Although the Samkhya and Yoga *darshanas* are not pantheistic, they follow a similar view in defining evil. It is a matter of how much one is caught in the psycho-mental illusions generated by the primordial substance (*prakriti*). Two of the three gunas (*rajas and tamas*), are causing the manifestations of what we call evil in the world, both in the physical and in the mental realm.

Evil in the Epics and Puranas

The writings of Hindu theism adopt a middle way in explaining evil, between the dictates of karma and the responsibility of the gods in producing it as sovereign agents in the universe. As these two elements are irreconcilable and mutually exclusive, the solutions to the problem of evil are themselves contradictory. The character of the gods becomes quite ambiguous in the *Epics* and the *Puranas*. They are responsible for producing both good and evil. Here are some examples:

Indra, the ex-hero of the Vedas, commits adultery in the *Skanda Purana* (2, 7, 23, 8-40) and justifies himself by the effect of his past karma. In the *Mahabharata* (12, 258, 42) he is excused for seducing Gotama's wife since he was in a process of working out his karma. No wonders that in the *Ramayana* (7, 30, 20-45) he is accused of having initiated adultery in our world by his bad example.

Although Krishna is to be followed as example according to the *Bhagavad Gita* (3, 23), when committing adultery in the Puranas he justifies himself in reference to human behaviour, saying: "Since even the sages are uncontrolled and act as they please, how one could possibly restrain Vishnu when he becomes voluntary incarnate?" (*Bhagavata Purana* 10, 33, 35).

Brahma, the creator god, is often accused of being creator of both good and evil. In one situation described in the *Mahabharata*, he grew jealous of people and their heavenly destiny and planned to delude them: "Formerly, all creatures were virtuous, and by themselves they obtained divinity. Therefore the gods became worried, so Brahma created women in order to delude men. Then women, who had been virtuous, became wicked witches, and Brahma filled them with wanton desires, which they in turn inspired in men. He created anger, and henceforth all creatures were born in the power of desire and anger (*Mahabharata* 13, 40, 5-12). According to the *Vishnu Purana* (1,5,1-18), evil precedes and accompanies Brahma's creation, this being the reason why mankind is evil: "His fourth creation produced creatures in whom darkness and passion predominated, afflicted by misery; these were mankind." In the *Markandeya Purana* (45, 40) it is said that he created both "cruel creatures and gentle creatures, dharma and adharma, truth and falsehood."

Not only is evil inevitable in creation, but it is said to be a good thing, a necessary dynamic factor in the universe. For instance, in the *Devibhagavata* (4, 13), Brihaspati, and the guru of the gods says: "All creatures, even gods, are subject to passions. Otherwise the universe, composed as it is of good and evil, could not continue to develop." According to the *Vishnu Purana* (1, 5, 59-65), the existence of evil in creation is both the will of Brahma the creator and the result of the obligation created by karma. In the same situation is Vishnu (*Linga Puranà* 2, 6, 1-57), who creates under the power of karma both good and evil, "good people and bad people, those who follow the right path, but also the heretics."

These ambiguous solutions to the problem of evil in Hindu mythology are caused by the fact that the gods cannot be at the same time sovereign, and in tune with karma. If the gods are responsible for the existence of evil in the world, they either create it willingly, or then are evil themselves, or are forced to create it by the higher law of karma, and then are weak.

Evil in Buddhism

Buddhism rejects the authority of the Vedas and of the other writings of Hinduism, explaining the nature of evil through the process of constant becoming. Evil is the perpetuation of illusion by the factors that fuel the chain of dependent origination (*paticca-samuppada*). Ignorance in perceiving that the world is impermanent, devoid of a self and in constant becoming leads to suffering. The Buddha proclaimed that in fact the whole of existence is suffering:

> The Noble Truth of Suffering (dukkha) is this: Birth is suffering; aging is suffering; sickness is suffering; death is suffering; sorrow and lamentation, pain, grief, and despair are suffering; association with the unpleasant is suffering; dissociation from the pleasant is suffering; not to get what one wants is suffering - in brief, the five aggregates of attachment are suffering (Samyutta Nikaya 56,11).

There are three fundamental defilements of the mind that combine and interact leading to suffering: greed (*raga*), aversion (*dvesha*) and ignorance (*avidya*). Their origin is desire to experience existence in personal form. As personhood is nothing but an illusory result of the temporary gathering together of five aggregates, the desire to perpetuate the illusion of personal existence produces suffering, so its extreme solution must be the abolition of personhood. There is no suffering if there is no person left to experience it.

Evil in Taoism

Since any aspect of the world is a manifestation of the Tao, corresponding to a different participation of the Yin and Yang principles, nothing can be considered to be essentially evil in the world. Even if Yin is termed as a negative principle, it never manifests itself alone. In the *Tao-te Ching* it is stated:

When beauty is abstracted
Then ugliness has been implied;
When good is abstracted
Then evil has been implied.

Every positive factor involves its negative or opposing one. What is usually called evil, as physical and mental manifestation, is the result of a lack of balance between the two opposing principles and corresponds to a bigger participation of the Yin principle. Evil belongs to the nature of the world, so humans have to subscribe to the universal harmony and respect the equilibrium of the two polarities. Tao is eternal and so are the two principles Yang and Yin, so that good and evil must be eternal, as necessary elements of our world.

Evil in Dualistic Religions

According to the dualistic religions there are two antagonist and coeternal deities involved in creation and in governing the destiny of humans. Zoroastrianism probably stated the first true religious dualism. Ahura Mazda and Angra Mainyu are the two coeternal gods responsible for the existence of good and evil in the world. The *Yasna* states: "There are two fundamental spirits, twins which are renowned to be in conflict. In thought and in word, in action, they are two: the good and the bad".

In the latter tradition of Zurvanism, Ohrmazd and Ahriman are twin brothers, each one creating according to his own nature:

The first of the good lands and countries which I, Ahura Mazda, created, was Paradise, by the good river Araxes.

Thereupon came Angra Mainyu, who is all death, and he counter-created by his witchcraft the serpent in the river and winter, a work of the devils.

The second of the good lands and countries which I, Ahura Mazda, created, was the plains in Samarkand. Thereupon came Angra Mainyu, who is all death, and he counter-created by his witchcraft the fly Skaitya, which brings death to the cattle. The third of the good lands and countries which I, Ahura Mazda, created, was the strong, holy Merv. Thereupon came Angra Mainyu, who is all death, and he counter-created by his witchcraft sinful lusts.... (Videvdad 1, 3-5). Humans are in the center of this eternal conflict, having the duty to choose always the good and thus help it defeat the evil.

After the 1st century AD the Western world witnessed the emergence of many dualistic religions. Their interpretation of the *Genesis* account of creation is sharply anti-Judaic and anti-Christian, being aimed at undermining their basic tenets. Marcionism, Gnosticism, Manicheism, Bogomilism and Catharism (as well as other dualistic religions that swept through the medieval world) all acknowledge the God of the Old Testament as creator, but take him as a minor deity among higher spiritual deities (the Aeons). He created the physical world out of his ignorance. It is therefore hazardous and generates nothing but problems. Contrary to the Bible, these religions see humans as superior to their creator because they are endowed with a higher spiritual essence by the Aeons. However, the physical body keeps them bound to a miserable condition, which perpetuates through reincarnation. The only way of escaping from this condition is the attainment of true knowledge (*gnosis*).

In Gnosticism the name of the creator god is Ialdabaot. He ignores the higher deities whose descendent he is and creates this world out of pre-existing matter. Then he boasts of being the only god. However, humans are superior to him, having received the spirit of life from a higher Aeon (Sophia, the mother of Ialdabaot). Satan and Jesus are the enemies of Ialdabaot and teach humans how to attain true knowledge that may save them from ignorance. A detailed study of Gnosticism, of its contradictions and incompatibilities with Christianity can be found in Irenaeus' treatise Against Heresies. A similar stand was adopted by *Manicheism,* a new religion that appeared in Persia in the 3rd century AD. Matter and the physical body are considered intrinsically evil as they derive from the bodies of the dead forces of evil (the Archons).

As a result of captivity in the bodily prison, the soul is overwhelmed by ignorance and forgets his true origin. Reincarnation occurs until the soul is released from its earthly sufferings. Manicheism was addressed by Augustine in many of his writings in the 4th century AD. See On the Morals of the Manichaeans and On the Nature of Good. In Catharism the god of the Old Testament is considered to be the ultimate representative of evil. He created the physical bodies of humans and locked angels inside them. According to radical Catharism, human souls are angels who served the good God but were tempted by Satan to experience earthly pleasures which they could not resist. The original bodies and spirits of these angels remained in heaven, but their souls fell into physical bodies. Reincarnation works until humans recognize their heavenly origin and purify themselves by the use of asceticism. Once cleansed of impurities they are accepted back in the heavenly world.

Evil in Christianity

According to Christianity, God created all things, but this doesn't make him the creator of evil. The Apostle John states: "God is light; in him there is no darkness at all" (*1 John* 1,5). When God finished his creation, he appreciated that "all that he had made was very good" (*Genesis* 1,31). However, anyone can clearly see that evil exists in our world, in awful measure. From here arises a major puzzle: If God is all-good, he should want to stop evil; if he is omnipotent, he could stop it; but evil exists in the world, so God lacks either all-goodness (if he can stop evil but does not want to) or omnipotence (if he wants to stop evil, but cannot), or both. As God is declared to be all-good (*1 John* 4,8) and all-powerful (*Revelation* 19,6), how can this puzzle be solved?

According to the Christian view, the origin of evil is to be found in the world of angels. God created them in time immemorial, as personal and immaterial beings endowed with free will. They were created ex nihilo, the same way as the material universe, and thus have a nature different from God's. These beings have minds (*Acts* 12, 7-10; *1 Peter* 1, 12), feelings (*Luke* 15, 10), and wills (*Jude* 6) and are not limited by a physical body. Their number was very large and there was a hierarchy among them (Hebrews 12, 22). Evil appeared in the world of angels when Lucifer, one of God's cherubs, rebelled against this order. In the book of the prophet Ezekiel we can read the following metaphorical description of this incident:

You were blameless in your ways from the day you were created till wickedness was found in you. Through your widespread trade you were filled with violence, and you sinned. So I drove you in disgrace from the mount of God, and I expelled you, O guardian cherub, from among the fiery stones. Your heart became proud on account of your beauty, and you corrupted your wisdom because of your splendour. So I threw you to the earth; I made a spectacle of you before kings (Ezekiel 28, 15-17).

This angel, who became Satan ("adversary") out of Lucifer ("angel of light"), was expelled from heaven together with all the others who joined him in his act of rebellion. The cause of his fall was pride, the desire to be independent from God, to refuse submission and inferiority to God. Lucifer wanted to be by himself more than his created status could permit him. Satan's fall couldn't have occurred without a real freedom of choice. He had the ability to choose either to obey God and recognize him as the ground of his being, or to follow a selfish way and seek autodetermination. His choice for the second alternative constitutes the origin of evil in the universe.

Therefore, evil is not created by God, but is a perversion of his creation, a result of using free will against the very purpose it was created for, against free-willed obedience to God in a communion relation based on love.

In order to have this kind of perfect communion with the creator, a personal being needs the possibility to choose it freely. This is why God allows starvation, disease, murder, war, and all other evils in our world to exist. Although such facts constitute reasons for atheism, they represent the cost of preserving our (misused) free will. However, evil was not intended by God and is not linked to the essence of God and creation. The destiny of Satan and demons is that of spiritual death, of irrevocable separation from the Source in which they should have found their fulfillment. This is hell, the realm where they are granted the liberty to eternally renew their wish to exist "by themselves." The doctrine of hell, as horrifying as it looks to be, points to the fact that evil has an end, that is has limited temporal power and influence in God's creation.

A few comments on the alleged illusory status of evil must be added here. To what extent can evil be termed as illusory? In terms of absolute existence, terms that characterize only God's being, we have seen that evil cannot exist by itself. This is what the Church Fathers meant by the fact that evil is without substance, reality, being or existence. For instance, in his writing On the Incarnation of the Word, Ch. 1, Athanasius says that "God alone exists, evil is non-being". This is not an affirmation of the illusory status of evil, but an ontological perspective on the fallen state of God's creatures that lost communion with God.

The context of his words is as following:

For the transgression of the commandment was making them turn back again according to their nature; and as they had at the beginning come into being out of nonexistence, so were they now on the way to returning, through corruption, to nonexistence again. The presence and love of the Word had called them into being; inevitably, therefore when they lost the knowledge of God, they lost existence with it; for it is God alone Who exists, evil is nonbeing, the negation and antithesis of good.

The same meaning is attached to the words of Gregory of Nyssa when mentioning that "there is no evil other than wickedness" in his Great Catechism, Ch. 7. The context here is his address to the heretics that claimed that man is the creation of an evil deity (in order to explain the fallen human nature). Gregory of Nyssa states that God is not responsible for man's turning away from him through sin. This act separates man from his presence and consequently from real existence, as only God is the source for it. Here is Gregory of Nyssa's commentary on the nature of evil:

Since, if their thoughts had taken a loftier view, and, withdrawing their minds from this disposition to regard the gratifications of the senses, they had looked at the nature of existing things dispassionately, they would have understood that there is no evil other than wickedness. Now all wickedness has its form and character in the deprivation of the good; it exists not by itself, and cannot be contemplated as subsistence. For no evil of any kind lies outside and independent of the will; but it is the nonexistence of the good that is so denominated. Now that which is not has no substantial existence and the Maker of that which has no substantial existence is not the Maker of things that have substantial existence. Therefore the God of things that are is external to the causation of things that are evil, since He is not the Maker of things that are nonexistent. He Who formed the sight did not make blindness.

According to Christianity, evil entered our world as a result of Satan's fall, so it has a personal character. Jesus Christ spoke directly to Satan at the moment of his temptation (*Matthew* 4, 1-11; etc.). He cast out demons (*Mark* 1, 21-28; etc.), and the apostles did also (*Acts* 5, 16; etc.), so they were not addressing illusions. The Apostle Peter warned his fellow Christians that Satan is a real and dangerous presence: "Be selfcontrolled and alert. Your enemy the devil prowls around like a roaring lion looking for someone to devour" (*1 Peter* 5, 8). Likewise, the Apostle Paul emphasizes that "Satan himself is masquerading as an angel of light" in order to deceive humans (*2 Corinthians* 11,14). Although belief in the existence of demons is old-fashioned, to say the least, such verses cannot be ignored and taken as mere childish bogus tales.

Although Satan is the initiator of evil, humans are responsible for spreading it into our world through sin. Thus we are not innocent victims lacking any responsibility. By misusing the freedom of choice that God has granted us, we became the perpetrators of evil in our world. Although we have real freedom to refuse evil, we don't do it, so evil continues to spread. The reason why God allows this situation and does not extinguish all evil in an instant is that such an act would necessarily involve the damnation of all those who perform it. This would cancel any possibility for them to repent and be reconciled with God. As he takes no pleasure "in the death of the wicked," but rather wants "that they turn from their ways and live" (*Ezekiel* 33, 11), a sudden extinction of evil would contradicts his love for mankind which one of us would pass the test of God's holiness if the extinction of evil were performed apart from his love?

God's attitude in tolerating evil in our world is perfectly expressed by Jesus in the Parable of the Weeds (Matthew 13, 24-43):

The kingdom of heaven is like a man who sowed good seed in his field. But while everyone was sleeping, his enemy came and sowed weeds among the wheat, and went away. When the wheat sprouted and formed heads, then the weeds also appeared. The owner's servants came to him and said, "Sir, didn't you sow good seed in your field? Where then did the weeds come from?" "An enemy did this," he replied. The servants asked him, "Do you want us to go and pull them up?" "No," he answered, "because while you are pulling the weeds, you may root up the wheat with them. Let both grow together until the harvest. At that time I will tell the harvesters: First collect the weeds and tie them in bundles to be burned; then gather the wheat and bring it into my barn" (13, 24-30).

The explanation to this parable is the following:

The one who sowed the good seed is the Son of Man. The field is the world, and the good seed stands for the sons of the kingdom. The weeds are the sons of the evil one, and the enemy who sows them is the devil. The harvest is the end of the age, and the harvesters are angels.

As the weeds are pulled up and burned in the fire, so it will be at the end of the age. The Son of Man will send out his angels, and they will weed out of his kingdom everything that causes sin and all who do evil. They will throw them into the fiery furnace, where there will be weeping and gnashing of teeth. Then the righteous will shine like the sun in the kingdom of their Father. He who has ears, let him hear (37-43).

God tolerates "weeds" among "wheat" until a certain moment. His purpose in doing so is that "weeds" could be properly differentiated from "wheat" and pulled up at the right moment. As the parable refers to humans, the people who may be called "weeds" still have the chance of converting and becoming "wheat." This can happen only as long as they can benefit from God's grace that is during their earthly lifetime. It is God's grace that allows evildoers to live, not his lack of justice or power that they may still have the chance to repent and return to a personal relationship with him. As a result, humans' attitude toward evil should be neither one of resignation, nor of rebellion against God, but of conscious and responsible participation in the world. Evil has an end, as does human suffering.

What is required from us while waiting for this end is to fight against evil and suffering, and especially against our sinful nature, which perpetuates both our suffering and that of our neighbours? Jesus descended in the midst of our problems and misery, and he urges for action in imitating him in daily living.

Although we are not spared from troubles and many times we do not understand their meaning, we should always remember that Jesus promised his help and power in order to conquer them. He said:

I have told you these things, so that in me you may have peace. In this world you will have trouble. But take heart! I have overcome the world" (John 16, 33).

Therefore there is no contradiction in God's character. God is omnipotent and all-good. Evil is not everlasting. God can stop it, and he will stop it one day forever (*Revelation* 20, 10). It is only sin that prevents us from understanding what evil really is and from doing what we can do in order to stop it spreading around us.

7

Holocaust Religion and Holocaust Industry

The Nazi Judeocide played and continues to play a major role in the Arab/Israeli conflict. On the one hand, it is unfortunately a commonly held Arab position that this Judeocide is merely one of many bogus Zionist postures to manipulate world public opinion. On the other hand, not less sadly, many Jews insist upon the uniqueness of this catastrophe (in Hebrew, 'shoa') and believe that it demonstrates beyond doubt the necessity of a Jewish state; and had there been one during WWII, this genocide would not have taken place. Moreover, it is claimed that only a militarily strong Israel can prevent such a catastrophe from recurring. Accordingly anybody not accepting these beliefs is considered to be Anti-Jewish.

Each of the above positions is the result of the same distorted mode of processing the past. This mode can be called religious, even though the usual definition of religion includes a god concept - one which is absent in this discussion. In all other ways, the necessary religious characteristics are in place: dogmas, commandments, rituals, shrines, prophets and priests and, of course, economic/financial structures. One can, therefore, speak of a "Holocaust Religion" and its "Satanic" arch enemy or twin, "Holocaust Denial". A third way to deal with the Judeocide, which should be defined as secular and scientific, is often identified with "Holocaust Denial." The use of the term "Holocaust", which means "A burnt- sacrifice or offering, the whole of which was consumed by fire," reflects the religious character of the dominant historiography of Judeocide.

Using the designation "Holocaust" for the extermination of the Jews implies accordingly the absurdity that the Nazis sacrificed Jews in a kind of a religious ritual. The birth of the Holocaust Religion is considered to have been triggered by the trial in Jerusalem of the Nazi criminal Adolf Eichmann in 1961. This show-trial was a spectacle meant to get the broader Jewish Israeli public, mainly the youngest generation, acquainted with the Judeocide. The trial did not succeed in the short run in achieving this aim not because this middle-ranking SS-officer, Eichman, was not adequate to represent the whole extermination machinery. Nor was the failure due to the impossibility of reducing the Nazi monstrous system to a single individual. The fundamental reason for the failure must be attributed to the central Zionist tenet: the "Negation of the Diaspora", a recurrent theme which made it thence very difficult for the young Jewish-Israelis to identify themselves with European Jewry.

Several generations of Israeli Jews were brought up to loathe Jewish existence abroad. In fact, the Jewish way of life in Europe was viewed as sick and to be overcome through Zionism. Young Jewish-Israelis were brainwashed, throughout the late 70s, to internalize typical Christian European prejudices against Jews and thus did not want to identify themselves with their own grandparents or even their parents, who had allegedly not resisted oppression in Europe. It is precisely owing to their role as victimizers that, even now, makes it is easier for Israeli soldiers to identify with the Nazis than with their own ancestors - the victims. Example: in 1982 after the bombing of Beirut and putting the city under siege, Israeli soldiers disgusted at what they had just done, told an excited and adoring German journalist who wanted to know how they were feeling: "we have just created a Warsaw ghetto."

Even though Eichmann's trial did not achieve the desired effect inside Israel, its impact abroad was enormous. Elie Wiesel, a former concentration camp inmate, who came to Jerusalem to report on the process, subsequently initiated a religious modality for handling the Judeocide. This religion was to become very dominant in the ensuing years. It came to be accepted not only by most Jews but also many non-Jews, especially in the industrialized countries. It was to become one of the most important tools of the Israeli propaganda machinery. The relevancy of the Holocaust Religion to the Middle East conflict cannot therefore be overlooked.

Its real breakthrough according to the Jewish theologian Marc Ellis, who defines it rather as a theology, came through the Israeli victory in 1967. "Holocaust theology yields three themes that exist in dialectical tension: suffering and empowerment, innocence and redemption, specialness and normalization." This war therefore was, according to this analysis, a kind of a religious messianic salvation. The Judeocide and the big 'threat' to Israel in 1967 is the suffering. The building of the State of Israel and especially the victory of 1967 is the redemption.

Of course Zionism lost its innocence long before 1967. Already in the 1930s, David Ben Gurion, the most important Zionist leader, realized the huge potential in Judeocide as he brought these religious elements together into a simple direct political motto for the instrumentalization of the Jewish sufferings in Europe. He declared: "Catastrophe is Power." Which means the Zionist movement should find ways to profit politically and financially from the agony. Yet the catastrophe became a real source of political power only after Israel became a military success in 1967, which means, a catastrophe as such is not necessarily a source of power. One must be powerful in order to be able to use and abuse a disaster. In their book "Dangerous Liaison", Andrew and Leslie Cockburn describe how only after 1967 did Israel becomes attractive to the US military establishment. Though Israel had, before that time, a burning desire to work for Washington, the US was not very enthusiastic until Israel demonstrated its strength on the battlefield.

The journalist J.J. Goldberg argues that the Jewish lobby became strong only after 1967. AIPAC, the best known lobby, became influential through the Israeli importance for the US foreign policy and not the other way around. This claim sounds very plausible when one considers that American Jewish organizations were not able to convince the Roosevelt administration to be more helpful towards European Jewry during the Nazi era. Although, for example, the New York Times was in Jewish ownership it did not dare, just like the mainstream US Jewish organizations, to oppose the anti-Jewish policy of the State Department. The lobby to establish a Zionist state in Palestine was anyway more effective than the one to save the Jews. This was the line dictated by Ben Gurion and executed by his delegate Abba Hillel Silver.

The Zionist influence at that period was less strong than perceived through the Arab lens. Still the leadership of the Jewish agency (JA), i.e., the government-in-formation, headed by the Zionist Labor movement, started very early to cash in on the Nazi persecution of the Jews. This "Holocaust Industry" had been founded even before the Judeocide was really launched. In the mid 30s the JA reached a deal with the Nazis, the so called Ha'avara (Transfer) agreement, which helped the Zionist movement not only to attract to Palestine very wealthy investors, but to get direct control of some of their money. According to the arrangement, rich Jews could get some of their properties out of Germany if they immigrated to Palestine and the Jewish Agency received a nice commission from these deals. This arrangement was, among others, the result of strong Nazi support for the Zionist project, since corresponding with the Zionist aims the main German objective at that time was "just" to expel the Jews from Europe. This policy coincided with the Zionist goals.

The collaboration with the Nazis brought the Zionists

the much needed capital for the colonization of Palestine ($40 million), which was "60% of capital invested in Palestine between 1933 and the war." This agreement practically saved the Zionist movement in Palestine from bankruptcy argues the journalist Lenni Brenner. The JA came thus to be the largest agent for German goods in the Middle East and sabotaged Jewish efforts to declare an effective boycott against the Nazis, of which they were very afraid. This fruitful cooperation between Nazis and Zionists came to an end in 1938 following Arab insurrections. After which the British tried to stop Jewish Immigration into Palestine. Besides, the German faction, which sought an anti-British alliance with the Arabs got stronger and blocked the export to Palestine of goods so needed at home. Still the pro-Zionist Nazi factions (Eichmann was a part of them) kept their contacts with the Jewish Agency.

According to the coordinator of the Zionist activities in occupied Europe, Nathan Dror-Schwalb, his people were working together with Eichmann in 1938 as he expelled the Austrian Jews. This is also documented by Jon and David Kimche. Zionist delegates, according to Schwalb, could operate without disturbance in Germany throughout the war and organize their cells of the youth movement Hehalutz. According to the Israeli historian S.B. Beit-Zvi, the JA-leadership did not hesitate to sabotage rescue efforts. This happened after it became clear that the British would not allow a Jewish mass immigration to Palestine. Beit-Zvi argues that the JA-leadership was afraid that a large number of Jews would be saved and sent to some other destinations rather than Palestine. This development was considered a political and economic danger to the Zionist project, as it would absorb resources needed to establish the state and would weaken the Zionist claim that Palestine is the only possible refuge for Jews.

According to Beit-Zvi, Golda Meir was responsible for sabotaging the concrete chances of rescue of the refugees which were discussed at the conference of Evian in 1938. Beit-Zvi claims that this was the real reason why this famous conference actually failed. In a very famous speech Ben Gurion formulated the JA rescue policy as follows: "If I knew that it would be possible to save all the children in Germany by bringing them over to England and only half of them by transporting them to Eretz Yisrael, then I would opt for the second alternative. For we must weigh not only the lives of these children but also the history of the People of Israel."

Ben-Gurion's apologists have tried to explain away this quotation. But an objective examination of the following activities of the JA, the protocols of JA-leadership and the factual low priority it gave to rescue operations, can only confirm the claim that this speech was emblematic of this attitude and that it basically never changed even after the scope of the catastrophe became clear. In the case of the Hungarian Jews, the charge of direct collaboration of the Labor party controlled JA leadership with the Nazis is raised by both Jewish Anti-Zionists and Ultra-Zionists (Likud and more radical parties). The Labor party representative, Israel Kastner is accused of making possible the efficient deportation of half a million Jews to Auschwitz through the cooperation of his committee with Eichmann. The defenders of Kastner argue that he actually tried to save the Hungarian Jews through negotiating with the Nazis. This last claim is probably basically true, but it is beyond discussion that these negotiations were sabotaged by the JA-leadership, the mainstream Jewish organizations in the USA and also by the Allies.

The JA-leadership had the same considerations as formulated by S.B. Beth Tzvi; it knew that there was no chance that if a large number of Jews were to be rescued by Kastner and his committee that they would be able to immigrate to Palestine. The sabotaging of this realistic rescue attempt by the JA got in return the British consent to build a Jewish brigade in the British army. The Israeli historian, Idith Zertal, claims that Ben Gurion was already before WWII mainly interested in the rescue operations only for national purposes. The saving of persecuted Jews was to be used primarily as a means of pressure on the British Empire to abolish its restrictions on Jewish immigration to Palestine. But even for these purposes, there were hardly any meaningful rescue activities during the war. There were very few Zionist delegates to coordinate such operations and they had hardly any financial resources to be effective. According to Zertal, the spectacular actions of the illegal immigration after the war, like the famous trip of the "Exodus", were mainly part of a very effective propaganda campaign.

She quotes the Jewish welfare organization "Joint" that claimed at that time, that the total number of immigrants including the illegal ones was smaller than the British quota. This means that if the Jewish refugees had been transported to Palestine legally, under normal conditions, it would have been cheaper, more comfortable and safer for them than using the shaky illegal ships and their number would not necessarily have been lower. But by using this legal way, the JA would have lost the propaganda effects of the pictures of British soldiers using excessive amounts of force against Jewish survivors. Though the Zionist leadership was not very active in saving Jews (to say the least), it had already started during WWII to prepare a restitution campaign. The JA felt itself empowered to make claims on Jewish properties without being bothered by such trivialities like whether or not the legitimate owners or their heirs were still alive. The Zionist project needed a lot of money and therefore it is not surprising that the JA did not have too many ethical considerations when they endeavored to save Nazi war criminals, that is, if the Nazis could pay enough for it. Thus the SS officer responsible for the robbery of the Hungarian Jewry, Kurt Becher, and some of his friends were saved.

The aforementioned Israel Kastner was sent in 1947 by the Israeli finance minister to Germany to save these Nazis from trial. In return, Becher gave orders to his Swiss trustee to transfer money to the Jewish Agency. This was also the case of the important Nazi agent Jaac van Harten, whose money financed in 1945/46 the illegal Jewish immigration to Palestine and acquisitions of weapons. Van Harten was crucial for the flight of Nazis out of Europe, but the agents of the Mossad Le'Aliyah Beth who protected him, could not care less. He himself found refuge later in Tel Aviv, where he got the protection of no less than Golda Meir, the de-facto foreign minister at that time (1947). Till the 60s Van Harten kept contacts with his former Nazi boss, Friedrich Schwend, who was then working in Peru with other famous Nazis like Josef Mengele and Klaus Barbie. Schwend was considered to be a kind of finance minister of the planned Fourth Reich.

The Zionist movement succeeded after WWII in getting restitution illegitimately in the name of the Nazi victims. At the last stages of the war representatives of the Jewish Agency gathered Jewish properties and were nominated as recipient for such assets at the Paris Reparation Conference (1945/46). The larger amount of money began to flow in the 50s as the USA intensified its efforts to reintegrate West Germany in its Cold War strategy. A German researcher reports about a meeting in Switzerland between the German chancellor Konrad Adenauer and the Israeli President Haim Weizmann. In this meeting Adenauer agreed to pay compensations if Israel gave it consent for the rearmament of West Germany.

These restitution and compensation monies were very crucial for building the Israeli economy and military. Some Israeli experts claim that without the German reparations the Israeli economy would have collapsed in the '50s. There is no doubt that the victory of 1967 would not have been possible without this support. Thus the suffering of the Jewish Nazi victims was used to finance Israeli military aggressions. After 1967 the influence of the Holocaust Industry and the Holocaust Religion increased as a result of the ever growing importance of Israel in terms of US interests. The Holocaust Religion was able to achieve a growing control over public opinion in Western countries. Its influence in the 90s reached an unexpected climax. Steven Spielberg's film "Schindler's List" and the ceremonies commemorating the Jubilee of the end of WWII functioned like a trigger for this outburst.

As an outcome of this memory-explosion the Holocaust Industry was in position to launch in 1995 a very effective restitution campaign against the Swiss banks, which has been expanded to include other countries. It was a mixture of a just claim, presented by the wrong organizations for the wrong purposes, fed through the fear of Judeophobes of the mythological 'Jewish Power' and its overestimated influence on the US government. Of course the Jewish organizations got the support of Clinton's administration in this campaign, but it is not clear how far the US would have gone on this issue against the Swiss banks. Thus the Swiss became 'victims' of their own prejudices against the Jews. From a rather unimportant organization looking rather helplessly for an issue, with this Swiss help, the World Jewish Congress and the affiliated organizations came to be a very influential factor. The undertaking has brought many billions of dollars and the story is not yet over.

Israel itself tries not to be involved directly in this campaign, in order not to get into any diplomatic complications with friendly countries like Switzerland. Instead the World Jewish Congress (WJC), the Jewish Claims Conference (JCC) and some other organizations are leading the activities. Israel just hopes in one way or another to get its share in any eventual booty. For example, after a certain compensation for survivors was paid by Switzerland, the Israeli government tried to cut the social security support to the Israeli recipients commensurate with what they'd receive from Switzerland. A step which means, that actually the money from Switzerland would have gone to the state of Israel and not to the victims.

In the meantime there is much more money in the restitution funds, but its distribution is delayed (Israel belongs to the slowest distributors) and the survivors have the feeling that the Jewish organizations 'representing' them, are just waiting for more of them to die, so that the funds will be distributed for other purposes. The survivors and the legitimate owners of robbed properties realized too late that their interests are being abused by the leading Jewish organizations (all of them with a strong Zionist influence). These survivors are too weak and too old to fight effectively against the mighty jet-setters of organized Jewry.

There was a series of articles in various papers in Israel, Switzerland, Germany and the USA demonstrating how the most important restitution organization, the Jewish Claims Conference, is robbing the legitimate heirs, as Joseph Wolff describes. Wolff, a former director of the Israeli oil firm Paz, after learning about the cruelty of the JCC, decided to try to help the twice victimized people.

The efforts of this influential and well connected person did not help much and still today there is not much clarity regarding the activities of the JCC. No outsider knows how much money it controls, how much is distributed, who are the recipients etc. The attacks of the US political scientist Norman Finkelstein against the JCC in his book "The Holocaust Industry" irritate the organized Jewry but in the short run do no more than that. This is because Finkelstein did not invest enough energy in the complicated investigations needed to prove his claims.

In a website "The Survivors vs. the Holocaust Industry", several old survivors tried to initiate the struggle against the JCC, but they did not get very far, as they did not have the necessary funds and power to finance the fight against the mighty organizations. They protested against the injustices and demanded that they should be able to decide how the money should be allocated. The protesting survivors claimed that the Jewish organizations were very slow in distributing the monies and that they are just waiting till all of them die. They noted that actually each and every month 1,000 survivors around the world die.

The survivor Gerhard Maschkowski, who was among the leaders of this struggle wrote: "After the war ended in 1945, Holocaust survivors were treated shabbily; most were forced to live in Displaced Persons Camps in Europe as the world was forced to deal with the stateless character of the Jewish people until the founding of the State of Israel in 1948 [he seems to forget to mention explicitly the role of the Jewish Agency in this postponement. The JA used once again the sufferings of the survivors as a political instrument - se]. Later, the "reparations and restitution" efforts established ostensibly for the benefit of Holocaust survivors in the United States, were inadequate and arbitrarily administered, resulting in a legacy of frustration and humiliation for American survivors. Today's abandonment is occurring in the context of settlements of class actions and disputes over Swiss bank accounts, looted Nazi gold, Nazi use of Jewish slave laborers, and European insurers' theft of Jews' insurance policies.

While the headlines cry with large dollar figures purporting to represent compensation for Holocaust victims, and the box quotes are full of lavish praise and gratitude for the settlements "as we enter a new millennium," the truth is, the interests of Holocaust survivors have received the lowest priority in these negotiations. From every perspective, the deals fall short of rendering meaningful justice or dignity to those who were victimized. "[...] the agreements were struck to provide immunity for vast numbers of European corporations that profited from the Holocaust, in most cases, without a true accounting for their World War II actions."

This last point is demonstrated perfectly by the Interhandel affair, the scandal of the foreign assets of the largest Nazi chemical combine I.G. Farben, who among other things produced the gas for the extermination of the Jews. These assets should have been confiscated during WWII and be used for the rehabilitation of war refugees. This did not happen, because Corporate America was interested in protecting these funds and the Swiss authorities and some banks were willing to help. This money, estimated to be of a present value of at least $5 billion, was in the 60s after a long legal fight misappropriated by the largest Swiss bank, Union Bank of Switzerland, (today United Bank of Switzerland - UBS) and the US government under Kennedy.

In 1995 I discovered in the Swiss federal archives highly classified documents proving clearly the dubious role of the UBS and the Swiss government in this affair. The Jewish organizations leading the restitution campaigns show an ostensive disinterest in this large amount of money stemming from the most important Nazi combine, whose direct involvement in the crimes in Auschwitz is well known. Recently an employee of the JCC confirmed my suspicions and said that the organizations do not want to raise the issue in order not to hurt the US interests involved.

The state of Israel itself refuses till today to return assets belonging to Jewish Nazi victims. These properties, mainly real estates in some very central locations, are worth according to estimations around $US 20 billion. Still the Holocaust Industry is hardly active on this issue, though it is obvious that the sum is much higher than in Switzerland and that the Israeli government, the institutions and corporations holding these possessions are more callous towards the victims and their heirs than their equivalents in Europe.

It is safe to argue that neither the Holocaust Industry nor Israel have ever represented the real interests of the Judeocide victims, although they keep trying to create the impression that they do. This lie serves Israel in many ways. It guarantees today the support of most of the Jews, who feel that Israel might be their redemption in the hour of an eventual need, a kind of an insurance against possible dangers paid by the blood and suffering of the Palestinians. With the Holocaust Religion, its institutions and priests it is possible to block an all too strong critique against Israel and its crimes against the Palestinians. Thus the Palestinians actually become indirectly victims of the Nazis and actually of the Judaeophobia. The Holocaust Industry helps to finance the aggressions against them and the Holocaust Religion assists in creating a negative public opinion of them and block the critique against the Israeli crimes. Thus the Palestinians have to pay the price for German crimes and Western hypocrisy. The exposure of the Zionist abuse of Judeocide is therefore an important element in the efforts to reach a real and just peace in the Middle East.

Beside the fact that such peace is also in the interest of many Jews, the dismantling of the Holocaust Religion due to their own efforts will benefit most of the Jews because as history teaches, the downfall of every power is bound to happen sooner or later. In this case one can reckon with a fierce Anti-Jewish black lash, which should be considered as a direct result of the arrogance and immorality of the pro-Israel lobbies propagating the Holocaust Religion. As the main sources of the extraordinary and abnormal influence of the Holocaust Industry are clearly the special relationships between the U.S. and Israel, once they come to an end, the situation will change dramatically for sure.

Already now there is a growing popular discomfort with the Holocaust Religion & Industry and their constant and inflammatory swinging of the Auschwitz and/or Judeophobia bludgeon. This strong irritation is canalized in many countries primarily by the radical right wing, which is not too afraid to formulate loudly a critique against this disproportional and hypocritical Zionist influence mixed with fiery Judaephobia. Thus the Holocaust Religion, with its constant display of power, causes among other factors, the rise of the extreme right wing movements.

Similar to the formulations of Israeli philosopher Adi Ophir, the dogmas of this Holocaust Religion can be articulated as religious commandments:

- *Remember what Amalek has done to thee!*

This compulsory directive is meant to cultivate and preserve for ever and ever the memory of all the wrongdoings of Amalek against the Jews. Amalek is the biblical collective designation for all the enemies of the Jews, who, in the 20th century came to be mainly the Nazis and the Arabs. It is in this sense not only a command to remember but also to distrust and hate all the non-Jews, the gentiles, who are potential or active Amalekites.

This attitude is based on the concept that the hate of the Jews, Judeophobia, is inherent in all other cultures. Any questioning of the real danger for the Jews in Europe or North America, for example, is considered blasphemy. Organizations like the Anti Defamation League (ADL) are zealously pursuing the supposed and the real sinners.

Activities like that of the ADL together with the everlasting commemorations of Judeocide are important elements for building the modern Jewish identity, especially for the secular Jews. Another consequence of this commandment is that the Jews are to be considered as the eternal victims. So even if they are the victimizers they are still to be conceived as victims.

- *Thou shall never compare The Holocaust with any other Genocide!*

The uniqueness of the Nazi Judeocide is a modern version of the old judeocentric concept of "choseness". Jewish sufferings are accordingly special and cannot and must never be compared with other miseries. Those who do it are accused of playing down this genocide.

This commandment is very important for the mythologizing of the Judeocide and for preventing a normal historical analysis, as one of the most common and important scientific methods are comparison. Comparison is also important if the Nazi Judeocide is to serve as a point of reference for every crime against humanity.

It is vital to note that while no two occasions are identical still they might possess certain structural similarities. The most chilling and deadly aspect of the Nazi crimes is the usage of modern technocratic methods in order to pursue immoral goals. The potential for technocrats, officers etc. to commit crimes is not some specific Nazi characteristic but is endemic to all modern systems.

The comparison can be partially or fully correct or can be completely wrong, but should not be forbidden. This commandment is very successful in the Western countries where the Judeophobia has a very long tradition and is still present.

Contemporary manifestation of the prejudices against Jews is sometimes very ingenious. It now camouflages itself commonly in an allegedly opposite attitude, "Judeophilia", a kind of 'positive' racism. The transformation from one to the other might happen often seamlessly.

- *Thou shall never compare the Nazi crimes with those of Israel!*

This prohibition is stronger outside Israel than inside. Even Israeli public figures dare from time to time to invade this taboo zone. The last example was given by Israeli right wing radicals who compared the evacuation of settlements from the Gaza strip with the deportation of Jews by the Nazis.

Some of them pointed out correctly that though in the broader public the Nazi crimes are identified with the extermination in concentration camps, the Nazis started their anti-Jewish politics with the aim "just" to deport Jews. In the years 1933-38 they tried to encourage the "voluntary" immigration (transfer or Ha'avara) and as of 1938 went over to mass expulsion. In 1941 the Nazis started with the systematic annihilation. The comparison of the right wingers is absurd, but should not be forbidden. On the other hand there are more founded reasons to compare the present Israeli policy and measures towards the Palestinians with those of the Nazis.

It is obvious that at least as of the beginning of the second Intifada in 2000, Israel, through its siege and frequent incursions, tries to induce a "voluntary" transfer of the Palestinians and looks for pretext to go over to mass expulsion. Several Israeli ministers declared openly that if there was a so called mega terrorist attack, i.e., a Palestinian attack with a high number of Jewish casualties, Israel would react with a second Naqba, which means, another mass expulsion respectively ethnic cleansing like in 1948. Actually we are already experiencing a "silent" and ever escalating ethnic cleansing.

There is no need to wait till a mass extermination in any form is initiated. Even before that the comparison is, with all the specific differences, valid and legitimate. Besides, there are obvious and strong anti-democratic tendencies in Israeli society not dissimilar to the situation in the Weimar Republic. The right wing radicals are very strong and getting stronger. Though they could not prevent the evacuation of settlements, they are bound sooner or later to try to take a complete control of the state.

- *Thou shall never doubt the number of 6 million Jewish victims!*

There is no real logical explanation for this figure being defended so desperately. The source of this statistic, the SS officer Wilhelm Hoettl, was certainly not the most reliable informant. If the number of the slaughtered Jews were lesser, would the Nazi crimes be less dreadful? Actually in the Jewish victims database by Yad Vashem there are only 3 millions names registered and many of them even appear several times.

- Thou shall never doubt the Nazi Judeocide!

This is one of the strongest prohibitions. While there is no convincing reason to doubt that the gassing of Jews took place, there is no compelling argument to forbid people from questioning the validity of the widely accepted historical description. Considering the widespread abuse of the Judeocide by Zionists and their followers and the obvious hypocrisy of many of these persons and organizations, it is understandable that their claims are mistrusted. On the other hand it cannot be overlooked that practically all the Holocaust deniers are racists. The problem is therefore not the denial as such but the racism and it is very doubtful if prohibition is the right means to fight against racism.

Skepticism towards any narrative or interpretation is legitimate as such and does not require hysterical reactions. The main problem with the Holocaust Denial is that it is accompanied by conspiracy theories and other anti-Jewish prejudices. These phenomena pose for the time being hardly a threat to Jews but rather to the propagators of these contents, who thus disqualify themselves to take part in the mainstream discourse.

Of course once the Holocaust Religion becomes weaker, as mentioned before, the situation will change dramatically for sure. To prevent the racists from profiting from this development it is the duty of democratic forces to do work towards the abolishment of this religion. For the time being the deniers and the Holocaust Religion followers and disseminators feed and need each other in order to catch more publicity in an effort to strengthen their own racist aims.

- *Thou shall never doubt the right of Israel to exist as the Jewish state!*

It is believed that as the Judeophobia will persist everywhere for ever, the Jews will need from now to eternity a secure refuge. Therefore so many Jews, though living in a greater security outside Israel, still believe that this country should function as a kind of anti-Judeocide insurance. Many of them are not very disturbed by the fact that this insurance is paid with Palestinian blood and suffering. Every anti-Zionist per this definition is a-priori a supporter of a potential Judeocide and is a Judeophobe. This is a myth. Israel has hardly served as a refuge and is not likely to become a real one. Today it endangers Jews all over the world more than it protects them.

- *Thou shall not criticize the leading Jewish organizations and the Israeli government!*

This commandment is reasoned by the above arguments. A career oriented politician, journalist or artist in Western countries will usually prefer to remain silent on these issues in public, as the potential punishment is viewed as very painful. This commandment, like some others on this list, applies mainly to non-Jews, but radical Jewish critics risk being branded as "self-haters", "Jewish Anti-Semites" etc.

- *Thou must never criticize Jewish organizations and the Zionist leadership for abandoning the European Jewry in the Nazi era!*

Most of the attempts to raise this issue are blocked by the argument that it will strengthen the Judephobes, who claim that the Jews alone bear the guilt for their fate in WWII.

Without trying to minimize the responsibility of the Nazis for their crimes, one should take into account the behaviour of a segment of the Jewish communities, most especially certain leaderships, inside and outside occupied Europe. The victims also have a duty and responsibility and the tragedy is always greater if a leadership betrays its own people. For all practical purposes, the Zionist leadership in Palestine and in the USA abandoned European Jewry, and in certain cases sabotaged rescue attempts and in some other cases even collaborated with the Nazis.

- *Thou shall not doubt the central Role of Hitler in the industrialization of the extermination of the Jews!*

The fact that there is no proof of a Hitler's order to build Auschwitz is one of the most emotional historical disputes. Even logical non-Hitler-centric descriptions are sometimes labelled as Holocaust Denial. This is one of the methods of preventing a political secular explanation of the Judeocide. One of the reasons for this commandment is that any other explanation implies that there might be some logical explanation for the Judeocide, there was a real possibility of saving the Jews and therefore the Zionist movement and the Allies are guilty of abandoning them.

RELIGION CAUSES NEGATIVE ACTS

Sometimes it seems as if one can't simply walk down the street without seeing some form of religious practice/worship/advertisement. It just begs the question, "Why?" Personally, it is my stellar opinion that religion does more harm than good. It sometimes disturbs me to think of all the horrors and misdeeds committed in the "name of God." I think just about every religion has at least one story that goes something like, "God says we must smite evildoers, so let's make genocide part of our practice." History is rife with examples such as the Crusades and the Spanish Inquisition to name a few. Look at the situation we have in the Middle East with all the bloodshed and senseless violence. Not only is most of it religiously motivated, but it just isn't good enough for different religions to fight each other — there has to be different factions of the same religion fighting over which one is right. Then you've got the worst bottom barrel of religions — the ones that practice fatalist beliefs.

If everything is predestined, what's the point of getting up in the morning and going to work/school? What's the point of doing anything if some cosmic, all-powerful force has already predetermined everything? I don't know about the rest of you, but the only reason that I've obtained anything in my life is because I worked for it. To me, religion just seems like a comfort blanket the people need. The world is often crazy and chaotic, and by subscribing to a particular faith, people seek to bring a certain order and balance to things. Why is it so hard to look within and find one's own strength and resolve to get through life's obstacles rather than bow to some deity who may or may not exist? There's nothing wrong with having a said religion or philosophy or spiritual belief system or whatever. The problem arises when a person or group of people go around preaching to others that their ideas are the only ones that are right, and then when talk and negotiations fail to simply digress to a might-makes-right belief system, either force others to convert to their ways or kill them outright. If one religion is truly the right way, then certainly the deity worshipped would be benevolent enough to grant his/her/its followers blessings which would in turn attract others.

The Social Problems of Religion

Religion achieves its highest social ministry when it has least connection with the secular institutions of society. In past ages, since social reforms were largely confined to the moral realms, religion did not have to adjust its attitude to extensive changes in economic and political systems. The chief problem of religion was the endeavor to replace evil with good within the existing social order of political and economic culture. Religion has thus indirectly tended to perpetuate the established order of society, to foster the maintenance of the existent type of civilization. But religion should not be directly concerned either with the creation of new social orders or with the preservation of old ones.

True religion does oppose violence as a technique of social evolution, but it does not oppose the intelligent efforts of society to adapt its usages and adjust its institutions to new economic conditions and cultural requirements. Religion did approve the occasional social reforms of past centuries, but in the twentieth century it is of necessity called upon to face adjustment to extensive and continuing social reconstruction. Conditions of living alter so rapidly that institutional modifications must be greatly accelerated, and religion must accordingly quicken its adaptation to this new and everchanging social order.

Religion and Social Reconstruction

Mechanical inventions and the dissemination of knowledge are modifying civilization; certain economic adjustments and social changes are imperative if cultural disaster is to be avoided. This new and oncoming social order will not settle down complacently for a millennium. The human race must become reconciled to a procession of changes, adjustments, and readjustments. Mankind is on the march toward a new and unrevealed planetary destiny. Religion must become a forceful influence for moral stability and spiritual progression functioning dynamically in the midst of these everchanging conditions and never-ending economic adjustments.

Urantia society can never hope to settle down as in past ages. The social ship has steamed out of the sheltered bays of established tradition and has begun its cruise upon the high seas of evolutionary destiny; and the soul of man, as never before in the world's history, needs carefully to scrutinize its charts of morality and painstakingly to observe the compass of religious guidance. The paramount mission of religion as a social influence is to stabilize the ideals of mankind during these dangerous times of transition from one phase of civilization to another, from one level of culture to another. Religion has no new duties to perform, but it is urgently called upon to function as a wise guide and experienced counselor in all of these new and rapidly changing human situations. Society is becoming more mechanical, more compact, more complex, and more critically interdependent.

Religion must function to prevent these new and intimate inter-associations from becoming mutually retrogressive or even destructive. Religion must act as the cosmic salt which prevents the ferments of progression from destroying the cultural savor of civilization. These new social relations and economic upheavals can result in lasting brotherhood only by the ministry of religion. A godless humanitarianism is, humanly speaking, a noble gesture, but true religion is the only power which can lastingly increase the responsiveness of one social group to the needs and sufferings of other groups. In the past, institutional religion could remain passive while the upper strata of society turned a deaf ear to the sufferings and oppression of the helpless lower strata, but in modern times these lower social orders are no longer so abjectly ignorant nor so politically helpless.

Religion must not become organically involved in the secular work of social reconstruction and economic reorganization. But it must actively keep pace with all these advances in civilization by making clearcut and vigorous restatements of its moral mandates and spiritual precepts, its progressive philosophy of human living and transcendent survival. The spirit of religion is eternal, but the form of its expression must be restated every time the dictionary of human language is revised.

Weakness of Institutional Religion

Institutional religion cannot afford inspiration and provide leadership in this impending worldwide social reconstruction and economic reorganization because it has unfortunately become more or less of an organic part of the social order and the economic system which is destined to undergo reconstruction. Only the real religion of personal spiritual experience can function helpfully and creatively in the present crisis of civilization. Institutional religion is now caught in the stalemate of a vicious circle. It cannot reconstruct society without first reconstructing itself; and being so much an integral part of the established order, it cannot reconstruct itself until society has been radically reconstructed.

Religionists must function in society, in industry, and in politics as individuals, not as groups, parties, or institutions. A religious group which presumes to function as such, apart from religious activities, immediately becomes a political party, an economic organization, or a social institution. Religious collectivism must confine its efforts to the furtherance of religious causes. Religionists are of no more value in the tasks of social reconstruction than non-religionists except in so far as their religion has conferred upon them enhanced cosmic foresight and endowed them with that superior social wisdom which is born of the sincere desire to love God supremely and to love every man as a brother in the heavenly kingdom. An ideal social order is that in which every man loves his neighbor as he loves himself.

The institutionalized church may have appeared to serve society in the past by glorifying the established political and economic orders, but it must speedily cease such action if it is to survive. Its only proper attitude consists in the teaching of non-violence, the doctrine of peaceful evolution in the place of violent revolution—peace on earth and good will among all men. Modern religion finds it difficult to adjust its attitude toward the rapidly shifting social changes only because it has permitted itself to become so thoroughly traditionalized, dogmatized, and institutionalized. The religion of living experience finds no difficulty in keeping ahead of all these social developments and economic upheavals, amid which it ever functions as a moral stabilizer, social guide, and spiritual pilot.

True religion carries over from one age to another the worthwhile culture and that wisdom which is born of the experience of knowing God and striving to be like him.

Religion and the Religionist

Early Christianity was entirely free from all civil entanglements, social commitments, and economic alliances. Only did later institutionalized Christianity become an organic part of the political and social structure of Occidental civilization. The kingdom of heaven is neither a social nor economic order; it is an exclusively spiritual brotherhood of God-knowing individuals. True, such a brotherhood is in itself a new and amazing social phenomenon attended by astounding political and economic repercussions. The religionist is not unsympathetic with social suffering, not unmindful of civil injustice, not insulated from economic thinking and insensible to political tyranny. Religion influences social reconstruction directly because it spiritualizes and idealizes the individual citizen. Indirectly, cultural civilization is influenced by the attitude of these individual religionists as they become active and influential members of various social, moral, economic, and political groups.

The attainment of a high cultural civilization demands, first, the ideal type of citizen and, then, ideal and adequate social mechanisms wherewith such a citizenry may control the economic and political institutions of such an advanced human society. The church, because of overmuch false sentiment, has long ministered to the underprivileged and the unfortunate, and this has all been well, but this same sentiment has led to the unwise perpetuation of racially degenerate stocks which have tremendously retarded the progress of civilization. Many individual social reconstructionists, while vehemently repudiating institutionalized religion, are, after all, zealously religious in the propagation of their social reforms. And so it is that religious motivation, personal and more or less unrecognized, is playing a great part in the present-day program of social reconstruction.

The great weakness of all this unrecognized and unconscious type of religious activity is that it is unable to profit from open religious criticism and thereby attain to profitable levels of self-correction. It is a fact that religion does not grow unless it is disciplined by constructive criticism, amplified by philosophy, purified by science, and nourished by loyal fellowship. There is always the great danger that religion will become distorted and perverted into the pursuit of false goals, as when in times of war each contending nation prostitutes its religion into military propaganda. Loveless zeal is always harmful to religion, while persecution diverts the activities of religion into the achievement of some sociologic or theological drive.

Religion can be kept free from unholy secular alliances only by:

1. A critically corrective philosophy.
2. Freedom from all social, economic, and political alliances.
3. Creative, comforting, and love-expanding fellowships.
4. Progressive enhancement of spiritual insight and the appreciation of cosmic values.
5. Prevention of fanaticism by the compensations of the scientific mental attitude.

Religionists, as a group, must never concern themselves with anything but *religion,* albeit any one such religionist, as an individual citizen, may become the outstanding leader of some social, economic, or political reconstruction movement. It is the business of religion to create, sustain, and inspire such a cosmic loyalty in the individual citizen as will direct him to the achievement of success in the advancement of all these difficult but desirable social services.

Transition Difficulties

Genuine religion renders the religionist socially fragrant and creates insights into human fellowship. But the formalization of religious groups many times destroys the very values for the promotion of which the group was organized.

Human friendship and divine religion are mutually helpful and significantly illuminating if the growth in each is equalized and harmonized. Religion puts new meaning into all group associations—families, schools, and clubs. It imparts new values to play and exalts all true humor. Social leadership is transformed by spiritual insight; religion prevents all collective movements from losing sight of their true objectives. Together with children, religion is the great unifier of family life, provided it is a living and growing faith.

Family life cannot be had without children; it can be lived without religion, but such a handicap enormously multiplies the difficulties of this intimate human association. During the early decades of the twentieth century, family life, next to personal religious experience, suffers most from the decadence consequent upon the transition from old religious loyalties to the emerging new meanings and values. True religion is a meaningful way of living dynamically face to face with the commonplace realities of everyday life. But if religion is to stimulate individual development of character and augment integration of personality, it must not be standardized. If it is to stimulate evaluation of experience and serve as a value-lure, it must not be stereotyped. If religion is to promote supreme loyalties, it must not be formalized.

No matter what upheavals may attend the social and economic growth of civilization, religion is genuine and worth while if it fosters in the individual an experience in which the sovereignty of truth, beauty, and goodness prevails, for such is the true spiritual concept of supreme reality. And through love and worship this becomes meaningful as fellowship with man and sonship with God. After all, it is what one believes rather than what one knows that determines conduct and dominates personal performances. Purely factual knowledge exerts very little influence upon the average man unless it becomes emotionally activated. But the activation of religion is superemotional, unifying the entire human experience on transcendent levels through contact with, and release of, spiritual energies in the mortal life.

During the psychologically unsettled times of the twentieth century, amid the economic upheavals, the moral crosscurrents, and the sociologic rip tides of the cyclonic transitions of a scientific era, thousands upon thousands of men and women have become humanly dislocated; they are anxious, restless, fearful, uncertain, and unsettled; as never before in the world's history they need the consolation and stabilization of sound religion. In the face of unprecedented scientific achievement and mechanical development there is spiritual stagnation and philosophic chaos. There is no danger in religion's becoming more and more of a private matter—a personal experience—provided it does not lose its motivation for unselfish and loving social service. Religion has suffered from many secondary influences: sudden mixing of cultures, intermingling of creeds, diminution of ecclesiastical authority, changing of family life, together with urbanization and mechanization.

Man's greatest spiritual jeopardy consists in partial progress, the predicament of unfinished growth: forsaking the evolutionary religions of fear without immediately grasping the revelatory religion of love. Modern science, particularly psychology, has weakened only those religions which are so largely dependent upon fear, superstition, and emotion. Transition is always accompanied by confusion, and there will be little tranquility in the religious world until the great struggle between the three contending philosophies of religion is ended:

1. The spiritistic belief (in a providential Deity) of many religions.
2. The humanistic and idealistic belief of many philosophies.
3. The mechanistic and naturalistic conceptions of many sciences.

And these three partial approaches to the reality of the cosmos must eventually become harmonized by the revelatory presentation of religion, philosophy, and cosmology which portrays the triune existence of spirit, mind, and energy proceeding from the Trinity of Paradise and attaining time-space unification within the Deity of the Supreme.

SOCIAL ASPECTS OF RELIGION

While religion is exclusively a personal spiritual experience—knowing God as a Father—the corollary of this experience—knowing man as a brother—entails the adjustment of the self to other selves, and that involves the social or group aspect of religious life. Religion is first an inner or personal adjustment, and then it becomes a matter of social service or group adjustment. The fact of man's gregariousness perforce determines that religious groups will come into existence. What happens to these religious groups depends very much on intelligent leadership. In primitive society the religious group is not always very different from economic or political groups. Religion has always been a conservator of morals and a stabilizer of society. And this is still true, notwithstanding the contrary teaching of many modern socialists and humanists.

Always keep in mind: True religion is to know God as your Father and man as your brother. Religion is not a slavish belief in threats of punishment or magical promises of future mystical rewards. The religion of Jesus is the most dynamic influence ever to activate the human race. Jesus shattered tradition, destroyed dogma, and called mankind to the achievement of its highest ideals in time and eternity—to be perfect, even as the Father in heaven is perfect. Religion has little chance to function until the religious group becomes separated from all other groups—the social association of the spiritual membership of the kingdom of heaven.

The doctrine of the total depravity of man destroyed much of the potential of religion for effecting social repercussions of an uplifting nature and of inspirational value. Jesus sought to restore man's dignity when he declared that all men are the children of God. Any religious belief which is effective in spiritualizing the believer is certain to have powerful repercussions in the social life of such a religionist. Religious experience unfailingly yields the "fruits of the spirit" in the daily life of the spirit-led mortal. Just as certainly as men share their religious beliefs, they create a religious group of some sort which eventually creates common goals. Someday religionists will get together and actually effect cooperation on the basis of unity of ideals and purposes rather than attempting to do so on the basis of psychological opinions and theological beliefs. Goals rather than creeds should unify religionists. Since true religion is a matter of personal spiritual experience, it is inevitable that each individual religionist must have own and personal interpretation of the realization of that spiritual experience.

Let the term "faith" stand for the individual's relation to God rather than for the creedal formulation of what some group of mortals have been able to agree upon as a common religious attitude. "Have you faith? Then have it to yourself." That faith is concerned only with the grasp of ideal values is shown by the New Testament definition which declares that faith is the substance of things hoped for and the evidence of things not seen. Primitive man made little effort to put his religious convictions into words. His religion was danced out rather than thought out. Modern men have thought out many creeds and created many tests of religious faith. Future religionists must live out their religion; dedicate themselves to the wholehearted service of the brotherhood of man. It is high time that man had a religious experience so personal and so sublime that it could be realized and expressed only by "feelings that lie too deep for words."

Jesus did not require of his followers that they should periodically assemble and recite a form of words indicative of their common beliefs. He only ordained that they should gather together to actually *do something*—partake of the communal supper of the remembrance of his bestowal life on Urantia. What a mistake for Christians to make when, in presenting Christ as the supreme ideal of spiritual leadership, they dare to require God-conscious men and women to reject the historic leadership of the God-knowing men who have contributed to their particular national or racial illumination during past ages.

Institutional Religion

Sectarianism is a disease of institutional religion, and dogmatism is an enslavement of the spiritual nature. It is far better to have a religion without a church than a church without religion. The religious turmoil of the twentieth century does not, in and of itself, betoken spiritual decadence. Confusion goes before growth as well as before destruction. There is a real purpose in the socialization of religion. It is the purpose of group religious activities to dramatize the loyalties of religion; to magnify the lures of truth, beauty, and goodness; to foster the attractions of supreme values; to enhance the service of unselfish fellowship; to glorify the potentials of family life; to promote religious education; to provide wise counsel and spiritual guidance; and to encourage group worship. And all live religions encourage human friendship, conserve morality, promote neighborhood welfare, and facilitate the spread of the essential gospel of their respective messages of eternal salvation. But as religion becomes institutionalized, its power for good is curtailed, while the possibilities for evil are greatly multiplied.

The dangers of formalized religion are: fixation of beliefs and crystallization of sentiments; accumulation of vested interests with increase of secularization; tendency to standardize and fossilize truth; diversion of religion from the service of God to the service of the church; inclination of leaders to become administrators instead of ministers; tendency to form sects and competitive divisions; establishment of oppressive ecclesiastical authority; creation of the aristocratic "chosen-people" attitude; fostering of false and exaggerated ideas of sacredness; the routinizing of religion and the petrification of worship; tendency to venerate the past while ignoring present demands; failure to make up-to-date interpretations of religion; entanglement with functions of secular institutions; it creates the evil discrimination of religious castes; it becomes an intolerant judge of orthodoxy; it fails to hold the interest of adventurous youth and gradually loses the saving message of the gospel of eternal salvation. Formal religion restrains men in their personal spiritual activities instead of releasing them for heightened service as kingdom builders.

Religion's Contribution

Though churches and all other religious groups should stand aloof from all secular activities, at the same time religion must do nothing to hinder or retard the social coordination of human institutions. Life must continue to grow in meaningfulness; man must go on with his reformation of philosophy and his clarification of religion. Political science must effect the reconstruction of economics and industry by the techniques it learns from the social sciences and by the insights and motives supplied by religious living. In all social reconstruction religion provides a stabilizing loyalty to a transcendent object, a steadying goal beyond and above the immediate and temporal objective. In the midst of the confusions of a rapidly changing environment mortal man needs the sustenance of a far-flung cosmic perspective.

Religion inspires man to live courageously and joyfully on the face of the earth; it joins patience with passion, insight to zeal, sympathy with power, and ideals with energy. Man can never wisely decide temporal issues or transcend the selfishness of personal interests unless he meditates in the presence of the sovereignty of God and reckons with the realities of divine meanings and spiritual values. Economic interdependence and social fraternity will ultimately conduce to brotherhood. Man is naturally a dreamer, but science is sobering him so that religion can presently activate him with far less danger of precipitating fanatical reactions. Economic necessities tie man up with reality, and personal religious experience brings this same man face to face with the eternal realities of an everexpanding and progressing cosmic citizenship.

RELIGION AND CASTE

It is an irony that we try to intermingle caste system with religion. It is also regrettable that we affix seal of religion on caste system and thereby we intentionally keep ourselves away from true religion. The truth happens to be that religion can never be, in any way, a helping hand to a system like caste system that is identified, as a factor of disintegration in society. Not only this, the aims and objects of any religious community are as distant from the caste system as the earth is away from the sun. Religion had originated with man's march on this earth. It can be put in this way - when the Creator sent man on earth in accordance with His action, He also sent religion along with him. As such, man and religion came on earth simultaneously. There is also a purpose behind the fact that both came together. A question is natural about purpose. We shall easily comprehend it if we comprehend meaning of religion in very simple terms.

As I hold, religion signifies adoption. What is to be adopted? As always, my reply is 'goodness' or 'niceness'. As such, religion consists in adopting goodness. It is only goodness owing to presence of which man could sustain his existence. He gradually developed non-violence and then adopted a path of mutual cooperation. Man came to earth with action in nature. In such a situation, man might have finished his existence in case religion was not with him. ...But, he not only maintained his existence, but also marched forward on the path of progress. This is the reason that human being and religion came together. When? Or what is the span of time in this respect? This can be a topic for research. ...However, both originated and grew up simultaneously.

We should know the meaning of religion in simple terms. It is clear that it stands for existence and welfare of man. Its basis is cooperation, affection and unity. It propagated message of 'Live and Let Live'. In this regard, any action, contrary to the spirit of cooperation, affection or unity cannot be religious. Religion is, as such, fully dedicated to welfare of all. According to circumstances pertaining to time and space, ways were established for salvation of man through many mediums from time to time. The establisher can be termed as Great man or

Learned man. He may also be God-incarnate or messenger of God. This established a way for a religious community. All religious communities that we know today as Islam, Christian, Confucian, Parsi, Boddh, Jews, Sikh or Hindu etc. are religious communities and give separate directives regarding lifestyle in case a man aspires for all sided development. Although their ways may be different, their aim is the same.

Difference between religion and religious community is that religion originated with man, while community came into existence afterwards. Situation of religion remained uniform in the whole world whereas establishment of religious community took place from time to time according to the circumstances pertaining to the region and era. A single force or element that can be adopted as per individual conviction was instrumental behind religion whereas there was more than one behind religious community. Religion is wholly dedicated to mutual cooperation, affection, unity, broadmindedness, equality and welfare of all. Contrary to it, a religious community irrespective of being dedicated to all-sided development of man is bound by circumstances relating to the region and era and all the facts enumerated above, it has a limited span in comparison to religion. However, religious community happens to be an indivisible part of religion.

After knowing religion and religious community we can conclude that both are dedicated to welfare and all-sided development of man: it is another matter that there is a difference as to their comprehension. A religious community also does not cherish all-sided development pertaining to its followers without cooperation, equality, affection and unity into them. In this regard any division amongst followers of a religious community, whatever may be the basis and whatsoever may be the argument in favour of such a division, is into against the aim of the religious community. The caste system, prevalent today in India, succeeds the varna system and is based on inequality, non-cooperation, short sightedness and division. Exploitation is at its base. The basic spirit behind caste system remains to ensure maximum possible gain akin to selfishness for self and group of self that is the people of one's own caste. It has accordingly caused harm to country and society for thousands of years. It has already divided us in about 3500 parts.

It is quite amazing that attempts are made to relate it to religion or religious community. However, one, who has even a little intelligence, shall certainly negativate it on the ground that purpose and meaning of religion and religious community is to keep existence of man safeguarded and achieve his objective. Caste obstructs all this process. As such, religion or religious community is quite non-related to caste system. Those, who try to affix seal of religion or religious community on caste system or wish to accord a footing to it, are ignorant of meaning and purpose of religion and religious community. Not only that, such persons, expressly or tacitly are not well wishers of society and nation. A perception of humanity happens to be incessantly far away from such persons.

Problems created by Mixed Faith Marriages

Those contemplating a mixed-religion marriage should consider the problems relating to the ideals of marriage before they take their vows. There is a big difference, for instance, between a Catholic and a non-Catholic's viewpoint of marriage. A Catholic recognizes marriage as a sacrament as well as a contract. This is not always the case with the non-Catholic, who more often than not permits divorce and remarriage. In mixed Catholic-Protestant marriages the rate of divorce and separation is about three times higher than in marriages where both parties are of the same faith. Three separate studies in Michigan, Maryland, and Washington, covering a total of 24,184 families have verified this condition. Mixed marriages are unstable and should be avoided at all costs.

Marriages between Catholics provide the children with a common spiritual relationship to their parents. Dr. Clifford Adams, directing the Marriage Counselling Service at Pennsylvania State College, School of Education, stated several years ago in an article in the Woman's Home Companion that

"My records show that 70 per cent of mixed marriages now end in divorce or separation." And Dr. Adams ought to know about this, for he counsels over 4000 students a year. Another problem soon to raise its head in marriage is the problem of birth control and the means used in spacing children. For the Catholic, contraception of any kind is forbidden under pain of mortal sin. The only method of birth control a Catholic may practice is selfcontrol or rhythm (which shall be discussed in detail later). In contrast to this position, a non-Catholic frequently condones contraceptive measures of family limitation.

The marriage of a Catholic to a non-Catholic is a rather drab affair, liturgically speaking. The priest officiating at the ceremony wears no liturgical vestments. There is no nuptial Mass, no nuptial blessing, and no mutual reception of Holy Communion. Not even the wedding rings are blessed before they are exchanged. Only the brief ceremony of pronouncing the mutual vows of marriage takes place before the communion rail (if in church) or in the rectory. All of this is the Church's way of expressing her disapproval of such a union. A mixed marriage creates many problems of living in marriage. The reason is that Catholicism permeates the entire life of the Catholic party. It is not just a Sunday affair. The use of sacramental such as holy water, statues, crucifix, and religious pictures are commonly found in Catholic homes.

In a mixed marriage, these religious articles and outward symbols of Catholicism could prove distasteful and embarrassing to the non-Catholic spouse. Even if they are accepted, they are tolerated, never fully understood by the non-Catholic party. This could have repercussions on the children's attitude toward sacramental. No matter how kind and considerate the couple may be, religious differences will eventually lead to quarrels. Intellectual disputes are bound to occur when two individuals differ in such an important life factor as religion. A popular non-Catholic columnist of some years ago pointed up the seriousness of this problem: "It is merely a fact that just as no wars have been so bloody as holy wars and no persecutions so cruel as those done in the name of religion, so there is nothing about which husbands and wives can quarrel so bitterly, nothing which can so completely estrange them as a difference in creed."

Before you follow through with a mixed marriage, sit down with your partner and weigh the costs and benefits of living as a mixed marriage couple.

Problems with Original Sin

The doctrine of the fall offers a reconciliation of the imperfection of the world and the perfection of its Creator. God's creation was originally good, according to this doctrine, but then the first man, Adam, sinned. As a result of this fall, sin entered the world, and now all suffer the affliction of original sin. This doctrine is an important part of the Christian tradition: not only does it exonerate God from responsibility for the existence of evil, it also grounds the idea that sin is universal and so that every one of us is in need of salvation. The doctrine of original sin does a lot of theological work.

There are at least three varieties of fall-theory, three ways in which original sin can be understood. First, it can be understood in terms of inherited guilt; second, in terms of inherited corruption; third, in terms of individual falls. Each of these forms of the doctrine, though, has its problems; it is very difficult to make sense of original sin, to explain it in plausible terms. It may be that the doctrine, despite its traditional importance, must be abandoned. If this is the case, then it is a massive blow to Christianity, and so a powerful weapon in the armoury of the atheist.

Some have proposed accounts of original sin in terms of inherited guilt, according to which mankind bears a corporate responsibility for the first sin of the first man. On this approach, each of us is guilty of Adam's sin, just as if we had committed that sin ourselves. How this can divide those who advance this version of the doctrine. Some appeal to the idea of corporate identity, suggesting that in some significant sense we and Adam are one and the same, and so that we bear the guilt for his sin. Others appeal to the idea of participation, suggesting that we were all in some sense in Adam at the time of the fall, and so that we fell along with him. Still others appeal to the idea of representation, suggesting that although we were not directly involved in Adam's sin, Adam was our representative in Eden and so in sinning acted for all of us.

Inherited Corruption

A second approach to original sin explains it in terms of inherited corruption. According to this approach, we are not sinful because we are guilty of the first sin of Adam, but rather we are corrupted as an effect of that transgression. In what sense we are thought to have been affected by Adam's sin varies. Some accounts of this kind hold that we are corrupted through physical heredity, that Adam's sin corrupted his nature and that this corruption was then passed on to us. Others describe the transmission of Adam's sinfulness in terms of social heredity, suggesting that Adam's sin set a bad example which humanity has subsequently persistently followed.

Individual Falls

A third group has pursued an altogether more mysterious line of thought. Groups within Christianity have long thought that the account of Genesis 3 does not tell the literal truth; the story of Adam in the Garden of Eden has often been taken to be an allegorical description of the real fall of mankind. This perspective leaves a lot of room to develop a different account of the real fall allegorized in Genesis.

Some have taken this opportunity. Typically, the accounts developed have postulated individual pre-natal falls for each of us. On these views, original sin is seen as the result of moral errors that each of us committed before our lives began, rather than as the result of a sin committed by a distant ancestor in Eden. Whether our moral errors are thought to have been made in a prior physical existence, in a prior spiritual existence, or somehow outside of time, depend on the particular version of the theory in question.

Religion is the root cause of society's problems. 'Religious belief can cause damage to a society, contributing towards high murder rates, abortion, sexual promiscuity and suicide. ....belief in and worship of God are not only unnecessary for a healthy society but may actually contribute to social problems. '... The Times (sept 27, 2005). These findings completely reverse the normally accepted effects of religiosity. The painstaking research which compared statistics from secular and sectarian countries around the world was undertaken by social scientist Gregory S. Paul and published in the academically respected Journal of Religion & Society.

Mr. Paul discovered that societal problems such as, homicide, early mortality, the prevalence of sexually transmitted diseases, teenage pregnancy and abortion were up to 300 times higher in countries whose morals and mores were driven by Religious models than in secular nations whose motives were based on common sense. It concludes with the bombshell:

'The widely held fear that a godless citizenry must experience societal disaster is therefore refuted.'

Has Science just made God obsolescent?

There is a link to the full online report below:

It shows that, despite chest-beating about finding solutions for crime and social deviance in our society, politicians will never succeed in curing these problems whilst they are hamstrung by the self-righteous religious morality they invariably pay allegiance to. In fact, the astounding conclusion from this report is that it is the politicians themselves who are causing society's problems by adhering to the wishes of religious activists.

What this ground-breaking research really means is that the tidal wave of dysfunction and suffering which is amply portrayed in the British Tabloid media every day will never be cured until there is a formal separation between church and state. The Church of England should be disestablished forthwith and all the influential power structures it has taken unto itself by claiming that it had a moral solution to society's problems should be dismantled. Then, when our politicians are more free to take decisions based on common-sense and the power of Religion has been set aside the people of the U.K. can benefit, like Japan, Sweden, Norway, and many other nations, from an improved and happier life based on humanitarian rather than religious ideals.

Fifteen years ago the SAFF identified a fundie strategy to attack science at its roots. The fundamentalists rightly saw that it was science, not some imagined pan-global satanic conspiracy, which was destroying the power base of religion. Children were being taught scientific materialism as an accepted part of the school curriculum and academe had all but dismantled the deity with its discoveries in physics. The anachronistic stories in the bible were rationalised for what they were, paranoid delusions caused by early man's ignorance of his world. The best the fundie machine could do at the time was to agree that the wrathful and vindictive legends were allegories containing spiritual insights whose meanings were still relevant to society today. In the renaissance the Christian Church persecuted scientists and materialist philosophers as heretics and regained control through torture and death.

However since the 18th Century the established churches (Catholic / Anglican / Methodists) had come to an arrangement of power with the establishment of science and had been largely detoothed. They had turned into 'apologists' for the bible. Later, other more extreme Protestant sects (Pentecostals, Baptists etc) decided that to fulfill their obligations to their deity science had to be met head on and defeated. They saw that the most dangerous (to them) precept of science was Darwin's Theory of Evolution because it condensed all scientific explanations of how we came to be and therefore flatly conflicted with biblical teachings.

So it was that the Christian Militia began its campaign against academe, infiltrating universities to question and undermine existing teaching; setting up rival biblical colleges, pressing for religion to be taught in schools, to enable them to countermand any scientific materialistic teachings, and getting their best minds to represent the idea of Creationism (the ludicrous idea that god made the world and everything in it in 7 days) as a theory which had the same validity as The Theory of Evolution. Creationism was taught alongside Evolution as a valid option in Bible State schools where prejudiced educationalists pushed their personal religious beliefs at the expense of the education of their young. This resulted in the recent court cases where independent educationalists tried to get a ruling to ban the pseudo science of Creationism from being taught in schools.

By this time the fundie machine had corralled heavy support in the shape of George Bush who when asked said that he thought there was nothing wrong in Creationism - he believed in it. By this time it was clear to the academic community that there was a battle going on and they were a good few steps behind. As usual provocation from religionists has caused the trouble, resulting in a breach of the uneasy peace between religion and science and now the gloves are off. Science has begun to actually do the job expected of it and to challenge the orthodox churches head on. About time! Let's face it, they've spent decades attacking New Age beliefs whilst ignoring the very same activities in the orthodox religions for fear of upsetting their cozy arrangement.

So, this new research is one of many which we hope to see hitting the headlines in the next few year or so as the battle for the minds of the masses continues apace. Because Mind Control is what this is all about. When the scientific community complained about the completely unscientific claims of the Creationists their response was that they had indeed undertaken scientific research with a survey which showed that most people in the U.S. believed God had made the earth in 7 days than believed we evolved from apes. If the majority of people know a thing to be true then it must be reality! Mind control pure and simple. However, the scientists who produced this amazing report have missed the point somewhat by sidestepping the really controversial implications of it.

It is not 'Religion' per se which is responsible for damaging western societies - the only religion which has had control over this society for the past two thousand years is Christianity. This research shows that all organised religions by qualification must affect their followers' deleteriously but the one clearly responsible for doing it throughout Europe and the New World is Christianity. Just as the holy writ of the Islamic religion has affected the other half of the world for centuries,. That is the unpalatable conclusion this report brings. We agree that the moderates in both Christianity and Islam try to work together amiably under the idea of Inter-Faith but no matter how many nice folk there are in Christianity and Islam they will never overcome the wicked, selfish nature of fundamentalism. It only needs a handful of people to destroy the best efforts of everyone else by misconstruing Holy Writ.

The SAFF we have always maintained that the idea of creating a Multi-Faith community was a facade due to the disproportionate power of the Church of England. Recently the Church of England insisted on its superiority by redefining the boundaries. Their shot across the bows of Islam was the public statement that 'Britain is not a multifaith community - it is a Multi-Cultural community'. A clear warning that the people who run Christianity taking precedence and having rights above any other religion in the U.K. Rights that they have no intention of relinquishing. So we applaud this new research which shows clearly what the SAFF has been saying for years - that the root cause of most of the world's problems is due to the impositions of Absolutist religions throughout history.

It is not a belief in spiritual things which causes evil; it is the unreasonable and almost impossible demands which the orthodox churches make upon their congregations. It is the wicked and superstitious fears which the orthodox religions inject into the minds of people at an impressionable age. The guilt, the intolerance and the unwillingness to allow any other form of spiritual belief to coexist on equal terms teaches people how to hate others who are different. Having a belief in spiritual things is part of the human condition. This is not an attack on people's chosen beliefs. It is a criticism of Orthodox Religion. Orthodox Religion is a harmful parasite still clinging to the soft underbelly of democracy; sucking the life out of it because the Priesthoods who lead it are unworthy or incapable. No wonder anything improves.

At a time when criticising religion is now considered a 'hate crime', eminent scientist Richard Dawkins' two-part Channel 4 programme, *The Root of All Evil?*, should have been a welcome riposte to backward-looking religiosity. Instead it was the type of crimson-inducing programme whereby peering through half-closed fingers seemed highly advisable. There is plenty to say about religious belief, why it emerges and what role it plays today. So it is depressing that Dawkins seems to have little to offer. And what he does say contains all the insight of a saloon-bar loudmouth. Dawkins' main presentation was reasonable enough. In primitive times, man's mercy at the hands of nature gave the impression that supernatural forces controlled the Earth. Religious worship arose as the need to appease what man saw as powerful Gods. So far, so good. Yet when explaining why religion continues to play a part in modern life, Dawkins' explanation is to flash the 'you must be stupid' card.

Religious worship, and with it religious symbols and texts, emerged as man began to realise there was something more important than the individual - the social group. In *The Elementary Forms of the Religious Life*, French sociologist Emile Durkheim pointed out that the symbols of God are often the symbols of society too. As Durkheim pondered: 'Is that not because the god and the society are only one?' In worshipping God, people are in fact worshipping the idea of society. Durkheim derived this proposition from how all societies divide the world into two categories, the sacred and the profane. Sacred things, often represented in religious symbols, are 'considered superior in dignity and power to profane things and particularly men'.

No doubt Dawkins would dismiss this behaviour as irrational madness at work. In fact, it is a fairly rational reflection of the relationship between the individual (profane) and society (sacred). As Durkheim argued: 'Primitive man comes to view society as something sacred because he is utterly dependent on it.' Religious worship - or the worship of the social group - creates values and beliefs that form the basis of social life. In pre-modern times collective worship enabled members of a social group to formulate and communicate bonds that helped forge social solidarity. Religion isn't 'the root of all evil' as such, but a primitive attempt to understand what it is to be human and thus provide meaning and purpose to our action. Ironically, Dawkins fails to appreciate how religion has contributed to the humanism he is seeking to defend. Instead he presents atheist humanism as something straight out of Aldous Huxley's *Brave New World* - all machine-like creatures bedazzled by reductive technology yet blind to what makes us truly human.

By fixating on irrational explanations, Dawkins ignores why values, beliefs and solidarities are a key plank of major religions. This is why he gets tongue-tied when arguing with an Islamic fundamentalist - amusingly a former New York hipster who looked like he had gone from worshipping The Strokes to worshipping Allah (perhaps he'd heard their new album). All this guy was interested in, was discussing the importance of values and why the West was devoid of them. Mulling over the existence of Allah was of no concern to this Cat Stevens-like convert. His concerns were rooted in society, not theology.

Religion for Diminished Humanism Sets Up

Dawkins' response here was revealing. For all his scientific arguments, he seems to take more exception to the concepts of truth, absolutes and commitment to a higher cause. Yet these are invaluable tramlines that can guide purposeful human action. Dawkins casts the existence of firm belief systems as being responsible for conflicts around the world. So for Dawkins, the dispute between Jewish settlers and Palestinians is reducible to religious dogma rather than more complex issues arising from politics and oppression. There is also a broader point to be made here. An understanding of religion, and the role it plays, cannot be isolated from the specific social and material conditions that give rise to it. To do so means you could end up reaching misanthropic conclusions about why individuals have attachments to religion.

For such an avowedly staunch humanist, Dawkins' own assessments can come across as anti-human. The other problem is that singling out religion for diminished humanism sets up a false battleground. In fact, even today religion expresses kernels of humanism that sometimes appear progressive compared to contemporary thinking. For example, the major religions recognise that as humans are capable of making moral choices, we are fundamentally different from animals. How many secularists share such views today? Elsewhere, religion's understanding of truth and selfless commitment to a wider community or cause appears preferable to today's culture of narcissism and navel-gazing.

There is a programme to be made on critically examining religion, but this was not it. Certainly, the irrationality of religious belief and how it has been a bulwark of reaction needs to be taken to task and at a time when a human-centered worldview is at the lowest-ever ebb, banging the drum for human subjectivity should be done as loudly and as stridently as possible. Unfortunately, not only does Dawkins fail to address the social climate responsible for shrill anti-humanism, he ends up dismissing the very qualities needed to reconstitute our place on the world's stage.

Bibliography

A.H. Armstrong, ed., *Classical Mediterranean Spirituality*, World Spirituality 15, New York: Crossroad, 1989.

Armstrong, Karen, *Muhammad: A Biography of the Prophet*, Victor Gollancz Ltd.: U.K. 1991

Babin, P., *The New Era in Religious Communication*, Minneapolis, MN: Fortress Press, 1991

Brasher, B., *Give Me That Online Religion*, San Francisco, CA: Jossey-Bass, 2001

Buddenbaum, J., *Reporting News about Religion: An Introduction for Journalists*, Ames, IA: Iowa State University Press, 1998

Coleman Barks, trans. *The Essential Rumi*, new expanded edition (San Francisco: Harper San Francisco, 2004

Daniel Chanan Matt, ed., *Zohar: The Book of Enlightenment*, Classics of Western Spirituality, New York: Paulist Press, 1988

Eichhoefer, Gerald W. *Enduring Issues in Philosophy*. San Diego: Greenhaven Press, Inc., 1995.

Geertz, C., *The Interpretation of Cultures*, London: Hutchinson, 1975

Hunt, Stephen J., *Alternative Religion: A Sociological Introduction*, Aldershot: Ashgate, 2003.

Jenkins, H., *Textual Poachers: Television Fans and Participatory Culture*, London: Routledge, 1992

Khan, Muhammad Zafrulla, (trans.) *The Qur'an*, Olive Branch Press: NY, 1997

Kintz, L. and J. Lesage, *Media, Culture, and the Religious Right*, Minneapolis, MN: University of Minnesota Press, 1998

L. S. Clark (eds), *Practicing Religion in an Age of Media*, New York: Columbia University Press, 2002

Malise Ruthven, *Islam: A Very Short Introduction*, New York: Oxford University Press, 2000

Mircea Eliade, ed., *The Encyclopedia of Religion*, 16 vol., New York: Macmillan, 1987

Nouwen, Henri J.M. *The Road to Daybreak: A Spiritual Journey*. New York: Doubleday, 1988

O'Flaherty, Wendy Doniger (ed. and trans.), *The Rig Veda: An Anthology*. Penguin Books, NY, 1981

Pritchard, James B. (ed.), *The Harper Concise Atlas of the Bible*, HarperCollins: NY, 1991

Roleff, Tamara L., ed. *Satanism*. San Diego: Greenhaven Press, Inc., 2002

Silk, M., *Unsecular Media*, Urbana, IL: University of Illinois Press, 1995

Steven Heine and Charles S. Prebish, eds., *Buddhism in the Modern World: Adaptations of an Ancient Tradition*, New York: Oxford University Press, 2003

Sushil Mittal & Gene Thursby, eds., *The Hindu World*, New York: Routledge, 2004

Takeuchi Yoshinori, ed., *Buddhist Spirituality I: Indian, Southeast Asian, Tibetan, and Early Chinese*, World Spirituality Series 8, New York: Crossroad Publishing, 1993

Tu Weiming & Mary Evelyn Tucker, eds., *Confucian Spirituality*, World Spirituality 11, New York: Herder & Herder, 2002

Veer, P. van der, 'Transnational Religion', paper presented at the Conference on Transnational Migration: Comparative Perspectives, Princeton, 2001

Warms, Richard, James Garber and Jon McGee, eds., *Sacred Realms: Essays in Religion, Belief & Society*, New York: Oxford University Press, 2004

Wilkins, W.J., *Hindu Mythology: Vedic and Puranic*, Rupa and Co.: Calcutta, 1986

William C. Chittick, *Sufism: A Short Introduction*, Oxford: One World, 2000

William C. Chittick, *The Sufi Path of Love: The Spiritual Teachings of Rumi*, New York: SUNY, 1983

Wise, Michael, Martin Abegg, Jr., Edward Cook, *The Dead Sea Scrolls: A New Translation*, HarperCollins: NY, 1996

Wuthnow, R., *Rediscovering the Sacred: Perspectives on Religion in Contemporary Society*, Grand Rapids, MI: Eerdmans, 1992

Xinzhong Yao, *An Introduction to Confucianism*, Cambridge: Cambridge University Press, 2000

Zaehner, R.C. (translation), *Hindu Scriptures*, J.M. Dent & Sons: London, 1966

Zaleski, J., *The Soul of Cyberspace: How New Technology is Changing our Spiritual Lives*, New York: HarperCollins, 1997

Index